# Ajax on Java

*Steven Douglas Olson*

O'REILLY®

Beijing • Cambridge • Farnham • Köln • Paris • Sebastopol • Taipei • Tokyo

**Ajax on Java**
by Steven Douglas Olson


Printed in the United States of America.

Published by O'Reilly Media, Inc., 1005 Gravenstein Highway North, Sebastopol, CA 95472.

O'Reilly books may be purchased for educational, business, or sales promotional use. Online editions are also available for most titles (*safari.oreilly.com*). For more information, contact our corporate/institutional sales department: (800) 998-9938 or *corporate@oreilly.com*.

**Editor:** Mike Loukides
**Executive Editor:** Mike Loukides
**Production Editor:** Lydia Onofrei
**Copyeditor:** Rachel Wheeler
**Proofreader:** Lydia Onofrei
**Indexer:** Johnna VanHoose Dinse
**Cover Designer:** Karen Montgomery
**Interior Designer:** David Futato
**Illustrators:** Robert Romano and Jessamyn Read

**Printing History:**

February 2007: First Edition.



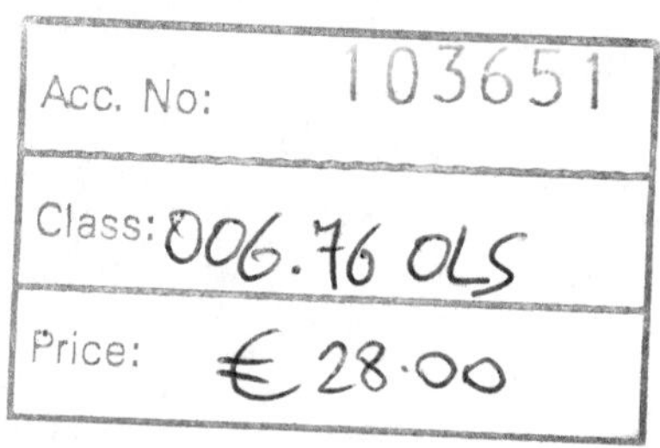

This book uses RepKover™, a durable and flexible lay-flat binding.

ISBN-10: 0-596-10187-2
ISBN-13: 978-0-596-10187-9
[M]

*To Erin, my best friend*
*and wife.*
*Thank you for believing in me.*

# Table of Contents

# Preface

"This is cool, look!" I told a group of coworkers.

"What is it?" one of them asked.

"It's Google Maps, and it uses Ajax," I said.

"What's Ajax?"

"It stands for Asynchronous JavaScript and XML. It allows a request from a web page to go to the server, get data, and display it without the user hitting submit and waiting for a page refresh."

"Wow, that could give my application the responsiveness of a desktop application!"

Until now, the choice for web developers has been between thin-client web applications and rich applications that require installs. With Ajax, you can build web applications that have the responsiveness of rich applications, without the overhead of keeping the end user up-to-date with the latest software. This is truly a great opportunity for web developers to write more responsive applications.

## Ajax: Some History

In the beginning there was HTML, and the world saw that it was good. Soon after came web applications, and the world was overjoyed with the ability to interact with data. There were search engines, online bill paying services, stock trading sites, interactive games, online shopping facilities, and much, much more.

So what's missing from the world of web applications? The answer is responsiveness. Back in 1984, I experienced my first real intuitive interaction with a computer. I was in college, and in the dorm was a study lab that had just been equipped with Apple Computer, Inc.'s new product: the Macintosh. These computers had a definite wow effect on the students. There was only one program, MacWrite, but that was enough for me. I was immediately sold on the friendly, easy-to-use experience that the MacWrite application gave me, as were many other students.

Until recently, browser-based web applications haven't been able to deliver the kind of experience users expect from desktop applications. Sure, some web applications do it with a rich client. But rich clients require overhead not present in browser-based applications. For ease of deployment and of keeping users current with the latest version, nothing beats a browser-based application. What would be ideal would be a browser-based application with a rich-client feel.

Meet Ajax.

Some of you probably know that Ajax technology has been around for a while, and that it wasn't always called Ajax. The term *Ajax* (Asynchronous JavaScript and XML) was coined by Jesse James Garrett of Adaptive Path in his article "Ajax: A New Approach to Web Applications" (*http://www.adaptivepath.com/publications/essays/archives/000385.php*). After that article appeared, there were plenty of comments about the fact that the approach wasn't really "new"; many developers were creating asynchronous applications before `XMLHttpRequest` became available. Java applets, despite their shortcomings, could deliver web applications that felt more like desktop applications. So could Flash applications.

So what's changed? What's the big deal? Well, now we at least have a name for the practice. That may not seem like much, but it gives us common ground to discuss it. Just as design patterns give us names to use when discussing programming techniques, the name *Ajax* instantly tells us which web programming technique is being used.

Since Garrett's article was published, there has been much discussion of how to use Ajax and of its capabilities and shortcomings. The appearance of articles, tools, and information relating to Ajax has lead to an explosion of interest. As information about Ajax becomes more and more widely available, Ajax techniques and usage will become more mainstream and will come to be expected by the users of the web applications we write.

That is the power of a name.

Ajax narrows the gap between a rich client application and a thin, browser-based client application. This book will introduce you to Ajax by illustrating how to create Ajax applications in a server-side Java environment: how to add Ajax features to servlet-based applications, JSPs, JSF applications, and so on.

So, join me in this exciting endeavor: let's strive to make our web applications more interactive, less boring, and more efficient by avoiding redundant data entry and long wait times between page loads—in short, to create a user experience closer to that of a real desktop application. These are some of the promises of Ajax technology.

## Audience

This book was written for progressive Java developers of all levels, especially those developing web applications. I say "progressive" because with the information provided in this book, you will be able to take your web programming to the next level. That next level is a higher level of usability for your customers, where clunky web applications are replaced with more-responsive, Ajax-enhanced applications.

## Assumptions This Book Makes

Java developers with web application experience should have no trouble understanding this book. I assume some experience with Java servlets, HTML, and JavaScript. Some experience with XML parsing is helpful, but not necessary.

## Contents of This Book

This book is divided into 10 chapters:

Chapter 1, *Setup*
: This chapter describes the environment that is needed to run the Ajax examples in this book. The examples use the Tomcat container, but if you are experienced with another J2EE container, you should be able to use that container as well.

Chapter 2, *JavaScript for Ajax*
: This chapter explains how to use JavaScript to access Ajax functionality and demonstrates how JavaScript is used to make asynchronous calls with the `XMLHttpRequest` object.

Chapter 3, *A Simple Ajax Servlet*
: This chapter explains how to service an Ajax client using a servlet. This is where this book differs from other Ajax books: it uses Java on the backend rather than another technology such as PHP, Perl, or Rails.

Chapter 4, *XML and JSON for Ajax*
: Although XML seems to be an integral part of Ajax, it is not required. This chapter discusses how to use XML to index the data coming back to the client and presents JSON as an attractive alternative to XML for performing the same function.

Chapter 5, *Getting Useful Data*
: This chapter illustrates how to store the data for Ajax applications in a database, as well as how to retrieve that data.

Chapter 6, *Ajax Libraries and Toolkits*
: A large number of frameworks and toolkits have appeared on the Ajax scene to help developers leverage some of the necessary functions that have to be written to support Ajax. This chapter explores several of those frameworks and toolkits: Dojo, Rico, Prototype, DWR, and Scriptaculous.

Chapter 7, *Ajax Tags*
: JavaServer Pages (JSPs) have the ability to reuse code through tag libraries. This chapter explains how to create Ajax tags for JSPs.

Chapter 8, *Ajax on Struts*
: Integrating Ajax into Struts applications is the subject of this chapter.

Chapter 9, *JavaServer Faces and Ajax*
: This chapter provides an example of how to use Ajax with JavaServer Faces.

Chapter 10, *Google Web Toolkit*
: The Google Web Toolkit, which allows for roundtrip debugging on Ajax code, offers a very exciting entry into using Ajax with Java. This chapter provides a tutorial for using this cutting-edge toolkit privided by Google for Ajax developers.

## Conventions Used in This Book

The following typographical conventions are used in this book:

Plain text
: Indicates menu titles, menu options, buttons, and keyboard accelerators (such as Alt and Ctrl).

*Italic*
: Indicates new terms, URLs, email addresses, filenames, file extensions, pathnames, directories, and Unix utilities.

`Constant width`
: Indicates commands, options, switches, variables, attributes, keys, functions, types, classes, namespaces, methods, modules, properties, parameters, values, objects, events, event handlers, XML tags, HTML tags, the contents of files, and the output from commands.

**`Constant width bold`**
: Shows commands or other text that should be typed literally by the user.

This icon signifies a tip, suggestion, or general note.

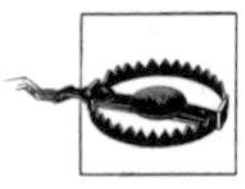

This icon indicates a warning or caution.

## Using Code Examples

This book is here to help you get your job done. In general, you may use the code in this book in your programs and documentation. You do not need to contact us for permission unless you're reproducing a significant portion of the code. For example, writing a program that uses several chunks of code from this book does not require permission. Selling or distributing a CD-ROM of examples from O'Reilly books does require permission. Answering a question by citing this book and quoting example code does not require permission. Incorporating a significant amount of example code from this book into your product's documentation does require permission.

We appreciate, but do not require, attribution. An attribution usually includes the title, author, publisher, and ISBN. For example: "*Ajax on Java* by Steven Douglas Olson. Copyright 2007 O'Reilly Media, Inc., 978-0-596-10187-9."

If you feel your use of code examples falls outside fair use or the permission given above, feel free to contact us at *permissions@oreilly.com*.

## How to Contact Us

Please address comments and questions concerning this book to the publisher:

O'Reilly Media, Inc.
1005 Gravenstein Highway North
Sebastopol, CA 95472
800-998-9938 (in the United States or Canada)
707-829-0515 (international or local)
707-829-0104 (fax)

We have a web page for this book, where we list errata, examples, and any additional information. You can access this page at:

*http://www.oreilly.com/catalog/9780596101879*

To comment or ask technical questions about this book, send email to:

*bookquestions@oreilly.com*

For more information about our books, conferences, Resource Centers, and the O'Reilly Network, see our web site at:

*http://www.oreilly.com*

## Safari® Enabled

When you see a Safari® Enabled icon on the cover of your favorite technology book, that means the book is available online through the O'Reilly Network Safari Bookshelf.

Safari offers a solution that's better than e-books. It's a virtual library that lets you easily search thousands of top tech books, cut and paste code samples, download chapters, and find quick answers when you need the most accurate, current information. Try it for free at *http://safari.oreilly.com*.

## Acknowledgments


I am very grateful for the help that I received while writing this book. In January 2004, when I read Jesse James Garrett's now famous article describing and coining the term *Ajax*, I felt that it was the start of a revolution in web development. Although some very innovative developers had already begun using Ajaxian techniques for a richer web experience, the movement really moved from a smoldering potential into a raging fire after early 2004. I am grateful to the army of developers who have crafted such frameworks as DWR (Joe Walker), Dojo, Rico (Richard Cowen, Bill Scott, Darren James), and Scriptaculous (Thomas Fuchs). Also, thanks to the Google Web Toolkit team and Ed Burns, Greg Murray, and Tor Norbye for their work on JavaServer Faces and Ajax.

Many evangelists have helped the movement as well. One site that has been a great source of information is Ajaxian.com, run by Ben Galbraith and Dion Almaer. Thanks to this site, much information and help for developers is available.

My editor, Mike Loukides, has been a huge help in this effort. Mike helped make many difficult subjects easy and turned some of my cryptic sentences into readable, understandable prose. He has been an invaluable resource.

The reviewers for this book have also been very helpful. Michael Davis examined much of the code and helped identify problems. David Lakis helped with the flow and helped make sure that the content was readable. Vimal Kansal reviewed many of the technical details.

Finally, I'm grateful to my family for putting up with me throughout this project. I'd like to thank my kids: Jordan, Erik, Stefani, Matthew, and Kyra. I couldn't have done this without the help and support of my wife, Erin; my thanks and love go especially to her.

—Steven Douglas Olson
*November 2006*

# CHAPTER 1
# Setup

To begin, you'll need to set up the environment for developing and deploying the Ajax examples in this book. This environment is different from that used for many other technologies.

## Requirements

To clarify, Ajax isn't a language or a software package; there is no single source of Ajax technology. If you're a Java developer, you probably already have many of the tools you need to work with Ajax.

Let's review the minimum requirements that you will need to develop an Ajax application with Java:

*Browser*
: You will need a browser that supports JavaScript (Internet Explorer, Safari, Mozilla, Opera, Firefox, etc.).

*Java Development Kit*
: You will need a Java compiler and libraries, preferably for Java 5 or Java 6.

*Apache Ant*
: You will need Apache Ant. You can get by without Ant, but only if you're a masochist. (An alternative is Maven. The examples in this book assume you're using Ant, but adapting them to Maven shouldn't be difficult.)

*Application server*
: The server piece can be any application server that can host Java servlets and can communicate via HTTP. The examples in this book have been developed using Sun's JDK 1.5 and Apache Tomcat 5.0, but there are many other application servers (such as JRun, JBoss, Resin, WebLogic, WebSphere, and Glassfish) that you can use with Ajax.

  If you are going to use a servlet container other than Tomcat, you can skip the "Installing Tomcat" section. However, I advise you to use Tomcat first; after you understand an example and have it running, then try it on a different server.

# Installing Tomcat

Start by downloading and installing the latest released version of Tomcat (browse to *http://jakarta.apache.org/tomcat/* and select the Current Releases link under the Downloads section). If you have never used Tomcat, you're in for a pleasant surprise. Tomcat is a great servlet engine that is used as the reference for the Java Servlet and JavaServer Pages technologies.

Tomcat is free, and Tomcat is mature. If you get a released production version, you will find that it is as stable as any production-version commercial application server. The Tomcat project also has good documentation; take advantage of it. If you're new to Tomcat, another good resource is Jason Brittain and Ian Darwin's *Tomcat: The Definitive Guide* (O'Reilly).

## A Minimalist Guide to Setting Up Tomcat

For Linux/Unix, download the *tar.gz* file and install it by running `tar -zxvf` in the directory where you want Tomcat to reside (e.g., */usr/local/tomcat*). For Windows, Tomcat ships as a self-extracting executable: just download and run *setup.exe* to install it.

Once you've installed Tomcat, start it running on Linux or Unix with the following command:

```
/<tomcat install directory>/bin/startup.sh
```

On Windows, use the following command:

```
\<tomcat install directory>\bin\startup.bat
```

Then start up a browser and browse to *http://localhost:8080* to see the Tomcat home page. From there you can run the example servlets to ensure that your installation is working correctly.

To shut down Tomcat, run the command `shutdown.sh` (Linux) or `shutdown.bat` (Windows) from your install directory.

## Setting TOMCAT_HOME

All the examples in this book will be built and deployed with Ant. (If you're not familiar with Ant and the concept of build files, you might want to take some time to familiarize yourself with them now.) The build files will require the `TOMCAT_HOME` environment variable to be set properly, to ensure that when you deploy your applications, *build.xml* will copy everything you need into the *webapps* directory of the Tomcat server.

To check the value of `TOMCAT_HOME` on a Windows machine, type `set` from a command prompt. Along with the other environment variables, you should see:

```
TOMCAT_HOME=c:\apps\Tomcat5.0
```

`TOMCAT_HOME` should be set to the location where you installed Tomcat. If it is not, set `TOMCAT_HOME` using the environment variables setup screen (Start → Control Panel → System Properties → Advanced → Environment Variables). If you don't know how to do this, open Help from the Start menu and search for "environment variables."

On Linux, from a command prompt type the command `set | grep TOMCAT`. You should see something like this:

```
TOMCAT_HOME=/usr/local/tomcat/Tomcat5.0
```

Again, the value of `TOMCAT_HOME` should be the directory where you installed Tomcat. If it isn't, you need to set it correctly. Usually this requires adding an `export` command such as the following to a resource file like *.bashrc*:

```
export TOMCAT_HOME=/usr/local/tomcat/Tomcat5.0
```

# Installing Ant

To run the examples in this book, you'll also need to download and install the Ant project. Browse to *http://ant.apache.org* and grab the latest version.

Make sure that the *bin* directory of your Ant installation is in your path, and then type `ant` at the command prompt. Ant should come back with the message "Build file does not exist." This message means that Ant is installed correctly and could not find the *build.xml* file when it tried to load it.

If you don't have Ant installed correctly, you will see an error such as "executable file ant not found." In this case, check to make sure that your `PATH` environment variable is set to include the *bin* directory of the Ant installation. As with `TOMCAT_HOME`, Windows users can set the `PATH` variable through System Properties (Start → Control Panel → System Properties → Advanced → Environment Variables), while Linux and Unix users must add lines such as the following to their shell's initialization file (most likely *.bashrc*):

```
export TOMCAT_HOME=/usr/local/tomcat/Tomcat5.0
export PATH=$PATH:$TOMCAT_HOME/bin
```

Once you have Ant installed correctly, you can use it to build the applications presented in this book. If you need more information on Ant, consult the documentation at *http://ant.apache.org* or one of the many books written about Ant. Steve Holzner's *Ant: The Definitive Guide* (O'Reilly) is the reference I use, and it has served me well.

# CHAPTER 2
# JavaScript for Ajax

Ajax is centered around the clever use of JavaScript. It isn't a web framework, like Struts or Tapestry, and it isn't some fancy new technology with a cool acronym; Ajax boils down to using JavaScript to interact directly with the web server, avoiding the submit/response cycle all too familiar to web users.

Java programmers have typically avoided JavaScript, sometimes for good reasons and sometimes for bad ones. Certainly, adding another layer of scripting to a JSP page can only add to the confusion. However, JavaScript runs entirely on the browser and is therefore very fast. There's no waiting for the server to generate a response: JavaScript can compute a result and update the page immediately.

Ajax adds server interaction, but without the Submit button. Whenever data is needed, the JavaScript in the web page makes a request, and the server replies with data—but not another HTML page. The server returns data that the JavaScript displays in the existing page. The result is that your web application feels a lot more like a desktop application. In short, you can achieve a rich application experience in your web pages by using Ajax.

This book won't attempt to teach JavaScript, or even to analyze its pros and cons. I assume that you have had some exposure to JavaScript. If you're new to it, check out *JavaScript: The Definitive Guide*, by David Flanagan (O'Reilly). This is the best JavaScript reference available. JavaScript isn't Java, though reading JavaScript code shouldn't be hard for any Java developer. You will find that the JavaScript used in this chapter is pretty easy; as long as you can get through the syntax, you shouldn't need to review or study JavaScript just yet.

## Creating the Application

We'll begin with the complete HTML and JavaScript code for our first application, a simple web page that displays the decimal value of any character. Then we'll break apart the JavaScript and examine it.

The HTML is presented in Example 2-1.

*Example 2-1. index.html*

```
<html>
<head>
    <link rel="stylesheet" type="text/css" href="style.css">
    <SCRIPT language="JavaScript" src="ajax.js"></SCRIPT>
    <title>Ajax On Java, Chapter 2 Example</title>
</head>
<body onload="focusIn( );">
    <h1> AJAX CHARACTER DECODER </h1>
    <h2> Press a key to find its value. </h2>
    <table>
        <tr>
            <td>
                Enter Key Here ->
                <input type="text" id="key" name="key"
                       onkeyup="convertToDecimal( );">
            </td>
        </tr>
    </table>
    <br />
    <table>
        <tr>
            <td colspan="5" style="border-bottom:solid black 1px;">
                Key Pressed:
                <input type="text" readonly id="keypressed">
            </td>
        </tr>
        <tr>
            <td> Decimal </td>
        </tr>
        <tr>
            <td><input type="text" readonly id="decimal"></td>
        </tr>
    </table>
</body>
</html>
```

For the most part, this is standard HTML. There are only two JavaScript references: `focusIn( )` and `convertToDecimal( )`. The `focusIn( )` function merely puts the cursor in the right input field when the page loads, so the user doesn't have to move it there with the mouse.

The `convertToDecimal( )` function will be our entry into the Ajax world. Example 2-2 lays out the JavaScript code that supports our web page, *ajax.js*.

*Example 2-2. ajax.js*

```
var req;

function convertToDecimal( ) {
    var key = document.getElementById("key");
```

*Example 2-2. ajax.js (continued)*

```
    var keypressed = document.getElementById("keypressed");
    keypressed.value = key.value;
    var url = "/ajaxdecimalcodeconverter/response?key=" + escape(key.value);
    if (window.XMLHttpRequest) {
        req = new XMLHttpRequest( );
    }
    else if (window.ActiveXObject) {
        req = new ActiveXObject("Microsoft.XMLHTTP");
    }
    req.open("Get",url,true);
    req.onreadystatechange = callback;
    req.send(null);
}

function callback( ) {
    if (req.readyState==4) {
        if (req.status == 200) {
            var decimal = document.getElementById('decimal');
            decimal.value = req.responseText;
        }
    }
    clear( );
}
function clear( ) {
    var key = document.getElementById("key");
    key.value="";
}
function focusIn( ) {
    document.getElementById("key").focus( );
}
```

Let's take a look at `convertToDecimal( )`, which is our entry point from *index.html*. The main JavaScript object we'll use is `XMLHttpRequest`. Unfortunately, one problem with JavaScript is that the code isn't the same on all browsers. In Mozilla, Firefox, and Safari, we get an `XMLHttpRequest` object like this:

```
new XMLHttpRequest( );
```

In Internet Explorer, we use an ActiveX object:

```
new ActiveXObject("Microsoft.XMLHTTP");
```

Because we can't tell in advance which browsers users will view our web page with, we have to write code that will work on any of the likely candidates. First, we must determine whether the user is using Internet Explorer or some other browser, such as Firefox or Mozilla. This task is handled by the following code:

```
if (window.XMLHttpRequest) {
    req = new XMLHttpRequest( );
}
else if (window.ActiveXObject) {
    req = new ActiveXObject("Microsoft.XMLHTTP");
}
```

That's basically it: req is now an object that we can use to build our Ajax page.

Now let's look at some code that does some real work. We will be using the code from *axax.js* in the next chapter, so examine it closely and pay special attention to the mechanism that talks to the server. Since we're Java developers, the backend will be a servlet, but the web page doesn't care.

The convertToDecimal( ) function first gets a String from the form and then sets the url variable to "/ajaxdecimalcodeconverter/response?key=...". Eventually, we'll send this URL to the server (in our case, a servlet) and expect a response (the decimal value of the key), but we're not going to send it in response to a Submit button press; we're going to send it asynchronously (that is, as soon as we have the keystroke that we want to convert).

After the if/else block, where we figure out which browser is being used and get an appropriate req object, we open a connection to the servlet with the call:

```
req.open("Get",url,true);
```

Let's look at the three parameters in the req.open( ) function:

"Get"
: The first parameter tells JavaScript whether to submit the request to the server using HTTPPost( ) or HTTPGet( ). The HTTPPost( ) method hides the parameters in the request; the HTTPGet( ) method puts the parameters in the URL for everyone to see. For this example, I chose HTTPGet( ) because it is easier to see what parameters are being passed, and the number of parameters is relatively small. If I were sending a complex set of parameters, I'd use "Post" instead.*

url
: The second parameter is the URL we're passing to the server. We created that URL earlier in the method.

true
: The last parameter determines whether or not the call is asynchronous. When this parameter is true, the request is sent asynchronously. When designing Ajax applications, you always want to set the asynchronous flag to true; basically, it means "don't stop anything, just notify me when the data comes back."

The alternative is to pass false for the third parameter to req.open( ). That will make the browser freeze until the server comes back—if it comes back (there's no guarantee). This never leads to a positive user experience, so you should always set the third parameter to true.

* I'm getting quite a ways ahead of the story, but it's a good idea to use Get only when the request doesn't make any changes to the data on the server. That's clearly the case here. Conversely, it's a bad idea to use Get when you are changing data on the server (for example, if you're sending new data, or deleting existing data); in this case, use Post instead.

Now, notice the next statement:

```
req.onreadystatechange=callback;
```

This line allows us to use the call asynchronously. We're telling the `req` object to call the `callback( )` function whenever a state transition occurs. Therefore, we can process data coming back from the server as soon as it arrives; whenever something happens, we'll be notified.

### What Is a Callback?

A *callback* is executable code that is passed as a parameter to another function. In our example, we pass code to the `XMLHTTPRequest` object, which tells us what function to call when it is ready.

The JavaScript code generates a request that is sent to a servlet. When the servlet returns with the information, the callback function is invoked; in turn, the callback function can display the new information to the user. We specified which function to call with the following JavaScript code:

```
req.onreadystatechange = callback;
```

This is really powerful. There's no more waiting on the page; when the data returns, the user will see it without having to wait for a page reload.

The last statement of `convertToDecimal( )` sends the request:

```
req.send(null);
```

Now, let's look at the `callback( )` function:

```
function callback( ) {
    if (req.readyState==4) {
        if (req.status == 200) {
            if (window.XMLHttpRequest) {
                nonMSPopulate( );
            }
            else if (window.ActiveXObject) {
                msPopulate( );
            }
        }
    }
    clear( );
}
```

This function checks the `readyState` and the status returned by the server. The `readyState` can have one of five values, listed in Table 2-1.

*Table 2-1. readyState values*

| Value | State |
|---|---|
| 0 | Uninitialized |
| 1 | Loading |
| 2 | Loaded |
| 3 | Interactive |
| 4 | Complete |

The `callback( )` function is called on every state change, but that's not exactly what we want. We don't want to do anything until our request has completed, so we wait until `req.readyState == 4`.

The next check, `req.status == 200`, ensures that the `HTTPRequest` returned a status of OK (`200`). If the page is not found, `status` will equal `404`. In this example, the code should be activated only when the request has been completed. Note that a `readyState` of `4` doesn't tell us that the request completed *correctly*; all we know is that it completed. We still have to check the `req.status` code.

For a complete list of HTTP status codes, see *http://www.w3.org/Protocols/rfc2616/rfc2616-sec10.html.*

## How Is Our JavaScript Function Called?

We've written a nice JavaScript function, `convertToDecimal( )`, that does some interesting things: it sends a request to the server without intervention by the user, and it arranges for the server's response to be added to the web page. But how does `convertToDecimal( )` get called? The browser calls it when it detects the `keyup` event on the "Enter Key Here ->" input field. Here is the complete HTML for the input field:

```
<input type="text" id="key" name="key" onkeyup="convertToDecimal( );">
```

`onkeyup="convertToDecimal( );"` tells the browser to call the JavaScript function `convertToDecimal( )` whenever the user presses and releases a key in the input field.

Why are we using the `onkeyup` trigger as opposed to `onkeypress`? This is a "gotcha" that you must understand. The `onkeypress` event seems like it should work for this application, but it doesn't. `onkeypress` and `onkeydown` trigger their actions before the character makes it into the field, sending whatever is in the field prior to the key press. Since we want to read the actual character, we need to use the `onkeyup` trigger instead.

## How Do We Get the Value of the Key Pressed?

Once control is passed to convertToXML( ), we make this call:

```
var key = document.getElementById("key");
```

At this point, the object with the id of key contains the decimal value of the key that was pressed. All that's left for us to do is retrieve the value that the object named key contains. This value is kept in the value parameter of the key element, so key.value contains the value of the key that was pressed.

Once we've retrieved it, we want to place this value in a field for display. That allows us to clear the field used to enter the key. We've named the field for displaying the key keypressed. Here's how to retrieve the keypressed field:

```
var keypressed = document.getElementById("keypressed");
```

The next step is to put the value of key into the value of keypressed:

```
keypressed.value = key.value;
```

## Formatting the Page

The final step in developing our application is to create a CSS file to give the page some formatting. This file is presented in Example 2-3.

*Example 2-3. style.css*

```
body {
    font-family: Arial, Helvetica, sans-serif;
    font-size: small;
    text-align:center;
    background:#cbdada;
}
#keypressed{
    width:30;
    border:none;
}
#key {
    width:20px;
    padding:0;
    margin:0;
    border:none;
    text-align:left
}
h1, h2 {
    font-size:120%;
    text-align:center;
}
```

*Example 2-3. style.css (continued)*

```
h2 {
    font-size:110%
}
table, input {
    margin-left:auto;
    margin-right:auto;
    padding:0px 10px;
    text-align:center;
    color:black;
    text-align:center;
    background: #a0f6f5;
    border:solid black 1px;
}
td {
    margin:10px 10px;
    padding: 0px 5px;
    border: none;
}
input {
    width: 80;
    border: none;
    border-top:solid #999999 1px;
    font-size: 80%;
    color: #555555;
}
```

## Running the Example

If you download the code for this example from this book's web site (*http://www.oreilly.com/catalog/9780596101879*), you can simply copy the files from the *ch02* directory. Some developers prefer to hand-type the example code, which does help solidify the examples in one's mind.

To run the example:

1. Save the HTML code from Example 2-1 in a file called *index.html*.
2. Save the JavaScript from Example 2-2 in a file called *ajax.js* in the same directory.
3. Save the CSS code from Example 2-3 in a file called *style.css* in the same directory.
4. Open *index.html* with a browser; you should see something similar to Figure 2-1.

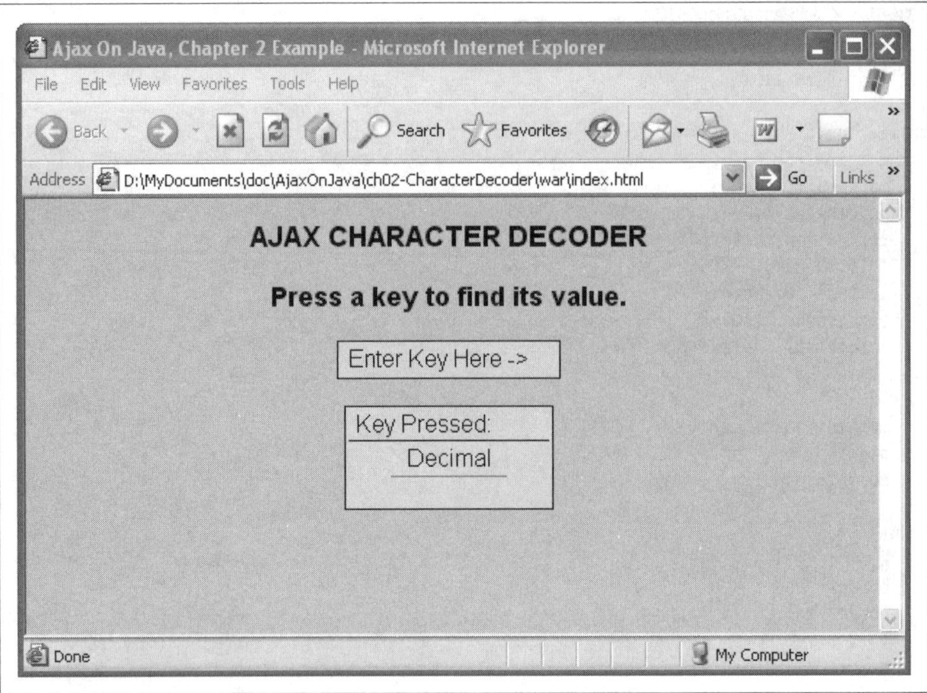


*Figure 2-1. The Ajax Character Decoder running in Internet Explorer*

When you press a key, the key will show up in the "Key Pressed:" field and the input field will be cleared. Since the server isn't implemented yet, you won't see the decimal value. In the next chapter, we'll hook up a servlet that populates the Decimal field.

CHAPTER 3

# A Simple Ajax Servlet

In the previous chapter, we wrote a JavaScript/HTML client for a system that converts keystrokes to the corresponding decimal values. Now we need to focus on the backend: the Java servlet that provides the client with the information it needs. The `XMLHTTPRequest( )` function in the client sends a request out into the ether; it doesn't care what kind of server replies. The response can come from a PHP server, a .NET server, a server hosting Ruby on Rails, a Java server, and so on. Any server that can receive an `HTTPRequest` and respond with an `HTTPResponse` will do.

Since this is a book for Java developers, we'll create a servlet that intercepts the request, converts the keystroke into its decimal representation, and sends the resulting data back to the client.

The first version of our servlet is very simple: it computes a single result (the value of the keystroke in decimal) and sends it back to the client. The complete servlet code is presented in Example 3-1.

*Example 3-1. The AjaxResponseServlet*

```
/*
 * Converts a character to decimal and sends back the
 * value in the response.
 */
package com.oreilly.ajax.servlet;

import java.io.IOException;
import javax.servlet.ServletException;
import javax.servlet.http.HttpServlet;
import javax.servlet.http.HttpServletRequest;
import javax.servlet.http.HttpServletResponse;

public class AjaxResponseServlet extends HttpServlet {
```

*Example 3-1. The AjaxResponseServlet (continued)*

```
    private static final long serialVersionUID = 1L;

    public void doGet(HttpServletRequest req, HttpServletResponse res)
            throws ServletException, IOException {

        String key = req.getParameter("key");
        if (key != null) {
            // extract the first character from key
            // as an int, then convert that int to a String
            int keychar = key.charAt(0);
            String decimalString = Integer.toString(keychar);
            // set up the response
            res.setContentType("text/xml");
            res.setHeader("Cache-Control", "no-cache");
            // write out the response string
            res.getWriter( ).write(decimalString);
        }
        else {
            // if key comes back as a null, return a question mark
            res.setContentType("text/xml");
            res.setHeader("Cache-Control", "no-cache");
            res.getWriter( ).write("?");
        }
    }
}
```

If you are experienced with servlets, you should understand what this code is doing. In case you haven't used servlets before, however, let's walk through the code.

The HTTP protocol allows the client and server to communicate with either a `POST` or a `GET` command. The `GET` command sends variables through the URL, as in *http://localhost/application?name=steve*. The `POST` command sends the data embedded in the client request.

For more information on the HTTP protocol, see Clinton Wong's *HTTP Pocket Reference* or *HTTP: The Definitive Guide*, by David Gourley et al. (both from O'Reilly).

When you write a servlet, you generally extend `HttpServlet` and override `doGet( )`, `doPost( )`, or both. Our client makes a simple `GET` request, so we only have to override one method:

```
doGet(request,response)
```

First we retrieve the key from the request:

```
String key = req.getParameter("key");
```

Next we check whether the key is `null`; if it is not `null`, we can begin to operate on it. In this case, we get its decimal value:

```
if (key != null) {
    // extract the first character from key
    // as an int, then convert that int to a String
    int keychar = key.charAt(0);
    String decimalString = Integer.toString(keychar);
```

Once we have the decimal value of the key, we set up the response and send a string containing the code:

```
    // set up the response
    res.setContentType("text/xml");
    res.setHeader("Cache-Control", "no-cache");
    // write out the response string
    res.getWriter( ).write(decimalString);
}
```

Again, this should be very familiar if you've worked with servlets before. We set the content type, tell the browser not to use caching, and write the result (a `String`) to the output stream (a `Writer`) we get from the response. That's all there is to it!

Now let's create a *web.xml* deployment descriptor and write an Ant build file to compile and run the code. The *web.xml* file is presented in Example 3-2.

*Example 3-2. web.xml*

```
<!DOCTYPE web-app
    PUBLIC  "-//Sun Microsystems, Inc.//DTD Web Application 2.2//EN"
    "http://java.sun.com/j2ee/dtds/web-app_2_2.dtd">
<web-app>
    <servlet>
        <servlet-name>AjaxResponseServlet</servlet-name>
        <servlet-class>
            com.AJAXbook.servlet.AjaxResponseServlet
        </servlet-class>
        <load-on-startup>1</load-on-startup>
    </servlet>
    <servlet-mapping>
        <servlet-name>AjaxResponseServlet</servlet-name>
        <url-pattern>/response</url-pattern>
    </servlet-mapping>
    <welcome-file-list>
        <welcome-file>index.html</welcome-file>
    </welcome-file-list>
</web-app>
```

There is only one servlet in this web application, the `AjaxResponseServlet`. That servlet is set to intercept requests at */response*. The `<servlet-mapping>` in *web.xml* must match the `url` value in the `convertToDecimal( )` function of *index.html*.

We'll place this *web.xml* file in the *war/WEB-INF* directory.

## Building and Deploying the Ajax Application

We now have all the components required to build the example. If you have never used Ant, you are about to be surprised by a powerful tool.

An Ant tutorial is beyond the scope of this book. If you don't understand the *build.xml* file in this section, you should refer to the Ant documentation at *http://ant.apache.org*.

The *build.xml* file presented in Example 3-3 builds the project and moves it to the *tomcat/webapps* directory; that's all Tomcat needs in order to begin running the web application. Make sure you have set TOMCAT_HOME to the directory where you installed Tomcat. Refer back to Chapter 1 for setup details.

*Example 3-3. build.xml*

```
<?xml version="1.0"?>
<project name="CH03 AJAX-CODECONVERTER" default="compile" basedir=".">

    <property environment="env"/>
    <property name="src.dir" value="src"/>
    <property name="war.dir" value="war"/>
    <property name="class.dir" value="${war.dir}/WEB-INF/classes"/>
    <property name="lib.dir" value="${war.dir}/WEB-INF/lib"/>
    <property name="webapp.dir"
              value="${env.TOMCAT_HOME}/webapps/ch03-ajaxcharacterconverter"/>

    <path id="ajax.class.path">
        <fileset dir="${lib.dir}">
            <include name="*.jar"/>
        </fileset>
    </path>

    <target name="init">
        <mkdir dir="${class.dir}"/>
    </target>

    <target name="compile" depends="init"
            description="Compiles all source code.">
        <javac srcdir="${src.dir}" destdir="${class.dir}" debug="on"
               classpathref="ajax.class.path"/>
    </target>

    <target name="clean" description="Erases contents of classes dir">
        <delete dir="${class.dir}"/>
    </target>

    <target name="deploy" depends="compile"
            description="Copies the contents of web-app to destination dir">
```

*Example 3-3. build.xml (continued)*

```
        <copy todir="${webapp.dir}">
            <fileset dir="${war.dir}"/>
        </copy>
    </target>

</project>
```

When you've created the *build.xml* file, you should be able to build and deploy the project with the following command:

```
ant deploy
```

## Directory Structure

For the build to work correctly, you must have the directory structure just right. Figure 3-1 shows the directory structure that I use with Eclipse. It can be modified, but *build.xml* should reflect the directory structure you are using.

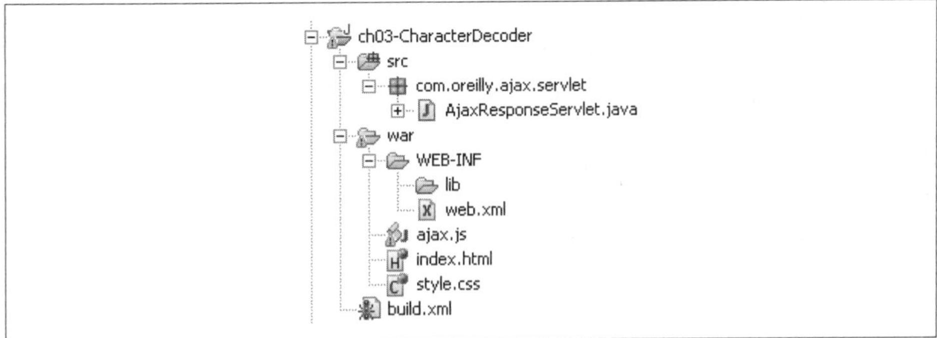


*Figure 3-1. Directory structure for Ajax Character Decoder (first version)*

# Running the Example

Start Tomcat and open a browser. Enter the address where you deployed the application. If you deployed it using the *build.xml* file in this book, the address should be *http://localhost:8080/ajax-decimal/index.html*.

Your browser should display the page shown in Figure 3-2. When you press a key, the JavaScript will move the key pressed to the "Key Pressed:" field, clear the input field, and make a request to the server to convert the key to its decimal value. The server then does the simple conversion and returns the value, which is picked up by the callback function and put into the Decimal field.

Congratulations! You've just completed a full Ajax-enhanced Java application. As simple as the application is, it demonstrates most of the major components you need in order to develop Ajax applications with Java.

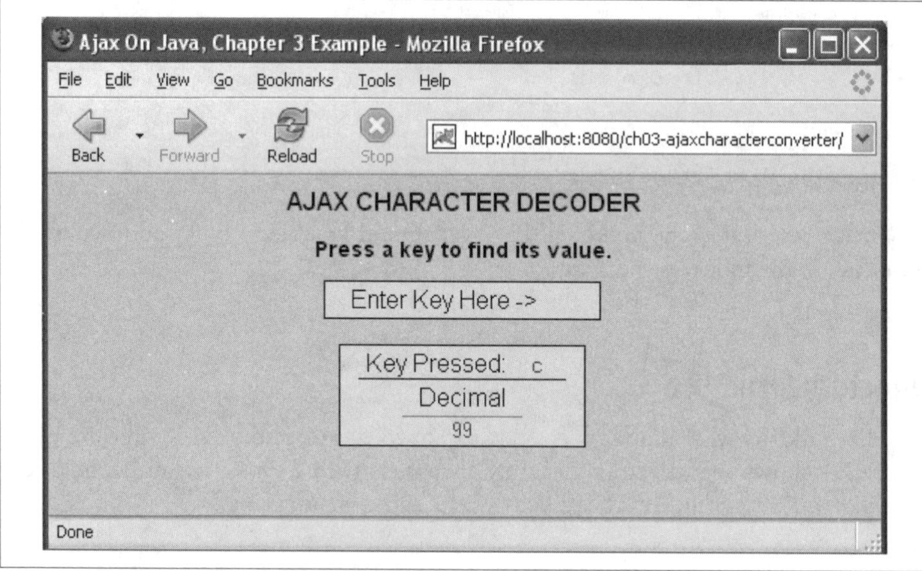


*Figure 3-2. Ajax Character Decoder running in Mozilla Firefox*

Notice that I said *most*, not all, of the components. We are still missing an important piece of Ajax: XML. And, to be sure, there are fancier, cleverer ways to do things: we can use JSF components and the like, and we can come up with better ways to handle the IE/Firefox differences. But still, we now have a working application. Everything else is icing on the cake.

## So Where's the XML?

It's true, there is no XML in this example. I avoided XML for two reasons: I wanted to keep the first example as simple as possible, and to show that you don't really have to use XML with Ajax.

So how does XML fit into Ajax? Because Ajax is about passing data back and forth between the browser and the server, there is a need to parse that data. In this very simple example, we only passed one field from the browser to the server and one field back from the server to the browser. In this case, XML is overkill. However, for real-world applications, you'll need to move more complex data, and you'll want a more structured way to represent your data.

The next chapter will illustrate how easy it is to use XML with Ajax to parse the data coming from the server. It will also demonstrate how to use JavaScript Object Notation (JSON), a native JavaScript data representation that you may find more convenient than XML.

CHAPTER 4

# XML and JSON for Ajax

Do you really need XML for an Ajax application? The previous chapter showed that you don't always need XML. In particular, if you only have one data point, XML is overkill. But the fact is, most web applications deal with multiple data points: usernames, passwords, addresses, cities, states, zip codes, etc. How will you decipher those fields when they're sent back from the server?

In some cases, passing a string of delimited values may seem like the simplest approach, but using XML has advantages. For one thing, XML is self-documenting. During debugging, you can look at the XML string and see exactly what goes where; that is a luxury you won't have with a string of comma-separated values.

Another reason for using XML is that an XML parser is built into most browsers. The parsing work has already been done for you; all you have to do is leverage the built-in parser. Sure, you could pass the data in other formats—Java properties files, comma or tab-separated values, YAML files, or a cute custom format that you've designed yourself—but then you would have to write your own parser in JavaScript.

There is another good way to send data to and from the server: JavaScript Object Notation (JSON). We will discuss JSON toward the end of this chapter.

## The Character Decoder

The example in this chapter is similar to the one in the previous chapter, but instead of the server returning one data point, it's going to return five. Retuning a small collection of data shows what happens when you go beyond a single data point and illustrates why most Ajax applications need XML or some other way to structure the data that is passed from the server to the client.

Figure 4-1 shows how the user interface of the application will look when we're done. The design is simple enough: we send a character to the server using

XMLHttpRequest( ), and the server responds with a String containing the five conversions in XML format (decimal, octal, hexadecimal, binary, and HTML). The callback( ) function in the client then calls a function to parse the XML and populate the fields in the browser.

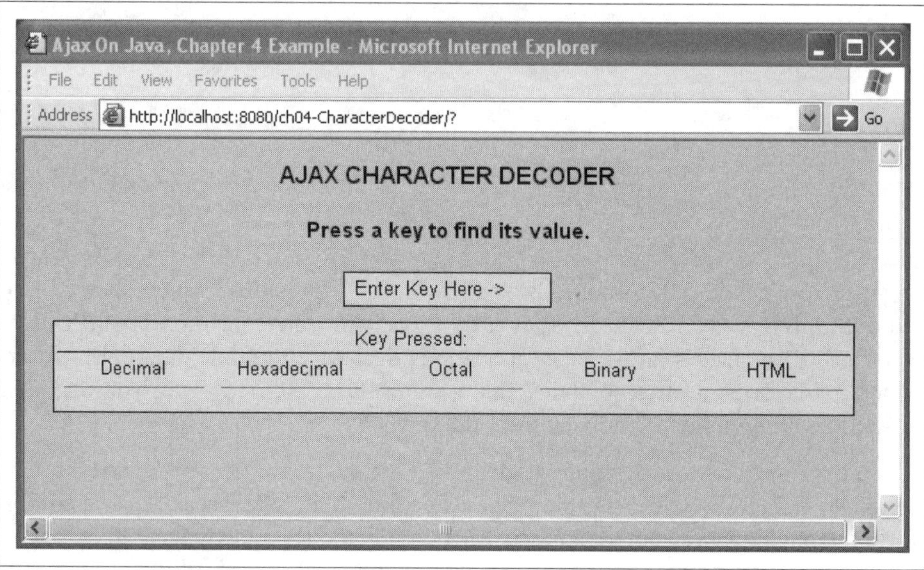


*Figure 4-1. The complete Ajax Character Decoder example*

Now it starts to get fun. One keystroke fills in all the data fields, and although it doesn't look like much is going on from the user's perspective, from the programmer's perspective we know that the application is communicating with the server without a clunky submit or reload or any waiting for the page to refresh.

## Setting Up a Simple XML Document

Before we delve into the code, we need to make some decisions. We're going to return data using XML, but how should that XML be structured? What should our XML response look like? We don't want anything complex, so we'll aim to create an XML document that looks like this:

```
<converted-values>
    <decimal>97</decimal>
    <hexadecimal>0x61</hexadecimal>
    <octal>0141</octal>
    <hyper>&amp;0x61;</hyper>
    <binary>1100001B</binary>
</converted-values>
```

With this format, the browser can use its document object model (DOM) parser to index and retrieve the data.

There are many ways to create this XML document. For the sake of simplicity, we'll first use a StringBuffer to wrap the data with XML tags. Later, we'll look at other ways to create the XML document.

When I talk about XML formatting, I'm referring to the server wrapping the data in XML. The client receives the XML-formatted string in the HTTPResponse and parses it for the individual data fields. The client passes data through the request using either HTTPPost( ) or HTTPGet( ). There is no reason for the client to send XML data to the server, because the data is already wrapped in the request as name/value pairs.

## Using a Servlet to Build an XML Document

Let's start by looking at the servlet code that wraps the data in XML. This servlet is shown in Example 4-1.

*Example 4-1. The AjaxResponseServlet*

```
/*
 * Converts a character to hex, decimal, binary, octal, and HTML, then
 * wraps each of the fields with XML and sends them back through the response.
 */
package com.AJAXbook.servlet;

import java.io.IOException;

import javax.servlet.ServletException;
import javax.servlet.http.HttpServlet;
import javax.servlet.http.HttpServletRequest;
import javax.servlet.http.HttpServletResponse;


public class AjaxResponseServlet extends HttpServlet {

    public void doGet(HttpServletRequest req, HttpServletResponse res)
          throws ServletException, IOException {
        // key is the parameter passed in from the JavaScript
        // variable named url (see index.html)
        String key = req.getParameter("key");
        StringBuffer returnXML = null;
        if (key != null) {
            // extract the first character from key
            // as an int, then convert that int to a String
            int keyInt = key.charAt(0);
            returnXML = new StringBuffer("\r\n<converted-values>");
            returnXML.append("\r\n<decimal>"+
                             Integer.toString(keyInt)+"</decimal>");
            returnXML.append("\r\n<hexadecimal>0x"+
                             Integer.toString(keyInt,16)+"</hexadecimal>");
            returnXML.append("\r\n<octal>0"+
                             Integer.toString(keyInt,8)+"</octal>");
```

*Example 4-1. The AjaxResponseServlet (continued)*

```
            returnXML.append("\r\n<hyper>&amp;0x"+
                            Integer.toString(keyInt,16)+";</hyper>");
            returnXML.append("\r\n<binary>"+
                            Integer.toString(keyInt,2)+"B</binary>");
            returnXML.append("\r\n</converted-values>");

            // set up the response
            res.setContentType("text/xml");
            res.setHeader("Cache-Control", "no-cache");
            // write out the XML string
            res.getWriter().write(returnXML.toString( ));
        }
        else {
            // if key comes back as a null, return a question mark
            res.setContentType("text/xml");
            res.setHeader("Cache-Control", "no-cache");
            res.getWriter( ).write("?");
        }
    }
}
```

This code is similar to the code from Chapter 3. The only thing that has been added is the code to wrap the data with XML tags:

```
returnXML = new StringBuffer("\r\n<converted-values>");
returnXML.append("\r\n<decimal>"+
                Integer.toString(keyInt)+"</decimal>");
returnXML.append("\r\n<hexadecimal>0x"+
                Integer.toString(keyInt,16)+"</hexadecimal>");
returnXML.append("\r\n<octal>0"+
                Integer.toString(keyInt,8)+"</octal>");
returnXML.append("\r\n<hyper>&amp;0x"+
                Integer.toString(keyInt,16)+";</hyper>");
returnXML.append("\r\n<binary>"+
                Integer.toString(keyInt,2)+"B</binary>");
returnXML.append("\r\n</converted-values>");
```

This code simply sets up a `StringBuffer` called `returnXML`. We then convert the incoming value to decimal, hex, etc.; wrap it with an appropriate XML tag; and append it to the buffer. When we've finished all five conversions and added the closing tag (`</converted-values>`), we send the response back to the Ajax client using `res.getWriter().write( )`. We return a question mark (without any XML wrapping) if the key we received was `null`.

## Other Ways to Build the XML Document

Building an XML document by appending to a `StringBuffer` is a common approach, but it's far from ideal, particularly if you need to generate a large document programmatically. Fortunately, there are alternatives.

### JDOM

One option is to use the JDOM library to write the XML. Download the *jdom.jar* file from *http://www.jdom.org*, and put it in your application's *WEB-INF/lib* directory. Then, instead of writing to a StringBuffer, use JDOM to build the XML, as shown in Example 4-2.

*Example 4-2. Using JDOM to create the XML document*

```
// additional imports needed for JDOM
import org.jdom.Document;
import org.jdom.Element;
import org.jdom.output.XMLOutputter;

public String createJdomXML(int key) throws IOException {
    Document document = new Document( );
    // create root node
    Element root = new org.jdom.Element("converted-values");
    document.setRootElement(root);

    // create your node
    org.jdom.Element element = new org.jdom.Element("decimal");
    // add content to the node
    element.addContent(Integer.toString(key));
    // add your node to root
    root.addContent(element);

    element = new org.jdom.Element("hexadecimal");
    element.addContent("0x" + Integer.toString(key, 16));
    root.addContent(element);
    element = new org.jdom.Element("octal");
    element.addContent("0" + Integer.toString(key, 8));
    root.addContent(element);
    element = new org.jdom.Element("hyper");
    element.addContent("&0x" + Integer.toString(key, 16));
    root.addContent(element);
    element = new org.jdom.Element("binary");
    element.addContent(Integer.toString(key, 2) + "B");
    root.addContent(element);

    // output JDOM document as a String of bytes
    XMLOutputter outputter = new XMLOutputter( );
    return outputter.outputString(document);
}
```

In the preceding code, we first create a Document (org.jdom.Document), then an Element named root with the String "converted-values" as its value. That element becomes the root of the XML document. Here's what the document looks like at this point:

```
<converted-values>
</converted-values>
```

To add child elements to the root, we create new elements and add them to the root element. The code that creates the `decimal` element and adds it to the root element looks like this:

```
org.jdom.Element element = new org.jdom.Element("decimal");
element.addContent(Integer.toString(key));
root.addContent(element);
```

We repeat this process until we've added all the elements to the root. Then we use an `XMLOutputter` to format the document into a `String` that we can send back to the client. The JDOM XML document now looks like this (with linefeeds and spaces added for readability):

```
<?xml version="1.0" encoding="UTF-8"?>
<converted-values>
    <decimal>97</decimal>
    <hexadecimal>0x61</hexadecimal>
    <octal>0141</octal>
    <hyper>&amp;0x61</hyper>
    <binary>1100001B</binary>
</converted-values>
```

## dom4j

dom4j is an XML library similar in intent to JDOM. After downloading dom4j from *http://www.dom4j.org/download.html* and installing it in your application's *WEB-INF/lib* directory, you can use it to create your XML document. As shown in Example 4-3, we create a document, add a root element to the document, add the elements and data to the root, and then return the document in a `String`.

*Example 4-3. Using dom4j to create the XML document*

```
// additional imports for dom4j
import org.dom4j.Document;
import org.dom4j.DocumentHelper;
import org.dom4j.DocumentException;
import org.dom4j.Element;
import org.dom4j.io.OutputFormat;
import org.dom4j.io.XMLWriter;

...

public String createDom4jXML(int key) throws IOException {
    Document document = DocumentHelper.createDocument( );
    Element root = document.addElement("converted-values");

    Element element = root.addElement("decimal").addText(
            Integer.toString(key));
    element = root.addElement("hexadecimal").addText(
            "0x" + Integer.toString(key, 16));
    element = root.addElement("octal").addText("0" + Integer.toString(key, 8));
    element = root.addElement("hyper").addText("&0x" + Integer.toString(key, 16));
```

*Example 4-3. Using dom4j to create the XML document (continued)*

```
    element = root.addElement("binary").addText(Integer.toString(key, 2) + "B");
    StringBuffer xmlDoc = null;

    StringWriter sw = new StringWriter( );
    OutputFormat outformat = OutputFormat.createPrettyPrint( );
    XMLWriter writer = new XMLWriter(sw, outformat);
    writer.write(document);
    writer.close( );
    xmlDoc = sw.getBuffer( );

    return xmlDoc.toString( );
}
```

The dom4j library uses the static method `DocumentHelper.createDocument( )` to create the XML document. The method `root.addElement( )` puts a child element on the root element, and `addText( )` puts the data in the elements. The `OutputFormat` class is then used to format the `XMLDocument`, so the document looks like this:

```
<?xml version="1.0" encoding="UTF-8"?>
<converted-values>
    <decimal>97</decimal>
    <hexadecimal>0x61</hexadecimal>
    <octal>0141</octal>
    <hyper>&amp;0x61</hyper>
    <binary>1100001B</binary>
</converted-values>
```

This step can be skipped, because it only formats the document for readability by adding linefeeds and spaces. Since humans shouldn't need to read this document (unless you are debugging), you won't need the formatting.

To use dom4j without the formatting, simply replace these two lines:

```
OutputFormat outformat = OutputFormat.createPrettyPrint( );
XMLWriter writer = new XMLWriter(sw, outformat);
```

with this line:

```
XMLWriter writer = new XMLWriter(sw);
```

## SAX

SAX, the Simple API for XML, provides another way to create an XML document for an Ajax application. It may be faster than JDOM or dom4J, because it doesn't require building a DOM tree for your document. Start by initializing a `StringWriter` and a `StreamResult`. Initialize the `StreamResult` with the `StreamWriter`, then get a `SAXTransformerFactory` and get a `TransformerHandler` from that. The `TransformerHandler` allows you to create an XML document by starting a document and appending elements and data to the `TransformerHandler`. Example 4-4 shows how it works.

*Example 4-4. Using SAX to write out the XML document*

```
// additional imports for writing XML with SAX
import java.io.*;
import org.xml.sax.helpers.AttributesImpl;
import javax.xml.transform.sax.SAXTransformerFactory;
import javax.xml.transform.sax.TransformerHandler;

public String createSAXXML(int key) {
    Writer writer = new StringWriter( );
    StreamResult streamResult = new StreamResult(writer);

    SAXTransformerFactory transformerFactory =
            (SAXTransformerFactory) SAXTransformerFactory.newInstance( );
    try {
        String data = null;
        TransformerHandler transformerHandler =
                transformerFactory.newTransformerHandler( );

        transformerHandler.setResult(streamResult);
        // start the document
        transformerHandler.startDocument( );
        // list all the attributes for element
        AttributesImpl attr = new AttributesImpl( );
        // start writing elements
        // every start tag and end tag has to be defined explicitly
        transformerHandler.startElement(null,null, "converted-values", null);
        transformerHandler.startElement(null,null,"decimal",null);
        data = Integer.toString(key, 10);
        transformerHandler.characters(data.toCharArray(),0,data.length( ));

        transformerHandler.endElement(null,null,"decimal");

        transformerHandler.startElement(null,null,"hexadecimal",null);
        data = "0x" + Integer.toString(key, 16);
        transformerHandler.characters(data.toCharArray(),0,data.length( ));

        transformerHandler.endElement(null,null,"hexadecimal");
        transformerHandler.startElement(null,null,"octal",null);
        data = "0" + Integer.toString(key, 8);
        transformerHandler.characters(data.toCharArray(),0,data.length( ));

        transformerHandler.endElement(null,null,"octal");
        transformerHandler.startElement(null,null,"binary",null);
        data = Integer.toString(key, 2)+"B";
        transformerHandler.characters(data.toCharArray(),0,data.length( ));

        transformerHandler.endElement(null,null,"binary");
        transformerHandler.startElement(null,null,"hyper",null);
        data = "&0x" +Integer.toString(key, 16);
        transformerHandler.characters(data.toCharArray(),0,data.length( ));

        transformerHandler.endElement(null,null,"hyper");
        transformerHandler.endElement(null,null, "converted-values");
```

*Example 4-4. Using SAX to write out the XML document (continued)*

```
            transformerHandler.endDocument( );
            transformerHandler.setResult(streamResult);
        } catch (Exception e) {
            return null;
        }
        return writer.toString( );
    }
```

After calling startDocument( ) to begin the document, we must create the elements and add data to them. We create an element by calling startElement( ):

```
transformerHandler.startElement(null,null,"binary",null)
```

The third element is the only element needed to set up the XML tag, <binary>.

The actual startElement( ) method declaration looks like this:

```
public void startElement(String uri, String localName, String
qName, Attributes atts)
```

The uri parameter is used for the namespace, but since this example does not use a namespace, a null is passed in.

The second parameter, localName, is also used for the namespace and not needed in this example.

The third parameter, qName, is the qualified name.

The last parameter, atts, is used when the element has attributes; pass in null if attributes are not used, as in this case.

To put the data after the element tag, we set a String, data, to the desired value:

```
data = Integer.toString(key, 2)+"B";
```

Then we convert the data to a CharArray and pass it into the characters( ) method. The second and third parameters show where processing starts and stops in the CharArray:

```
transformerHandler.characters(data.toCharArray(),0,data.length( ));
```

Finally, we terminate the element with a call to endElement( ):

```
transformerHandler.endElement(null,null,"binary");
```

Each element is created with startElement( ), characters( ), and endElement( ). When all of the elements for the documents have been completed, a call to endDocument( ) is executed and the result is sent to the StreamResult that was set up at the start of the method:

```
transformerHandler.endElement(null,null, "converted-values");
transformerHandler.endDocument( );
transformerHandler.setResult(streamResult);
```

Finally, the `StreamResult` is converted to a `String` by calling `toString()` on the `StringWriter`. The `StreamResult` wraps the `StringWriter` that was set up at the beginning of this method:

```
return writer.toString();
```

The `String` can then be returned to the calling method.

Using SAX is purportedly a faster and less memory-intensive way to create XML documents than using DOM-based libraries such as JDOM and dom4j. If your testing shows that speed is an issue, or if the SAX API is more natural for your application, you should consider using it.

There are other ways to create an XML document. For example, the Apache project's Element Construction Set (ECS) allows you to create an XML document, but there is no method to add data to the document at this time, so for this application ECS is not useful.

## Back on the Client: Mining the XML

Here's where the fun begins. The client code in Example 4-5 shows how to mine the data fields from the XML document that the server sends.

*Example 4-5. The client code*

```
<!DOCTYPE HTML PUBLIC "-//w3c//dtd html 4.0 transitional//en">
<html>
<head>
    <STYLE type="text/css">
        .borderless { color:black; text-align:center; background:powderblue;
                border-width:0;border-color:green; }
    </STYLE>

    <title>function</title>
    <SCRIPT language="JavaScript" type="text/javascript">
        var req;

        function convertToXML() {
            var key = document.getElementById("key");
            var keypressed = document.getElementById("keypressed");
            keypressed.value = key.value;
            var url = "/ajaxcodeconverter-lab2/response?key=" + escape(key.value);
            if (window.XMLHttpRequest) {
                req = new XMLHttpRequest();
            }
            else if (window.ActiveXObject) {
                req = new ActiveXObject("Microsoft.XMLHTTP");
            }
            req.open("Get",url,true);
            req.onreadystatechange = callback;
            req.send(null);
        }
```

*Example 4-5. The client code (continued)*

```
function nonMSPopulate( ) {
    xmlDoc = document.implementation.createDocument("","", null);
    var resp = req.responseText;
    var parser = new DOMParser( );
    var dom = parser.parseFromString(resp,"text/xml");

    decVal = dom.getElementsByTagName("decimal");
    var decimal = document.getElementById('decimal');
    decimal.value=decVal[0].childNodes[0].nodeValue;

    hexVal = dom.getElementsByTagName("hexadecimal");
    var hexadecimal = document.getElementById('hexadecimal');
    hexadecimal.value=hexVal[0].childNodes[0].nodeValue;

    octVal = dom.getElementsByTagName("octal");
    var octal = document.getElementById('octal');
    octal.value=octVal[0].childNodes[0].nodeValue;

    hyperVal = dom.getElementsByTagName("hyper");
    var hyper = document.getElementById('hyper');
    hyper.value=hyperVal[0].childNodes[0].nodeValue;

    binaryVal = dom.getElementsByTagName("binary");
    var bin = document.getElementById('bin');
    bin.value=binaryVal[0].childNodes[0].nodeValue;
}

function msPopulate( ) {
    var resp = req.responseText;

    var xmlDoc=new ActiveXObject("Microsoft.XMLDOM");
    xmlDoc.async="false";
    xmlDoc.loadXML(resp);

    nodes=xmlDoc.documentElement.childNodes;

    dec = xmlDoc.getElementsByTagName('decimal');
    var decimal = document.getElementById('decimal');
    decimal.value=dec[0].firstChild.data;

    hexi = xmlDoc.getElementsByTagName('hexadecimal');
    var hexadecimal = document.getElementById('hexadecimal');
    hexadecimal.value=hexi[0].firstChild.data;

    oct = xmlDoc.getElementsByTagName('octal');
    var octal = document.getElementById('octal');
    octal.value=oct[0].firstChild.data;

    bin = xmlDoc.getElementsByTagName('binary');
    var binary = document.getElementById('bin');
    binary.value=bin[0].firstChild.data;
```

*Example 4-5. The client code (continued)*

```
            hypertextml = xmlDoc.getElementsByTagName('hyper');
            var hyper = document.getElementById('hyper');
            hyper.value=hypertextml[0].firstChild.data;
        }

        function callback( ) {
            if (req.readyState==4) {
                if (req.status == 200) {

                    if (window.XMLHttpRequest) {
                        nonMSPopulate( );
                    }
                    else if (window.ActiveXObject) {
                        msPopulate( );
                    }
                }
            }
            clear( );
        }

        function clear( ) {
            var key = document.getElementById("key");
            key.value="";
        }

    </SCRIPT>
</head>

<body>
    <H1>
        <CENTER>AJAX CHARACTER DECODER</CENTER>
    </H1>
    <H2>
        <CENTER>Press a key to find its value.</CENTER>
    </H2>
    <form name="form1" action="/ajaxcodeconverter-lab2" method="get">

    <table border="2" bordercolor="black" bgcolor="lightblue" valign="center"
           align="center">
        <tr>
            <td align="center">
                Enter Key Here ->
                <input type="text" id="key" name="key" maxlength="1" size="1"
                       onkeyup="convertToXML( );">
            </td>
        </tr>
    </table>
    <br>
```

*Example 4-5. The client code (continued)*

```
    <table class="borderless" border="1" valign="center" align="center">
        <tr>
            <td align="center" colspan="5">
                Key Pressed: 
                <input class="borderless" type="text" readonly id="keypressed"
                        maxlength="1" size="1">
            </td>
        </tr>
        <tr>
            <td align="center">  Decimal  </td>
            <td align="center">Hexadecimal</td>
            <td align="center">   Octal   </td>
            <td align="center">
                    Binary    
            </td>
            <td align="center">
                    HTML    
            </td>
        </tr>
        <tr>
            <td align="center"><input class="borderless" type="text" readonly
                id="decimal" maxlength="6" size="6"></td>
            <td align="center"><input class="borderless" type="text" readonly
                id="hexadecimal" maxlength="6" size="6"></td>
            <td align="center"><input class="borderless" type="text" readonly
                id="octal" maxlength="6" size="6"></td>
            <td align="center"><input class="borderless" type="text" readonly
                id="bin" maxlength="8" size="8"></td>
            <td align="center"><input class="borderless" type="text" readonly
                id="hyper" maxlength="6" size="6"></td>
        </tr>
    </table>

    </form>
</body>
</html>
```

Wow, that's a chunk of code. Let's break it up into two parts: first we'll look at the XML parsing, then at writing the data to the fields.

## XML Parsing with JavaScript

Remember, it all starts with our callback( ) function in JavaScript:

```
function callback( ) {
    if (req.readyState==4) {
        if (req.status == 200) {
```

```
                if (window.XMLHttpRequest) {
                    nonMSPopulate( );
                }
                else if (window.ActiveXObject) {
                    msPopulate( );
                }
            }
            clear( );
        }
    }
```

Remember how convertToXML( ) had to determine whether the browser was Internet Explorer or something else? We have the same problem again here. When callback( ) is invoked, it must check to see whether we are running ActiveXObject (Internet Explorer) or XMLHttpRequest (all other major browsers).

If the browser is Internet Explorer, we run msPopulate( ) to strip out the data from the XML. Otherwise, we run nonMSPopulate( ). What's the difference? It has to do with how we get an XML parser and with the API that parser presents to us. Firefox, Mozilla, and Safari all use new DOMParser( ) to get a built-in parser that can parse XML, and it's rumored that Opera will support this soon. Internet Explorer, on the other hand, uses new ActiveXObject("Microsoft.XMLDOM") to get the Microsoft XML parser.

Although Ajax works on most browsers in their current released states, it's entirely fair to say that the problem of cross-browser compatibility is the Achilles' heel of web applications.

## Populating the Form on a Microsoft Browser

The msPopulate( ) function is reproduced in Example 4-6.

*Example 4-6. The msPopulate() function*

```
function msPopulate( ) {
    var resp = req.responseText;

    var xmlDoc=new ActiveXObject("Microsoft.XMLDOM");
    xmlDoc.async="false";
    xmlDoc.loadXML(resp);

    dec = xmlDoc.getElementsByTagName('decimal');
    var decimal = document.getElementById('decimal');
    decimal.value=dec[0].firstChild.data;

    hexi = xmlDoc.getElementsByTagName('hexadecimal');
    var hexadecimal = document.getElementById('hexadecimal');
    hexadecimal.value=hexi[0].firstChild.data;

    oct = xmlDoc.getElementsByTagName('octal');
    var octal = document.getElementById('octal');
    octal.value=oct[0].firstChild.data;

```

*Example 4-6. The msPopulate() function (continued)*

```
20      bin = xmlDoc.getElementsByTagName('binary');
21      var binary = document.getElementById('bin');
22      binary.value=bin[0].firstChild.data;
23
24      hypertextml = xmlDoc.getElementsByTagName('hyper');
25      var hyper = document.getElementById('hyper');
26      hyper.value=hypertextml[0].firstChild.data;
27 }
```

Here, we use the built-in browser functions that I have touted as a programmer power play. We start by getting the `ActiveXObject` called `Microsoft.XMLDOM` (line 4). Next, we load the response from the servlet into the XML document (line 6).

Now we can mine the document for the data. First we get the data between the `<decimal></decimal>` tags. To do this, we first retrieve the XML data field information, by calling `getElementsByTagName(elementName)` (line 8); this function returns the array of child nodes belonging to the element (parent node) associated with the given tag. After we get the array of child nodes, we can reference the first element in the child node by calling `firstChild`. We then obtain the value of the child node by referencing the `data` field. So, to sum it up, we get our decimal value from `dec[0].firstChild.data`.

> If you are parsing a document that contains multiple tags with the same tag name, you can access any of the values by indexing the array. For example, if you had another `<decimal>value</decimal>` entry, you would index it with this call: `dec[1].firstChild.data`.

After obtaining the decimal value from the XML, line 10 updates the `decimal` form element. We've now retrieved one value from the XML and displayed it on the page. We continue on in this fashion until all of our data fields are updated with the values retrieved from the XML DOM sent from the servlet.

## Populating the Form on Other Browsers

The code for handling non-Microsoft browsers, shown in Example 4-7, is similar; there are some minor differences in the parser API, but that's about it.

*Example 4-7. The nonMSPopulate() function*

```
function nonMSPopulate( ) {
    var resp = req.responseText;
    var parser = new DOMParser( );
    var dom = parser.parseFromString(resp,"text/xml");

    decVal = dom.getElementsByTagName("decimal");
    var decimal = document.getElementById('decimal');
    decimal.value=decVal[0].childNodes[0].nodeValue;

```

*Example 4-7. The nonMSPopulate() function (continued)*

```
10         hexVal = dom.getElementsByTagName("hexadecimal");
11         var hexadecimal = document.getElementById('hexadecimal');
12         hexadecimal.value=hexVal[0].childNodes[0].nodeValue;
13
14         octVal = dom.getElementsByTagName("octal");
15         var octal = document.getElementById('octal');
16         octal.value=octVal[0].childNodes[0].nodeValue;
17
18         hyperVal = dom.getElementsByTagName("hyper");
19         var hyper = document.getElementById('hyper');
20         hyper.value=hyperVal[0].childNodes[0].nodeValue;
21
22         binaryVal = dom.getElementsByTagName("binary");
23         var bin = document.getElementById('bin');
24         bin.value=binaryVal[0].childNodes[0].nodeValue;
25 }
```

We create a new DOMParser (line 3), then we create a DOM on line 4 from the XML string that we received from the servlet. Next, we get the element between the <decimal></decimal> tags (line 6) by calling dom.getElementByTagName("decimal"). After retrieving the decimal form element from our HTML document, we retrieve the value sent to us in the XML and use it to set the appropriate field:

```
decimal.value=decVal[0].childNodes[0].nodeValue;
```

The reference to decVal[0] gets the data between the <decimal></decimal> tags. If we had two sets of <decimal></decimal> tags, we would reference the second set as decVal[1].

This is what the data should look like in the response sent from the servlet:

```
<converted-values>
    <decimal>97</decimal>
    <hexadecimal>0x61</hexadecimal>
    <octal>0141</octal>
    <hyper>&amp;0x61;</hyper>
    <binary>1100001B</binary>
</converted-values>
```

# Building the Application

Now that we have reviewed the code, let's build it and try it out. It's very similar to the example in the previous chapter, and because I don't like to overwrite my work, I put the new application in its own directory tree. The directory structure I used is shown in Figure 4-2.

This is just a guide so you can see how I built the sample. You can name your directories differently as long as you know how to configure the application server properly.

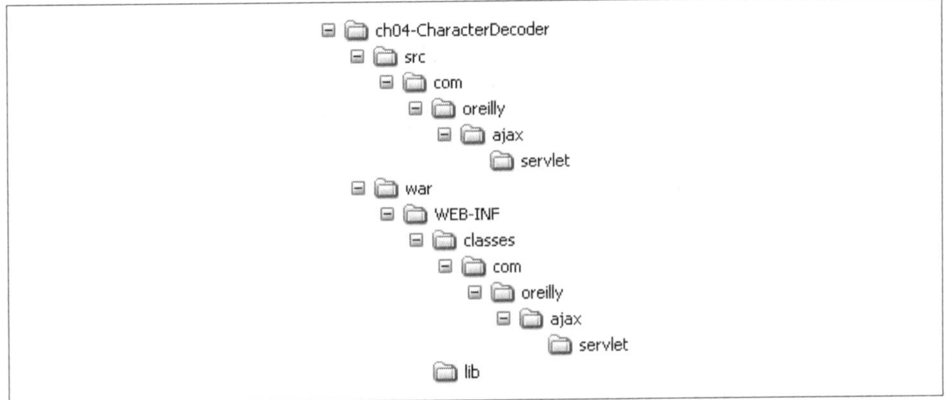


*Figure 4-2. Directory structure for Ajax Character Decoder (second version)*

The *web.xml* file for the project is presented in Example 4-8.

*Example 4-8. web.xml*

```
<!DOCTYPE web-app
    PUBLIC  "-//Sun Microsystems, Inc.//DTD Web Application 2.2//EN"
    "http://java.sun.com/j2ee/dtds/web-app_2_2.dtd">
<web-app>
    <servlet>
        <servlet-name>AjaxResponseServlet</servlet-name>
        <servlet-class>
            com.AJAXbook.servlet.AjaxResponseServlet
        </servlet-class>
        <load-on-startup>1</load-on-startup>
    </servlet>
    <servlet-mapping>
        <servlet-name>AjaxResponseServlet</servlet-name>
        <url-pattern>/response</url-pattern>
    </servlet-mapping>
    <welcome-file-list>
        <welcome-file>index.jsp</welcome-file>
    </welcome-file-list>
</web-app>
```

The *build.xml* file for the project is shown in Example 4-9.

*Example 4-9. build.xml*

```
<?xml version="1.0"?>
<project name="AJAX-CODECONVERTER " default="compile" basedir=".">

    <property environment="env"/>
    <property name="src.dir" value="src"/>
    <property name="test.dir" value="test"/>
    <property name="war.dir" value="war"/>
```

*Example 4-9. build.xml (continued)*

```
    <property name="db.dir" value="db"/>
    <property name="class.dir" value="${war.dir}/WEB-INF/classes"/>
    <property name="test.class.dir" value="${test.dir}/classes"/>
    <property name="lib.dir" value="${war.dir}/WEB-INF/lib"/>
    <property name="webapp.dir"
              value="${env.TOMCAT_HOME}/webapps/ajaxcodeconverter-lab2"/>

    <path id="ajax.class.path">
        <fileset dir="${lib.dir}">
            <include name="*.jar"/>
        </fileset>
    </path>

    <target name="testenv">
        <echo message="env.TomcatHome=${env.TOMCAT_HOME}"/>
        <echo message="env.ANT_HOME=${env.ANT_HOME}"/>
    </target>

    <target name="init">
        <mkdir dir="${class.dir}"/>
        <mkdir dir="${test.class.dir}"/>
    </target>

    <target name="compile" depends="init"
            description="Compiles all source code.">
        <javac srcdir="${src.dir}" destdir="${class.dir}" debug="on"
               classpathref="ajax.class.path"/>
    </target>

    <target name="clean" description="Erases contents of classes dir">
        <delete dir="${class.dir}"/>
        <delete dir="${test.class.dir}"/>
    </target>

    <target name="deploy" depends="compile"
            description="Copies the contents of web-app to destination dir">
        <copy todir="${webapp.dir}">
            <fileset dir="${war.dir}"/>
        </copy>
    </target>

</project>
```

## Running the Application on Tomcat

If you are running your application on the Tomcat server, you can use the Tomcat Web Application Manager (accessible through the URL *http://localhost:8080/manager/html*) to check whether it was deployed. The application manager is shown in Figure 4-3. As you can see in this figure, two versions of our Ajax converter have been deployed successfully and are currently running. The directory in which you installed the application becomes part of the path.

*Figure 4-3. Tomcat Web Application Manager*

Click the link under Applications to open a browser window that accesses the directory of your application. Then click the "index.html" link to see the application.

## Passing Data with JSON

Now that you've seen how to use XML as the data vehicle, we must talk about some of the problems with XML. One major drawback is speed. XML requires two tags per data point, plus extra tags for parent nodes and so on. All this extra data in transmission slows down the data exchange between the client and server. You can easily end up with a long document that contains only a few bytes' worth of data. Constructing the document can also be a rather elaborate process that requires a lot of memory on the server.

Fortunately, there is another way to send data to the client that is easier to parse and more compact. That alternative is JSON (pronounced Jason). JSON objects are typically smaller than the equivalent XML documents, and working with them is more memory-efficient.

The other great benefit of JSON is that you can parse it with JavaScript's `eval()` function. You don't need other libraries, and you don't need to worry as much about cross-browser functionality. As long as your browser has JavaScript enabled and supports the `eval()` function, you will be able to interpret the data.

You may still need to use XML (and now you know how), but if you have the option, there are compelling reasons to use JSON. In most cases, you will be better off with a JSON implementation.

This is our data object represented in JSON:

```
{"conversion":{
"decimal": "120",
"hexadecimal": "78",
"octal": "170",
"hyper": "&amp;0x78",
"binary": "1111000B"}
}
```

There are programmatic ways to build the JSON object, but to keep it simple we'll use a `StringBuffer` again and glue together the strings that will form the conversion object. Example 4-10 illustrates how we build the data object in the servlet.

*Example 4-10. AjaxJSONServlet.java*

```
package com.oreilly.ajax.servlet;

import java.io.IOException;

import javax.servlet.ServletException;
import javax.servlet.http.HttpServlet;
import javax.servlet.http.HttpServletRequest;
import javax.servlet.http.HttpServletResponse;

public class AjaxResponseServlet extends HttpServlet {

    private static final long serialVersionUID = 1L;

    public void doGet(HttpServletRequest req, HttpServletResponse res)
            throws ServletException, IOException {
        // key is the parameter passed in from the JavaScript
        // variable named url (see index.html)
        String key = req.getParameter("key");
        if (key != null) {
            // extract the first character from key
            // as an int, then convert that int to a String
            int keyInt = key.charAt(0);
            // set up the response
            res.setContentType("text/xml");
            res.setHeader("Cache-Control", "no-cache");
            // write out the XML string
            String outString = createStringBufferJSON(keyInt);
            res.getWriter( ).write(outString);
        }
        else {
            // if key comes back as a null, return a question mark
            res.setContentType("text/xml");
            res.setHeader("Cache-Control", "no-cache");
            res.getWriter( ).write("?");
        }
    }
```

*Example 4-10. AjaxJSONServlet.java (continued)*

```
    public String createStringBufferJSON(int keyInt) {
        StringBuffer returnJSON = new StringBuffer("\r\n{\"conversion\":{");
        returnJSON.append("\r\n\"decimal\": \""+
                          Integer.toString(keyInt)+"\",");
        returnJSON.append("\r\n\"hexadecimal\": \""+
                          Integer.toString(keyInt,16)+"\",");
        returnJSON.append("\r\n\"octal\": \""+
                          Integer.toString(keyInt,8)+"\",");
        returnJSON.append("\r\n\"hyper\": \"&0x"+
                          Integer.toString(keyInt,16)+"\",");
        returnJSON.append("\r\n\"binary\": \""+
                          Integer.toString(keyInt,2)+"B\"");
        returnJSON.append("\r\n}}");
        return returnJSON.toString( );
    }
}
```

That wasn't all that different from creating an XML document with a `StringBuffer`.

An alternative approach is to use the JSON library. Download *json_simple.zip* from *http://www.JSON.org/java/json_simple.zip*, and unzip it. Copy the *json_simple.jar* file from the *lib* directory into your *WEB-INF/lib* directory, and then add to it the import from `json_simple`:

```
import org.json.simple.JSONObject;
```

Now the code from Example 4-10 can be written as shown in Example 4-11.

*Example 4-11. Writing JSON support with the json_simple library*

```
public String createJSONwithJSONsimple(int keyInt) {
    JSONObject obj = new JSONObject( );
    JSONObject obj2 = new JSONObject( );

    obj2.put("decimal",Integer.toString(keyInt));
    obj2.put("hexadecimal",Integer.toString(keyInt,16));
    obj2.put("octal",Integer.toString(keyInt,8));
    obj2.put("hyper","&0x"+Integer.toString(keyInt,16));
    obj2.put("binary",Integer.toString(keyInt,2)+"B");

    obj.put("conversion",obj2);
    return(obj.toString( ));
}
```

The first `JSONObject`, `obj`, encapsulates the second object to product the result. The JSON object built with *json_simple.jar* looks like this:

```
{"conversion":{"decimal":"103","hyper":"&0x67","octal":"147","hexadecimal":"67",
"binary":"1100111B"}}
```

You can nest objects with the `json_simple` library. As a matter of fact, you can nest objects in a JSON array. You'll learn more about JSON arrays and JSON objects in Chapter 5.

Another JSON library, called `jsontools`, is located at *http://developer.berlios.de/projects/jsontools/*. The manual for the `jsontools` project does a really great job of explaining JSON and how to use the `jsontools` library, so you may want to download it if you're looking for a good primer on JSON.

Also, don't forget to look at the documentation at *http://www.JSON.org*.

## Changing the JavaScript for JSON

Now let's look at the client JavaScript code. I've replaced two functions with one: I removed `msPopulate( )` and `nonMSPopulate( )`, and now all browsers use the `populateJSON( )` function shown in Example 4-12.

*Example 4-12. The populateJSON() function*

```
function populateJSON( ) {
    var jsonData = req.responseText;

    var myJSONObject = eval('(' + jsonData + ')');

    var decimal = document.getElementById('decimal');
    decimal.value=myJSONObject.conversion.decimal;

    var hexadecimal = document.getElementById('hexadecimal');
    hexadecimal.value=myJSONObject.conversion.hexadecimal;

    var octal = document.getElementById('octal');
    octal.value=myJSONObject.conversion.octal;

    var binary = document.getElementById('bin');
    binary.value=myJSONObject.conversion.binary;

    var hyper = document.getElementById('hyper');
    hyper.value=myJSONObject.conversion.hyper;
}
```

# Summary

Remember that Ajax isn't a technology: it's a group of ideas that, used together, have proven very powerful. When you combine form manipulation with JavaScript, asynchronous callbacks with `XMLHTTPRequest`, and built-in XML with JSON parsers, you have something revolutionary—even though the individual pieces have been around for a while.

Combine these client-side technologies with Java's established server-side technologies, such as servlets, Struts, and JSF, and you've got a really powerful basis for building a new generation of interactive web applications.

CHAPTER 5

# Getting Useful Data

Google Suggest was one of the first Ajax applications: it's actually older than the name Ajax. Google Suggest alters the experience of filling in an HTML form. Normally, you fill in your data, click Submit, and cross your fingers; more than likely, you'll find out that you've requested a username that already exists, made a typo in your area code, or made some other simple error that you have to correct. Google Suggest changes all that: as you type in a field, it continuously shows you possible completions that match entries in the database.

## Form Entry with Ajax

Order-entry applications aren't sexy, but they're everywhere—and Ajax could be one of the best things that's ever happened to them. In the world of web applications, it's all about ease of use and saving time. Google Suggest suggests a way of making the web experience much easier: using Suggest as a model, we can write web applications that tell users immediately when they have requested usernames that are already in use, that fill in a city and state automatically on the basis of a zip code, and that make it simpler to enter names (product names, customer names, etc.) that are already in the database.

That's what we'll do in this chapter, while exploring ways to make a signup page easier to use and manage. We'll start with a Customer Sign-up page, shown in Figure 5-1. This page has two fields that get special treatment: the username field and the zip code field. We'll call these fields *suggestion fields*. For the username field, we'll notify users immediately if they enter usernames that have already been taken, rather than waiting until the form is submitted to validate this data. We'll also utilize the value entered into the zip code field to autopopulate the city and state fields with the values that correspond to that zip code, saving users some work.

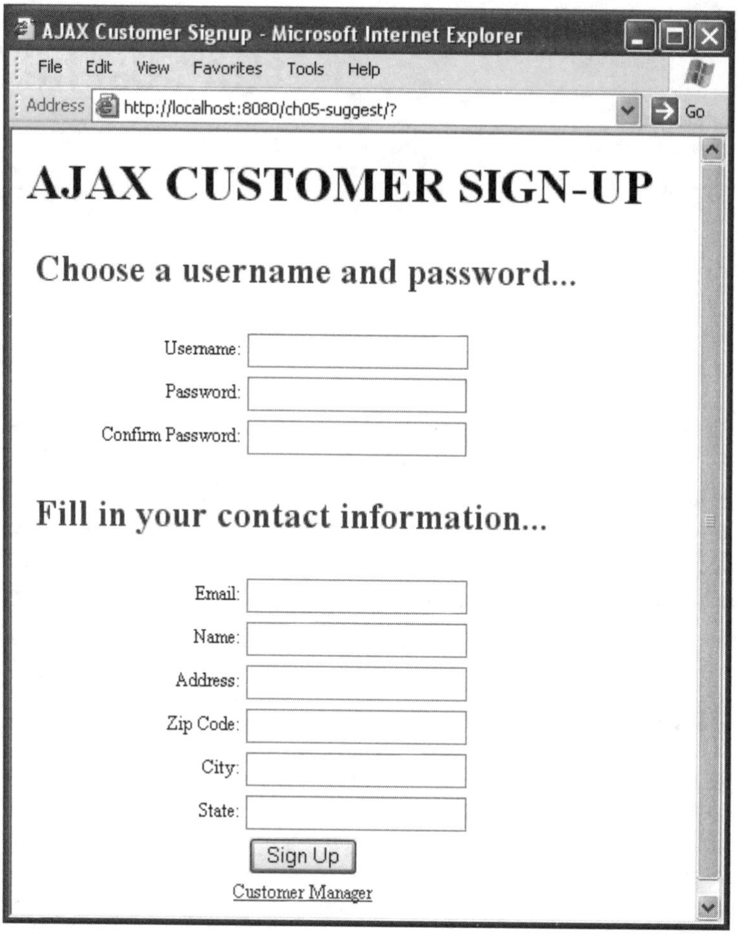

*Figure 5-1. The Ajax Customer Sign-up page*

## Validating the Username

We'll begin by validating the username to ensure that it does not currently exist in the database. To accomplish this, all we have to do is register the `onblur` JavaScript control with the username field:

```
<td>User Name:</td>
<td align="left">
    <input type="text" id="ajax_username" name="ajax_username"
           onblur="validateUsername( );">
</td>
```

The JavaScript `onblur` event fires whenever the field loses focus—for example, when the user presses Tab to move the cursor to the next field or clicks anywhere outside of the input field. When onblur fires, it transfers control to the validateUsername( ) JavaScript function:

```
function validateUsername( ) {
    var username = document.getElementById("ajax_username");
    var url = "/ajax-customer-lab5-1/username?username=" + escape(username.value);
    if (window.XMLHttpRequest) {
        req = new XMLHttpRequest( );
    }
    else if (window.ActiveXObject) {
        req = new ActiveXObject("Microsoft.XMLHTTP");
    }
    req.open("Get",url,true);
    req.onreadystatechange = callbackUsername;
    req.send(null);
}
```

This code should look familiar. validateUsername( ) retrieves the username from the field and puts it in a URL, calling escape(username.value) to ensure that any special characters in the username are escaped properly. It then sends the URL to the server in an HTTPGetRequest. When the request returns, the browser invokes the callback function, callbackUsername( ):

```
function callbackUsername( ) {
    if (req.readyState==4) {
        if (req.status == 200) {
            usernameCheck( );
        }
    }
}
```

The callbackUsername( ) function is simple. It waits for the response and sends control to the usernameCheck( ) method, which checks whether the entered username currently exists in the database and, if so, brings up an alert box informing the user that the name is already in use:

```
function usernameCheck( ) {
    // we only want a boolean back, so no parsing is necessary
    userExists = req.responseText;
    var username = document.getElementById("ajax_username");
    if (userExists == "true") {
        alert("Choose another username, "+username.value+" exists already");
        username.value="";
        username.focus( );
    }
}
```

This is not an elegant solution, but it illustrates the basic idea. You could embellish the code by displaying the text off to the side and disabling the Signup button until the user enters a unique username, or by looking ahead as the user types and enabling the Signup button only when the entered username is unique.

Note that the server sends a simple `true` or `false` value. Since we only need one value, there's no need to wrap it in XML or JSON. The simplest solution is almost always best.

## Creating the Database

Now that we've written the client code for checking the username, we need to support it with a database. These examples will use MySQL, which is freely available from *http://www.mysql.org*, but you can use any database with a JDBC driver. Create a database for this example with the following command:

```
mysql> create database AJAX;
```

Now the application will need a table to store the users for the suggest application (not to be confused with the database user we just set up).

Here is the SQL that creates the table to store the users:

```
USE AJAX;
CREATE TABLE USERS(USERNAME VARCHAR(50) PRIMARY KEY,
    PASSWORD VARCHAR(50),
    EMAIL VARCHAR(50),
    FIRST_NAME VARCHAR(50),
    LAST_NAME VARCHAR(50),
    ADDRESS VARCHAR(50),
    ZIPCODE VARCHAR(5),
    CITY VARCHAR(50),
    STATE VARCHAR(2),
    JOINED DATE,
    LAST_LOGIN DATE);
```

Now we need to create another table to store zip codes for the application. This table should store all the known U.S. zip codes. (If you are in another country, you can adapt the table, but I'll assume you want to get it working with U.S. zip codes.) Here is the SQL for creating the zip code table:

```
CREATE TABLE ZIPCODES (ZIPCODE VARCHAR(5) PRIMARY KEY,
    CITY VARCHAR(50),
    STATE VARCHAR(2));
```

`VARCHAR(5)` is the minimum size for a U.S. zip code, and `VARCHAR(2)` is big enough for an abbreviated U.S. state name. After you get this example running, you can adapt these values to your circumstances.

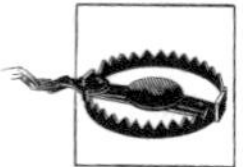

MySQL table names are case-sensitive on Linux but not on Windows, so use care when creating tables. If you create a table called `USERS` in a Linux environment, you must access it with `SELECT * from USERS`. However, if you create a table called `users` on a Windows machine, you can access it with `SELECT * from users` or `SELECT * from USERS`. This can be misleading if you start your project on Windows and later migrate your code to Linux. To avoid confusion, I always keep my table names uppercase.

Now we need to be able to log in to the database from the web application. Use the GRANT command to create a username and a password for the web application:

```
mysql> GRANT ALL ON AJAX.* to 'ajax'@'localhost' IDENTIFIED BY 'polygon';
```

This command sets up a new user with the username ajax, allows the user ajax to connect only from the local machine (localhost), and gives the user the password polygon. You will need this information when connecting to the database through JDBC.

To populate the database with zip code data, we'll use the file *ZIPCODES.sql*, which you can download with the source code for this book from *http://www.oreilly.com/catalog/9780596101879*. To load the data into your database, use the *mysqlimport* tool included with MySQL. You will need to be in MySQL's *bin* directory or have the *bin* directory of MySQL in your path. The import command looks like this:

```
mysqlimport -d -u root -p AJAX C:\ZIPCODES.sql
Enter password: ******
```

This command reads in all of the data from *ZIPCODES.sql* and stores it in the ZIPCODES table. The -d option deletes any rows that are already in the table. This won't have any effect the first time you import the file, but if for some reason the first attempt fails and you need to run the script again, -d will prevent duplicate rows by deleting the rows that were imported on the first run.

The -u option defines the user to use when importing the rows. In this case, the user is root. -p is the password option; you'll be prompted for the password. AJAX is the name of the database to import into, and the last parameter is the file to import: *C:\ZIPCODES.sql*.

Notice that the file prefix, *ZIPCODES*, is the same as the table name. mysqlimport requires the table name to match the filename.

If the rows are imported successfully, you will see something similar to this:

```
Ajax.ZIPCODES: Records: 41905  Deleted: 0 Skipped: 0 Warnings: 41912
```

## Servicing the Ajax Request: Servlets

Now that the database is ready, we return to the coding at hand: the servlets that bridge the gap between the database and the client. A few pages ago we set up the client to check for preexisting usernames. In the servlet, we merely have to get the username from the request and query the database for a matching name. We'll keep the servlet simple by just using a JDBC connection; we won't do any connection polling, Object-Relational Mapping, or any of the other fancy tricks you'd probably see in a real application.

Example 5-1 presents the code to get the username and check it against the database to see whether it already exists.

*Example 5-1. The AjaxUsernameServlet*

```
public class AjaxUsernameServlet extends HttpServlet {
    public void doGet(HttpServletRequest req, HttpServletResponse res)
            throws ServletException, IOException {
        String username = req.getParameter("username");
        if (username != null) {
            if (existsUsername(username)) {
                res.setContentType("text/xml");
                res.setHeader("Cache-Control", "no-cache");
                res.getWriter( ).write("true");
            }
        } else {
            // if key comes back as a null, return a message
            res.setContentType("text/xml");
            res.setHeader("Cache-Control", "no-cache");
            res.getWriter( ).write("Username null");
        }
    }
    private boolean existsUsername(String username) {
        ResultSet result = null;
        try {
            Statement select = DatabaseConnector.getConnection().createStatement( );
            result = select.executeQuery("SELECT USERNAME from USERS where
                                         USERNAME = '" + username + "';");
            if (result == null || result.next( )) {
                return true;
            }
        } catch (SQLException e) {
            // use log4j or handle this how you want
        }
        return false;
    }
}
```

The doGet( ) method intercepts the request and checks for the username parameter. The parameter is sent to the existsUsername( ) method, which checks the database and returns true if the user exists. If the user exists, doGet( ) sends the string "true" back to the user; otherwise, it sends the string "Username null". Again, we're not using any XML here, just simple strings.

The DatabaseConnector class, presented in Example 5-2, is a singleton. If there is no JDBC connection currently stored in the connection field, a new one is created, stored, and returned. If there is an existing connection, it is simply returned.

*Example 5-2. The DatabaseConnector class*

```
public class DatabaseConnector {
    private static Connection connection;

    public static Connection getConnection( ) {
        if (connection != null)
            return connection;
        Connection con = null;
        String driver = "com.mysql.jdbc.Driver";
```

*Example 5-2. The DatabaseConnector class (continued)*

```
        try {
            Class.forName(driver).newInstance( );
        } catch (Exception e) {
            System.out.println("Failed to load mySQL driver.");
            return null;
        }
        try {
            con = DriverManager.getConnection(
                    "jdbc:mysql:///AJAX?user=ajax&password=polygon");
        } catch (Exception e) {
            e.printStackTrace( );
        }
        connection = con;
        return con;
    }
}
```

That covers it for username validation: a full round trip is made to the database to check for username collision. Next, we'll start working on the zip codes, using the database to populate the city and state fields automatically.

## Loading City and State by Zip Code

We've already loaded the zip codes into the database. Now we are going to hook up the client. We have to access the database again to validate the zip code and retrieve the city/state data. We'll use the same approach that we did for validating the username: we'll wait until the user has entered the whole zip code in the field and then, when the cursor leaves the field, we'll populate the city and state fields with the matching values. (Implementing this as a lookahead field wouldn't be particularly helpful; the user will either know the zip code or not.)

First, we need to add the JavaScript `onblur` trigger to the zip code field:

```
<td>Zip Code:</td>
<td align="left">
    <input type="text" id="zipcode" name="zipcode"
            onblur="retrieveCityState( )">
</td>
```

There's nothing new here. The `retrieveCityState( )` function is called whenever the zip code field loses focus. This function sets up the `XMLHttpRequest` and sends it to the `AjaxZipCodesServlet`:

```
var req;

function retrieveCityState( ) {
    var zip = document.getElementById("zipcode");
    var url = "/ajax-customer-lab5-1/zipcodes?zip=" + escape(zip.value);
    name.value="?"+name.value;
    if (window.XMLHttpRequest) {
        req = new XMLHttpRequest( );
    }
```

```
        else if (window.ActiveXObject) {
            req = new ActiveXObject("Microsoft.XMLHTTP");
        }
        req.open("Get",url,true);
        req.onreadystatechange = callbackCityState;
        req.send(null);
    }
```

Because we are getting a good number of JavaScript functions, we'll extract the JavaScript and place it in a separate file called *oreillyAJAX.js*, which is loaded by *index.html*:

```
<title>AJAX Customer Sign-up</title>
<script language="JavaScript" src="oreillyAJAX.js"></script>
```

The servlet for looking up zip codes, presented in Example 5-3, is simple. The `doGet( )` method extracts the zip parameter from the request; that parameter contains the zip code the user typed. The zip code is passed to the `getCityState( )` method, which queries the database for the city and state. Take a look at the format used to return data to the client. Is it XML or JSON?

*Example 5-3. The AjaxZipCodesServlet*

```
public void doGet(HttpServletRequest req, HttpServletResponse res)
        throws ServletException, IOException {
    String responseString = null;

    String zipCode = req.getParameter("zip");
    if (zipCode != null) {
        HashMap location = getCityState(zipCode);
        responseString = JSONUtil.buildJSON(location, "location");
    }
    if (responseString != null) {
        res.setContentType("text/xml");
        res.setHeader("Cache-Control", "no-cache");
        res.getWriter( ).write(responseString);
    } else {
        // if key comes back as a null, return a question mark
        res.setContentType("text/xml");
        res.setHeader("Cache-Control", "no-cache");
        res.getWriter( ).write("?");
    }
}

private HashMap getCityState(String zipCode) {
    Connection con = DatabaseConnector.getConnection( );
    HashMap cityStateMap = new HashMap( );
    cityStateMap.put("zip", "zipCode");
    String queryString = "";
    try {
        queryString = "SELECT CITY, STATE FROM ZIPCODES where ZIPCODE="
                + zipCode + ";";
        Statement select = con.createStatement( );
        ResultSet result = select.executeQuery(queryString);

        while (result.next( )) { // process results one row at a time
            String city;
```

*Example 5-3. The AjaxZipCodesServlet (continued)*

```
                String state;

                city = result.getString("CITY");
                if (result.wasNull( )) {
                    city = "";
                }
                cityStateMap.put("city", city);
                state = result.getString("state");
                if (result.wasNull( )) {
                    state = "";
                }
                cityStateMap.put("state", state);
            }
        } catch (Exception e) {
            System.out.println("exception caught getting city/state:"
                               + queryString + " " + e.getMessage( ));
        } finally {
            if (con != null) {
                try {
                    con.close( );
                } catch (SQLException e) {
                }
            }
        }
        return cityStateMap;
    }
```

We use the JSON format to pass data back to the client because it is simpler to process and therefore less error-prone. Using the zip code, we look up the corresponding city and state in the database and store them in a `HashMap`. We then pass that `HashMap` into the `buildJSON( )` method. An `Iterator` then goes through all of the entries in the `HashMap` and builds a JSON-formatted `String` from the key/value pairs in the `HashMap`:

```
public static String buildJSON(HashMap map, String title) {
    StringBuffer returnJSON = new StringBuffer("\r\n{\"" + title + "\":{");
    String key = "";
    String value = "";
    // loop through all the map entries
    Iterator it = map.entrySet().iterator( );

    while (it.hasNext( )) {
        Map.Entry e = (Map.Entry) it.next( );
        value = (String) e.getValue( );
        key = (String) e.getKey( );
        returnJSON.append("\r\n\"" + key + "\": \"" + value + "\",");
    }
    // remove the last comma
    int lastCharIndex = returnJSON.length( );
    returnJSON.deleteCharAt(lastCharIndex - 1);
    returnJSON.append("\r\n}}");
    return returnJSON.toString( );
}
```

This isn't production-quality code: the exceptions aren't handled very well, the database connections aren't managed well, there's no logging, and so on. In a real application, you'd want to fix these weaknesses. What we have accomplished in this example, though, is quite important. We've built an Ajax application that couldn't have been implemented entirely with client-side code. We didn't really need a trip to the server to look up the decimal value of a character, but we do need to communicate with the server to find out whether someone has requested a username that's already in use, or to find out the city and state associated with a zip code.

Now let's get more ambitious: let's build a suggestion field that helps an administrator enter a user's name.

## Building a Suggestion Field

Building the suggestion field is the most fun but also the most complicated part of the next sample application. Our form will look like Figure 5-2.

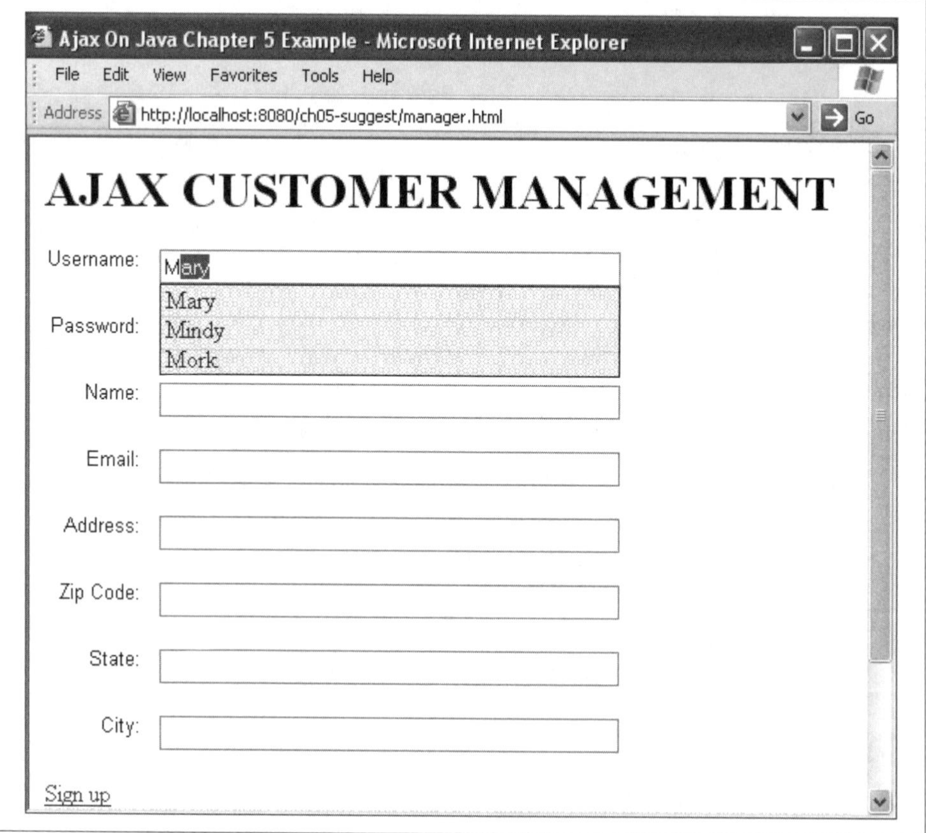


*Figure 5-2. The Ajax Customer Management page*

When you type "M," the application finds all the names in the database starting with the letter M; in this case, there are three. If you type "Ma," the selection displays only "Mary." Hitting Return then calls up the record for Mary, as shown in Figure 5-3.

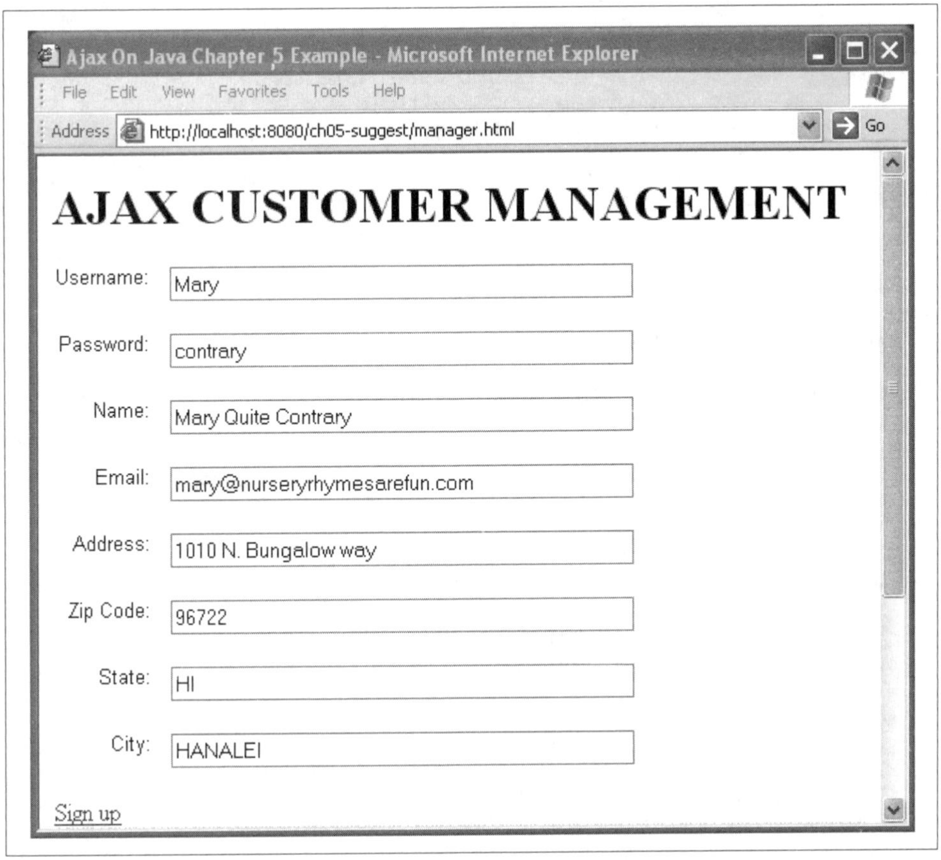

*Figure 5-3. Ajax suggestion field lookup for one record*

This application takes a few shortcuts. The first is the lookup: it doesn't go to the database and look up the matching set of names for every character that's typed. We could implement it that way, but it wouldn't improve the application and it would require more requests to the database, which has the potential for creating efficiency problems.

Even though Ajax applications are more responsive than traditional web applications, it's easy to imagine users cursing an application that makes a round trip to the server with every character that is typed. Instead, this application loads all of the usernames at the beginning. This approach wouldn't be ideal if there were hundreds or thousands of users, but if the application is only pulling a small amount of data, this simpler, single-query design is more efficient. For a bigger database, you could trigger the query with `onkeyup()` and get the result set for the letters in the suggestion field.

The HTML code for the form is presented in Example 5-4.

*Example 5-4. The Ajax Customer Management code*

```
<!DOCTYPE html PUBLIC "-//W3C//DTD HTML 4.01 Transitional//EN">
<html>
<head>
    <LINK REL="stylesheet" TYPE="text/css" HREF="oreillyajax.css">
    <title>Ajax on Java Customer Management Page</title>
    <script language="JavaScript" src="oreillySuggest.js"></script>
    <script language="JavaScript">
        window.onload = function () {
            init("ajax_username");
        }
    </script>
</head>
<body >
    <h1>AJAX CUSTOMER MANAGEMENT</h1>

    <form name="form1" action="/ch05-suggest" method="get">

    <label for="ajax_username">Username:</label>
    <input  class="cm_label" type="text" id="ajax_username" autocomplete="off">
    <br /><br />

    <label class="cm_label" for="password">Password:</label>
    <input class="cm_input" type="text" id="password" name="password"><br /><br />

    <label class="cm_label" for="confirmpassword">Name:</label>
    <input class="cm_input" type="text" id="name" name="name"><br /><br />

    <label class="cm_label" for="email">Email:</label>
    <input class="cm_input" type="text" id="email" name="email"><br /><br />

    <label class="zlabel" for="address">Address:</label>
    <input class="cm_input" type="text" id="address" name="address"><br /><br />

    <label class="cm_label" for="zipcode">Zip Code:</label>
    <input class="cm_input" type="text" id="zipcode" name="zipcode"><br /><br />

    <label class="cm_label" for="state">State:</label>
    <input class="cm_input" type="text"  id="state" name="state"><br /><br />

    <label class="cm_label" for="city">City:</label>
    <input class="cm_input" type="text" id="city" name="city"><br /><br />

    </form>

    <a href="index.html">Sign up</a>

</body>
</html>
```

A Cascading Style Sheet is used to set up the div that is needed for the suggestion field. Here's the code from *oreillyajax.css*:

```
div.suggestions {
    position: absolute;
    -moz-box-sizing: border-box;
    box-sizing: border-box;
    border: 1px solid blue;
}

div.suggestions div {
    cursor: default;
    padding: 3px;
}

div.suggestions div.current {
    background-color: #3366cc;
    color: white;
}
```

A *div* (short for division) is an HTML tag for a generic block object to which formatting can be applied.

The suggestion div is set up for absolute positioning; that is, it is positioned according to fixed coordinates. Those coordinates are set in the *oreillySuggest.js* JavaScript file, based on the location of the username input field. So, the div's initial values are set in the CSS file, but the final values are set by the JavaScript functions. This strategy gives the program flexibility to adapt to changes in the HTML: the div remains anchored to the bottom of the username input field, even if that field moves around as the application grows. Figure 5-4 shows how the suggestion field looks on the screen.

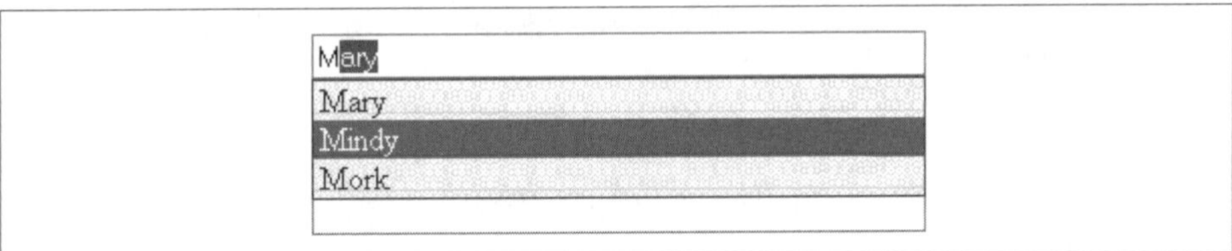


*Figure 5-4. Suggestion field on the Customer Management page*

Now the JavaScript file, *oreillySuggest.js*, comes into play. This file is loaded and the `init( )` function is called to set up the `ajax_username` field:

```
window.onload = function () {
    init("ajax_username");
}
```

The init( ) function does a lot of the groundwork: it requests the list of usernames from the server; sets up handlers for trigger events such as onkeyup, onkeydown, and onblur; and sets up the div for displaying suggestions. We'll look at these three tasks next. Here's the code for the init( ) function:

```
function init(field) {
    inputTextField = document.getElementById(field);
    cursor = -1;
    createDebugWindow( );
    fillArrayWithAllUsernames( );
    inputTextField.onkeyup = function (inEvent) {
        if (!inEvent) {
            inEvent = window.event;
        }
        keyUpHandler(inEvent);
    }
    inputTextField.onkeydown = function (inEvent) {
        if (!inEvent) {
            inEvent = window.event;
        }
        keyDownHandler(inEvent);
    }
    inputTextField.onblur = function ( ) {
        hideSuggestions( );
    }

    createDiv( );
}
```

## Retrieving the Usernames

The init( ) function loads the usernames by calling fillArrayWithAllUsernames( ), which sets up the call to the server:

```
function fillArrayWithAllUsernames( ) {
    var url = "/ajax-customer-lab5-1/lookup?username=*"+"&type="+ escape("3");
    if (window.XMLHttpRequest) {
        req = new XMLHttpRequest( );
    }
    else if (window.ActiveXObject) {
        req = new ActiveXObject("Microsoft.XMLHTTP");
    }
    req.open("Get",url,true);
    req.onreadystatechange = callbackFillUsernames;
    req.send(null);
}
```

Nothing really new is happening here. We create a URL, get an XMLHttpRequest object to communicate with the server, register callbackFillUsernames( ) as the callback function, and send the URL to the server. The URL /ajax-customer-lab5-1/lookup?username=*&type=3 passes control to the AjaxLookupServlet. type=3 tells the servlet to call getAllUsers( ), which executes a wildcard lookup on the USERS table and returns a list of all usernames in the database:

```
private String getAllUsers( ) {
    Connection con = DatabaseConnector.getConnection( );
    ResultSet result = null;
    StringBuffer returnSB = null;
    try {
        Statement select = con.createStatement( );
        result = select.executeQuery("SELECT USERNAME from USERS;");
        returnSB = new StringBuffer( );
        while (result.next( )) {
            returnSB.append(result.getString("username") + ",");
        }
        returnSB.deleteCharAt(returnSB.length( ) - 1);
        catch (SQLException e) {
            // you could pop up a window with Ajax to let users know
            // there is a problem
        } finally {
            if (con != null) {
                try {
                    con.close( );
                } catch(SQLException e) {
                }
            }
        }
        return returnSB.toString( );
    }
}
```

The usernames are then collected into one long comma-separated string, using a `StringBuffer`. The resulting string is then sent back to the client as is: no XML, no JSON wrapping. It's simple and effective.

When the server returns the data, the browser calls `callbackFillUsernames( )`:

```
function callbackFillUsernames( ) {
    if (req.readyState==4) {
        if (req.status == 200) {
            populateUsernames( );
        }
    }
}
```

The next step, the call to `populateUsernames( )`, occurs only if the request has reached the ready state (i.e., the server has returned a result) and the request's status is `200` (success). `populateUsernames( )` parses out the usernames from a comma-separated string and loads them into a JavaScript array. The `String.split( )` JavaScript function does the conversion:

```
function populateUsernames( ) {
    var nameString = req.responseText;
    debugInfo('name array'+nameString);
    var nameArray = nameString.split(',');

    lookAheadArray = nameArray;
}
```

At this point, the lookAheadArray is loaded with usernames; the program is ready to interpret the characters entered into the username field and open a div if there are any matches.

## Creating the Div

init( )'s final act is to call createDiv( ), which sets up the div:

```
function createDiv( ) {
    suggestionDiv = document.createElement("div");
    suggestionDiv.style.zIndex = "2";
    suggestionDiv.style.opacity ="0.8";
    suggestionDiv.style.repeat = "repeat";
    suggestionDiv.style.filter = "alpha(opacity=80)";
    suggestionDiv.className = "suggestions";
    suggestionDiv.style.visibility = "hidden";
    suggestionDiv.style.width = inputTextField.offsetWidth;
    suggestionDiv.style.backgroundColor = "white";
    suggestionDiv.style.autocomplete = "off";
    suggestionDiv.style.backgroundImage = "url(transparent50.png)";
    suggestionDiv.onmouseup = function( ) {
        inputTextField.focus( );
    }
    suggestionDiv.onmouseover = function(inputEvent) {
        inputEvent = inputEvent || window.event;
        oTarget = inputEvent.target || inputEvent.srcElement;
        highlightSuggestion(oTarget);
    }
    suggestionDiv.onmousedown = function(inputEvent) {
        inputEvent = inputEvent || window.event;
        oTarget = inputEvent.target || inputEvent.srcElement;
        inputTextField.value = oTarget.firstChild.nodeValue;
        lookupUsername(inputTextField.value);
        hideSuggestions( );
        debugInfo("textforLookup"+oTarget.firstChild.nodeValue);
    }
    document.body.appendChild(suggestionDiv);
}
```

Most of this code sets various properties of the div, including:

zIndex
: The depth. A higher number places it on top of an element with a lower number, so our div, which has a zIndex of 2, will appear on top of a div with a zIndex of 0 or 1.

opacity
: The transparency. This controls the extent to which the elements below it show through. A value of 1 allows nothing through, while a value of 0 effectively makes the element invisible.

visibility
: The visibility. The value hidden removes the element from the view. We can use this setting to hide the suggestion box when it is empty and show it when there is a match.

autocomplete
: When autocomplete is set to off, the browser does not offer suggestions. This must be set to off, or the browser will drop down its own suggestion box!

onmouseup, onmouseover, *etc.*
: JavaScript functions that are called when events occur.

For a full list of the properties that can be set, refer to *Cascading Style Sheets: The Definitive Guide*, by Eric A. Meyer (O'Reilly).

Ajax techniques become even more portable and powerful when combined with style sheets and when using the DOM to modify the characteristics of the HTML page.

## Handling the Events

Now we're looking at the heart of the JavaScript: the event handlers that actually make the suggestion field work. The first event we'll investigate is onkeyup. Back in init( ), we registered the keyUpHandler( ) function as an event handler to be called whenever a key-up event (i.e., when a key is pressed and released) occurs in ajax_username. The keyUpHandler( ) function looks like this:

```
function keyUpHandler(inEvent) {

    var potentials = new Array( );
    var enteredText = inputTextField.value;
    var iKeyCode = inEvent.keyCode;
    debugInfo("key"+iKeyCode);

    if (iKeyCode == 32 || iKeyCode == 8
                       || ( 45 < iKeyCode && iKeyCode < 112)
                       || iKeyCode > 123) /*keys to consider*/
    {
        if (enteredText.length > 0) {
            for (var i=0; i < lookAheadArray.length; i++) {
                if (lookAheadArray[i].indexOf(enteredText) == 0) {
                    potentials.push(lookAheadArray[i]);

                }
            }
            showSuggestions(potentials);
        }

        if (potentials.length > 0) {
            if (iKeyCode != 46 && iKeyCode != 8) {
                typeAhead(potentials[0]);
```

```
            }
            showSuggestions(potentials);
        }
        else {
            hideSuggestions( );
        }
    }
}
```

The keyUpHandler( ) function saves the current value of the input field in the enteredText variable and saves the last key pressed in iKeyCode. It then checks whether this key was valid; if so, it executes a loop that checks enteredText against the strings in the lookAheadArray. Strings matching the beginning of enteredText are saved in the array potentials. If there are potential matches, the suggestion div is displayed with the call showSuggestions(potentials). Otherwise, the suggestion div is hidden.

Other handlers come into effect when the div is shown. The program keeps track of mouseover, mousedown, up-arrow, and down-arrow events to highlight the selected item. For presses of the arrow keys and Return key, the onkeydown event works well. In init( ), we registered the keyDownHandler( ) function as the event handler to be called whenever a key-down event occurs. The code for the keyDownHandler( ) function follows:

```
function keyDownHandler(inEvent) {

    switch(inEvent.keyCode) {
        /* up arrow */
        case 38:
            if (suggestionDiv.childNodes.length > 0 && cursor > 0) {
                var highlightNode = suggestionDiv.childNodes[--cursor];
                highlightSuggestion(highlightNode);
                inputTextField.value = highlightNode.firstChild.nodeValue;
            }
            break;
        /* down arrow */
        case 40:
            if (suggestionDiv.childNodes.length > 0 &&
                    cursor < suggestionDiv.childNodes.length-1) {
                var newNode = suggestionDiv.childNodes[++cursor];
                highlightSuggestion(newNode);
                inputTextField.value = newNode.firstChild.nodeValue;
             }
             break;
        /* Return key = 13 */
        case 13:
            var lookupName = inputTextField.value;
            hideSuggestions( );
            lookupUsername(lookupName);
            break;
    }
}
```

The down-arrow and up-arrow keys change the highlighted element in the suggestion div. Pressing the up-arrow key decrements the cursor index, and retrieves the indexed node and highlights it. The contents of that node (a complete username) are then copied into the text field. The down-arrow key behaves similarly. The highlightSuggestion( ) function does all the highlighting work, as you'll see momentarily.

If the user presses Return, we do a lookup on the name that was selected and hide the suggestions, which are no longer needed. The code for the lookupUsername( ) function follows:

```
function lookupUsername(foundname) {

    debugInfo('looking up :'+foundname);
    var username = document.getElementById("ajax_username");
    var url = urlbase+"/lookup?username=" + escape(foundname)+"&type="+
            escape("2");
    alert('url submitting:'+url);
    if (window.XMLHttpRequest) {
        req = new XMLHttpRequest( );
    }
    else if (window.ActiveXObject) {
        req = new ActiveXObject("Microsoft.XMLHTTP");
    }
    req.open("Get",url,true);
    req.onreadystatechange = callbackLookupUser;
    req.send(null);
}
```

### Highlighting a suggestion

The highlightSuggestion( ) function is simple. Its argument is the node that's currently selected, which we want to highlight. The method loops through all the nodes in the div. When it finds a node that matches the selected node, it sets the CSS class name for the background to "current", which is a CSS style we've designed for setting the background color. Nodes that don't match have their background classes set to "", which gives them the default background. Here's code for highlightSuggestion( ):

```
function highlightSuggestion(suggestionNode) {
    for (var i=0; i < suggestionDiv.childNodes.length; i++) {
        var sNode = suggestionDiv.childNodes[i];
        if (sNode == suggestionNode) {
            sNode.className = "current";
        }
        else if (sNode.className == "current") {
            sNode.className = "";
        }
    }
}
```

The onmouseover and onmousedown events were set up back in the init( ) function. The onmouseover event highlights the element that fired the trigger by calling highlightSuggestion(sugTarget):

```
suggestionDiv.onmouseover = function(inputEvent) {
    inputEvent = inputEvent || window.event;
    sugTarget = inputEvent.target || inputEvent.srcElement;
    highlightSuggestion(sugTarget);
}
```

The onmousedown event selects the current node. It looks up the information associated with the current username, populates the form with that information, and hides the suggestion box:

```
suggestionDiv.onmousedown = function(inputEvent) {
    inputEvent = inputEvent || window.event;
    sugTarget = inputEvent.target || inputEvent.srcElement;
    inputTextField.value = sugTarget.firstChild.nodeValue;
    lookupUsername(inputTextField.value);
    hideSuggestions( );
}
```

## Configuring the Servlets

All that's left is the setup for the servlet, but that is really just a repeat of what we have done in previous chapters.

The *web.xml* file, shown in Example 5-5, sets up the servlets that this application uses, which are:

- AjaxZipCodesServlet
- AjaxSignupServlet
- AjaxLookupServlet
- AjaxUsernameServlet

*Example 5-5. The web.xml file for the Ajax customer application*

```
<!DOCTYPE web-app PUBLIC  "-//Sun Microsystems, Inc.//DTD Web Application 2.2//EN"
    "http://java.sun.com/j2ee/dtds/web-app_2_2.dtd">
<web-app>
    <servlet>
        <servlet-name>AjaxZipCodesServlet</servlet-name>
        <servlet-class>
            com.oreilly.ajax.servlet.AjaxZipCodesServlet
        </servlet-class>
        <load-on-startup>1</load-on-startup>
    </servlet>
    <servlet-mapping>
        <servlet-name>AjaxZipCodesServlet</servlet-name>
        <url-pattern>/zipcodes</url-pattern>
    </servlet-mapping>
    <servlet>
        <servlet-name>AjaxSignupServlet</servlet-name>
```

*Example 5-5. The web.xml file for the Ajax customer application (continued)*

```
        <servlet-class>
            com.oreilly.ajax.servlet.AjaxSignupServlet
        </servlet-class>
        <load-on-startup>4</load-on-startup>
    </servlet>
    <servlet-mapping>
        <servlet-name>AjaxSignupServlet</servlet-name>
        <url-pattern>/signup</url-pattern>
    </servlet-mapping>
    <servlet>
        <servlet-name>AjaxLookupServlet</servlet-name>
        <servlet-class>
            com.oreilly.ajax.servlet.AjaxLookupServlet
        </servlet-class>
        <load-on-startup>3</load-on-startup>
    </servlet>
    <servlet-mapping>
        <servlet-name>AjaxLookupServlet</servlet-name>
        <url-pattern>/lookup</url-pattern>
    </servlet-mapping>
    <servlet>
        <servlet-name>AjaxUsernameServlet</servlet-name>
        <servlet-class>
            com.oreilly.ajax.servlet.AjaxUsernameServlet
        </servlet-class>
        <load-on-startup>2</load-on-startup>
    </servlet>
    <servlet-mapping>
        <servlet-name>AjaxUsernameServlet</servlet-name>
        <url-pattern>/username</url-pattern>
    </servlet-mapping>
    <welcome-file-list>
        <welcome-file>index.jsp</welcome-file>
    </welcome-file-list>
</web-app>
```

We've now created a complete Ajax application with a database on the backend. The application does a lot of visual processing, using JavaScript to manipulate the DOM. Yes, the database access is old-school, but it's generic enough to allow you to plug in your own backend access: JDO, Hibernate, or whatever other technology you choose.

A lot can be done to improve this application. For example, the JavaScript is very flat; it could be improved using an object-oriented approach in which all the functions are associated with a JavaScript object created by the `init( )` function. Still, this application is typical of what you'll do with Ajax.

Don't be afraid to play with the JavaScript. That is where most of the visual power lies. In the past, you would have had to spend time learning Swing or another graphical library, but JavaScript's ability to manipulate the browser's DOM tree makes it in many respects as powerful as the other graphics APIs out there.

CHAPTER 6

# Ajax Libraries and Toolkits

When the term *Ajax* was first coined, many developers were surprised by the power of JavaScript. They had been using JavaScript for years but hadn't figured out that they could use it to create web applications with functionality that rivaled that of native desktop applications. That "eureka" moment led to hype, which in turn created the energy that has allowed Ajax to mature. When Ajax was getting started, developers had to build their applications without any help (as we have done in the past few chapters): they had to write all the JavaScript, parse the XML or JSON by hand, and create servlets to handle the asynchronous interaction with the client. That's no longer the case. The number of frameworks that exist now to simplify the task of creating Ajax applications is solid proof that Ajax is more than just hype: it's a valid, thriving architecture.

All I can say is, "Cool, bring it on!" As web developers, we have waited a long time to bring this functionality to our web applications. Swing developers, beware: Ajax levels the playing field.

Up until now, we've been building our Ajax applications with `XMLHttpRequest`. We have used `XMLHttpRequest` to send requests to the server, and we have set up callback methods to intercept the responses coming back from the server.

We can make that portion of our code more resilient by using libraries. An Ajax toolkit or library can help us build the request object and set up the callback function. Using a toolkit also eliminates one of the ugliest parts of our JavaScript code: the separate code we have to write to handle Internet Explorer and the other browsers.

This chapter will introduce the following Ajax libraries:

- The Dojo Toolkit
- The Rico Toolkit
- The DWR Toolkit
- Scriptaculous
- Prototype

## Using the Dojo Toolkit

We'll start our look at Ajax frameworks with the Dojo Toolkit. Dojo is an open source DHTML toolkit written in JavaScript. It includes many utilities that go beyond Ajax. The libraries that we are most interested in include:

`dojo.io`
: Platform-independent input/output APIs

`dojo.rpc`
: RPC, the Dojo way

`dojo.json`
: JSON, the Dojo way

Although we are only going to use the `dojo.io` library for this example, you should look at the Dojo manual (*http://manual.dojotoolkit.org*) for information on `dojo.rpc` and `dojo.json`.

The other libraries that Dojo contains are:

`dojo.lang`
: Utility routines to make JavaScript easier to use

`dojo.string`
: String manipulation routines

`dojo.dom`
: DOM manipulation routines

`dojo.style`
: CSS style manipulation routines

`dojo.html`
: HTML-specific operations

`dojo.event`
: Aspect Oriented Programming-inspired event system

`dojo.reflect`
: Reflection API

`dojo.date`
: Date manipulation

`dojo.logging.Logger`
: Logging library

`dojo.profile`
: JS Profiler

`dojo.regexp`
: Regular expression generators

`dojo.collections`
: Contains `Dictionary`, `ArrayList`, `Queue`, `SortedList`, `Stack`, and `Set` sub-parts

`dojo.animation.Animation`
: Animation support

`dojo.dnd`
: Drag-and-drop support

`dojo.validate`
: Data validation methods (`isText`, `isNumber`, `isValidDate`, etc.)

`dojo.fx`
: Fading, exploding visual effects

`dojo.graphics.Colorspace`
: Colorspace manipulation

`dojo.graphics.color`
: Color manipulation

`dojo.svg`
: SVG library

`dojo.crypto`
: Cryptographic routines

`dojo.math.Math`
: Math library

`dojo.math.curves`
: Curve-generation library

`dojo.math.matrix`
: Linear algebra

`dojo.math.points`
: Point manipulations

`dojo.storage`
: Storage system that implements a local durable cache

`dojo.xml.Parse`
: First-pass XML to JS parser

`dojo.uri`
: URI/URL manipulation routines

That's a handful. You can accomplish a lot with Dojo, and it is worth exploring further, but doing so is outside the scope of this book. Again, consult the Dojo manual for more information on the Dojo libraries.

Now, back to the task at hand: using Dojo to set up an Ajax call. In the previous chapter, we used the following code to retrieve the state and city corresponding to a user-entered zip code:

```
function retrieveCityState( ) {
    var zip = document.getElementById("zipcode");
    var url = "/ajax-customer-lab5-1/zipcodes?zip=" + escape(zip.value);
    name.value="?"+name.value;
    if (window.XMLHttpRequest) {
        req = new XMLHttpRequest( );
    }
    else if (window.ActiveXObject) {
        req = new ActiveXObject("Microsoft.XMLHTTP");
    }
    req.open("Get",url,true);
    req.onreadystatechange = callbackCityState;
    req.send(null);
}
```

Most of the `retrieveCityState( )` function has to do with initializing the `XMLHttpRequest` object. This code is fragile: if the test for `XMLHttpRequest` ever changes, you'll have to modify the application (and every other application you've created that uses code like this). Therefore, it makes sense to initialize `XMLHttpRequest` in a library function. You could create your own library, but why go to the trouble when someone's already done it for you? Here's the `retrieveCityState( )` method rewritten to use Dojo:

```
function retrieveCityState( ) {
    zip = document.getElementById("zipcode");
    dojo.io.bind({
        url: "/ch06-Frameworks/zipcodes?zip=" + escape(zip.value),
        load: function(type, data, evt){ displayCityAndState(data); },
        error: function(type, data, evt){ reportError(type,data,evt); },
        mimetype: "text/plain"
    });
}
```

This revised version of `retrieveCityState( )` uses the `dojo.io.bind( )` function to set up the `XMLHttpRequest` object and the callback and error-handling functions.

The parameters that are passed to `dojo.io.bind( )` are:

`url`
: The URL of the Ajax service that handles the request.

`load`
: The JavaScript callback function that is called when the response arrives.

`error`
: The JavaScript function that is called in case of any errors.

`mimetype`
: The MIME type that is used to interpret the response coming back from the server. The type will almost always be `text/plain`. This parameter does not set an outgoing MIME header for HTTP transports.

To use `dojo.io.bind( )`, you must first install the Dojo Toolkit. Point your browser to *http://www.dojotoolkit.org* and download the library. Extract the file *dojo.js* and put it in your web application so you can import the JavaScript library:

```
<script language="JavaScript" src="dojo.js"></script>
```

That's all there is to it. To handle errors, add a `reportErrors( )` function, as indicated by the `error:` key in the `dojo.io.bind( )` call:

```
function reportError(type,data,evt) {
    alert('error retrieving a city and state for that zip code.');
}
```

That's all it takes to use the Dojo Toolkit to take care of the `XMLHTTPRequest` communication for you.

Example 6-1 presents the revised HTML file for our Customer Sign-up page, including the JavaScript for using `dojo.io.bind( )` to retrieve the city and state information.

*Example 6-1. The HTML and JavaScript code for dojoindex.html*

```
<html>
<head>
    <meta name="generator" content="HTML Tidy, see www.w3.org">
    <LINK REL="stylesheet" TYPE="text/css" HREF="oreillyajax.css">
    <title>AJAX Customer Sign-up</title>
    <script language="JavaScript" src="scripts/dojo.js"></script>
    <script language="JavaScript" type="text/javascript">

    function retrieveCityState( ) {
        zip = document.getElementById("zipcode");
        dojo.io.bind({
            url: "/ch06-Frameworks/zipcodes?zip=" + escape(zip.value),
            load: function(type, data, evt){ displayCityAndState(data); },
            error: function(type, data, evt){ reportError(type,data,evt); },
            mimetype: "text/plain"
        });
    }

    function displayCityAndState(data) {
        var jsonData = data;
        var myJSONObject = eval('(' + jsonData + ')');
        if (myJSONObject.location.city== null) {
            alert('no entry in database for zip code: '+myJSONObject.location.zip);
            var city = document.getElementById('city').value="";
            var city = document.getElementById('state').value="";
        }
        else {
            var city = document.getElementById('city').
                    value=myJSONObject.location.city;
            var city = document.getElementById('state').
                    value=myJSONObject.location.state;
        }
    }
```

*Example 6-1. The HTML and JavaScript code for dojoindex.html (continued)*

```
    function reportError(type,data,evt) {
        alert('error retrieving a city and state for that zip code.');
    }

    </script>
</head>
<body>
    <h1>AJAX Zip Code Lookup with Dojo</h1>
    <form name="form1" action="signup" method="get">
    <table align="left" class="borderless">
        <tr>
            <td colspan="2">
            <table class="borderless">
                <tr>
                    <td class="headtext">
                        <h2>Choose a username and password...........</h2>
                    </td>
                </tr>
            </table>
            </td>
        </tr>
        <tr>
            <td>User Name:</td>
            <td align="left">
                <input type="text" id="ajax_username" name="ajax_username"
                       autocomplete="off" onblur="validateUsername( )">
            </td>
        </tr>
        <tr>
            <td>Password:</td>
            <td align="left">
                <input type="password" id="password" name="password">
            </td>
        </tr>
        <tr>
            <td>Confirm Password:</td>
            <td align="left">
                <input type="password" id="confirmpassword" name="confirmpassword">
            </td>
        </tr>
        <tr>
            <td> </td>
        </tr>
        <tr>
            <td colspan="2">
                <table align="left" class="borderless">
                    <tr>
                        <td class="headtext">
                            <h2>Fill in your contact information...</h2>
                        </td>
                    </tr>
                </table>
            </td>
        </tr>
```

*Example 6-1. The HTML and JavaScript code for dojoindex.html (continued)*

```
        <tr>
            <td>Email:</td>
            <td align="left"><input type="text" id="email" name="email"></td>
        </tr>
        <tr>
            <td>Name:</td>
            <td align="left">
                <input type="text" id="customername" name="customername">
            </td>
        </tr>
        <tr>
            <td>Address:</td>
            <td align="left"><input type="text" id="address" name="address"></td>
        </tr>
        <tr>
            <td>Zip Code:</td>
            <td align="left">
                <input type="text" id="zipcode" name="zipcode"
                        onblur="retrieveCityState( )">
            </td>
        </tr>
        <tr>
            <td>City:</td>
            <td align="left"><input type="text" id="city" name="city"></td>
        </tr>
        <tr>
            <td>State:</td>
            <td align="left"><input type="text" id="state" name="state"></td>
        </tr>
        <tr>
            <td>Error:</td>
            <td align="left">
                <input type="text" id="ziperror" name="ziperrorstate">
            </td>
        </tr>
        <tr>
            <td colspan="2" align="center">
                <input type="submit" value="Sign Up">
            </td>
        </tr>
        <tr>
            <td colspan="2" align="center">
                <a href="manager.html">Customer Manager</a>
            </td>
        </tr>
    </table>
    </form>
</body>
</html>
```

As browsers evolve, and as JavaScript itself evolves, the toolkits will evolve, too. Libraries such as Dojo let you take advantage of improvements made to browsers and to JavaScript without rewriting your existing code. These libraries insulate you from changes while at the same time enabling you to take advantage of the advances in technology.

## Using the Rico Toolkit

To experiment with Rico, download the latest version from *http://openrico.org/rico/downloads.page*. The Rico Toolkit depends on the Prototype library, so start by importing the *prototype.js* and *rico.js* files into your HTML page:

```
<script language="JavaScript" src="scripts/prototype.js"></script>
<script language="JavaScript" src="scripts/rico.js"></script>
```

Then you need to register a request handler:

```
ajaxEngine.registerRequest('zipRequestHandle', 'rico');
```

The first parameter, `zipRequestHandle`, is the handle we'll use to make the Ajax request. The second parameter is the string `rico`, which is registered with the `ajaxEngine`. That is the relative URL used when the `zipRequestHandle` is invoked. Therefore, we need to map the servlet to this URL in *web.xml*:

```
<servlet>
    <servlet-name>RicoZipCodesServlet</servlet-name>
    <servlet-class>
        com.oreilly.ajax.servlet.RicoZipCodesServlet
    </servlet-class>
    <load-on-startup>5</load-on-startup>
</servlet>
<servlet-mapping>
    <servlet-name>RicoZipCodesServlet</servlet-name>
    <url-pattern>/rico</url-pattern>
</servlet-mapping>
```

Everything is now set up. Back in the HTML page, the zip code text field uses the Ajax engine to send the request to the server, using the `zipRequestHandle`:

```
<td>Zip Code:</td>
<td align="left" colspan="2">
    <input type="text" id="zipcode" name="zipcode"
           onblur="ajaxEngine.sendRequest('zipRequestHandle',
           'zip='+escape(this.value));">
</td>
```

The `onblur` JavaScript event is set to call `ajaxEngine.sendRequest( )`, sending the `zipRequestHandle` that we initialized earlier and passing in the value of the input field, which should be a zip code.

When the user enters a zip code and presses the Tab key to move the cursor to the next field, the onblur event triggers the Rico ajaxEngine to send a request to the specified URL. The server should then respond with an XML-formatted document that looks like this:

```
<ajax-response>
    <response type="element" id="cityDiv">some content for the city</response>
    <response type="element" id="stateDiv">some content for the state</response>
</ajax-response>
```

The root of the XML response must be <ajax-response>. Each element within the response must be wrapped in a <response> tag, with the id and type attributes defined.

When an <ajax-response> document comes back from the server, Rico matches the id attributes in the document with the fields in the HTML form and populates the form accordingly. In this document, we have two IDs: cityDiv and stateDiv. The data from these XML elements is used to populate the HTML tags with the cityDiv and stateDiv IDs in our HTML document:

```
<tr>
    <td>City:</td>
    <td align="left">
        <div id="cityDiv">
            <input type="text" id="inputcity" name="inputcity">
        </div>
    </td>
</tr>
<tr>
    <td>State:</td>
    <td align="left" colspan="2">
        <div id="stateDiv">
            <input type="text" id="inputstate" size="2" name="inputstate">
        </div>
    </td>
</tr>
```

So, if an HTML element has an id that matches an id in the response, Rico updates that HTML element with the content from the XML document.

What goes in the <response> elements? It would be simplest if we could just insert the city and state names, but Rico replaces everything inside the tags with the cityDiv and stateDiv IDs with the content from the XML document. In our HTML, the cityDiv and stateDiv IDs are assigned to <div> elements. Therefore, we need to supply new <input> tags to replace the contents of the divs in the HTML document.

Why not use HTML input fields for the state and city rather than wrapping the input fields with a div? The XML is less complex (we can just ship the city and state names back to the browser rather than shipping the entire <input> tags), and Rico can just fill in the fields. If the user-entered zip code does not have a corresponding entry in the database, the user can manually enter the state and city.

That won't work on all browsers, though (particularly Internet Explorer). Rico uses the innerHTML JavaScript method to replace the content of the elements. On Internet Explorer, the <input> element does not work with the innerHTML method.

Instead of directly entering the text into the <input> element, we wrap it with a <div> tag and have the servlet return the complete HTML code to create the <input> element.

So, the buildRicoXML( ) method needs to generate the content for a div that includes the HTML inputs. Also, we want to add a div to hold a message in case the zip code is not in the database:

```
public static String buildRicoXML(HashMap map,String element, String message) {
    StringBuffer ricoXML = new StringBuffer("<ajax-response>");
    String key = "";
    String value = "";
    // loop through all the map entries
    Iterator it = map.entrySet().iterator();

    while (it.hasNext()) {
        Map.Entry e = (Map.Entry) it.next();
        value = (String) e.getValue();
        key = (String) e.getKey();
        ricoXML.append("\r\n <response type=\"element\" id=\"" + key + "\">" +
                "<input type=\"text\" id=\"inner"+key+"\" name=\"inner"+key+"\"
                value=\""+value+"\" /></response>");
    }
    ricoXML.append("\r\n <response type=\"element\" id=\"message\"
            name=\"message\">"+message+"</response>");
    ricoXML.append("\r\n</ajax-response>");
    return ricoXML.toString();
}
```

Now the zip code lookup application is ready. You'll first see a browser with three empty fields (Figure 6-1).

If a user enters a zip code that is not in the database, the message div instructs that user to manually enter the city and state (Figure 6-2).

Here's the code that creates the Rico response for the unsuccessful zip code lookup and message:

```
<ajax-response>
    <response type="element" id="state">
        <input type="text" id="innerstate" name="innerstate" value=" " />
    </response>
```

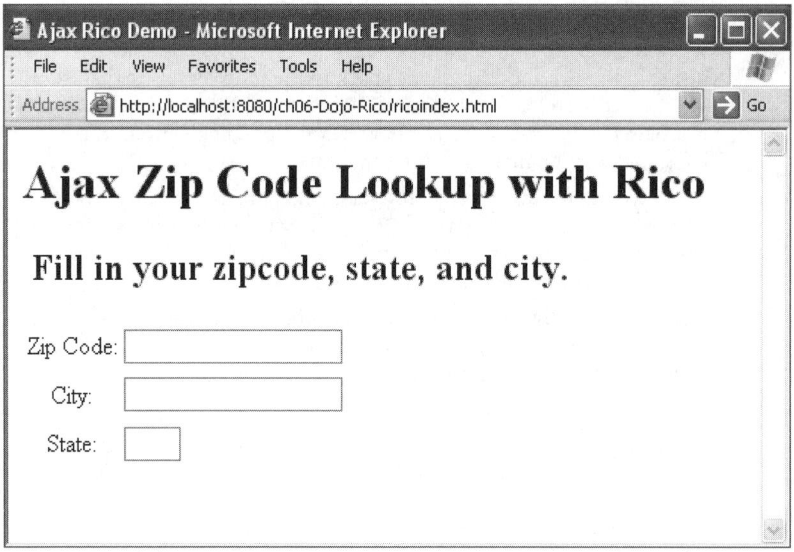

Figure 6-1. Rico zip code lookup

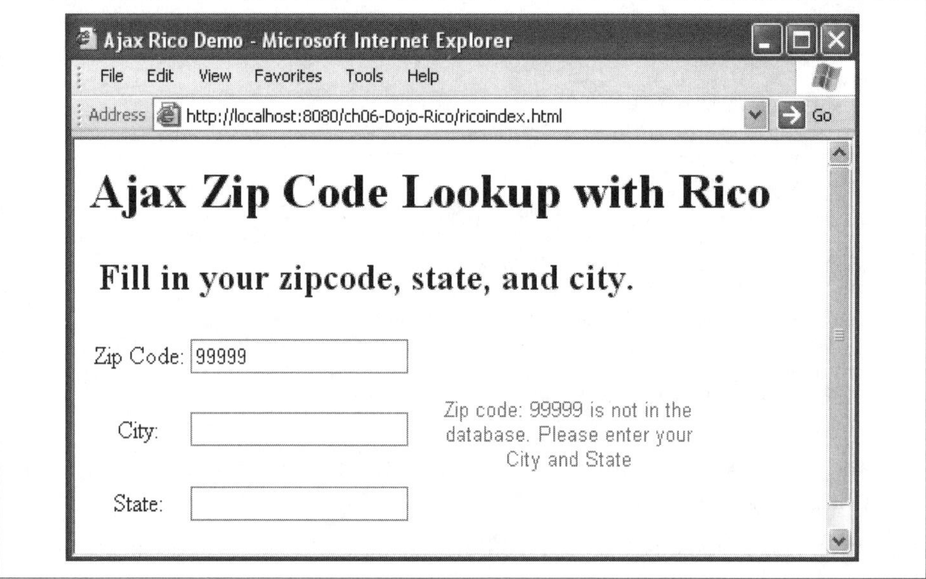


Figure 6-2. Unsuccessful zip code lookup with message

```
    <response type="element" id="city">
        <input type="text" id="innercity" name="innercity" value=" " />
    </response>
    <response type="element" id="message" name="message">
        Zip code: 99999 is not in the database. Please enter your City and State
    </response>
</ajax-response>
```

When the user enters the city and state, you can capture that information, verify it, and add it to your zip code database. That goes beyond what we'll demonstrate here, but it would be a useful endeavor.

What if the zip code is in the database? In that case, we don't really need to provide input fields; it may be cleaner to just display the city and state. To accomplish this, we could use a different method that doesn't fill the div with an input field but instead simply returns the city and state wrapped in the Rico response:

```
public static String buildRicoXML(HashMap map, String message) {
    StringBuffer ricoXML = new StringBuffer("<ajax-response>");
    String key = "";
    String value = "";
    // loop through all the map entries
    Iterator it = map.entrySet().iterator( );

    while (it.hasNext( )) {
        Map.Entry e = (Map.Entry) it.next( );
        value = (String) e.getValue( );
        key = (String) e.getKey( );
        ricoXML.append("\r\n <response type=\"element\" id=\"" +
                key + "\">" + value + "</response>");
    }
    ricoXML.append("\r\n <response type=\"element\" id=\"message\"
            name=\"message\">"+message+"</response>");
    ricoXML.append("\r\n</ajax-response>");
    return ricoXML.toString( );
}
```

Now, the XML we're returning looks like this:

```
<ajax-response>
    <response type="element" id="state">CA</response>
    <response type="element" id="city">FRESNO</response>
    <response type="element" id="message" name="message"></response>
</ajax-response>
```

That results in the div containing only the bare text with no input fields for the user. The resulting page is shown in Figure 6-3.

Rico requires a bit more setup, but it's worth it because you don't have to write a callback function: Rico automatically populates the fields you need with the data that comes back.

This approach works fine if you want to fill document elements with values coming back from an `HTTPRequest`, but what if you need to look at the data or modify it? That's where Rico's Object Response Type comes into play.

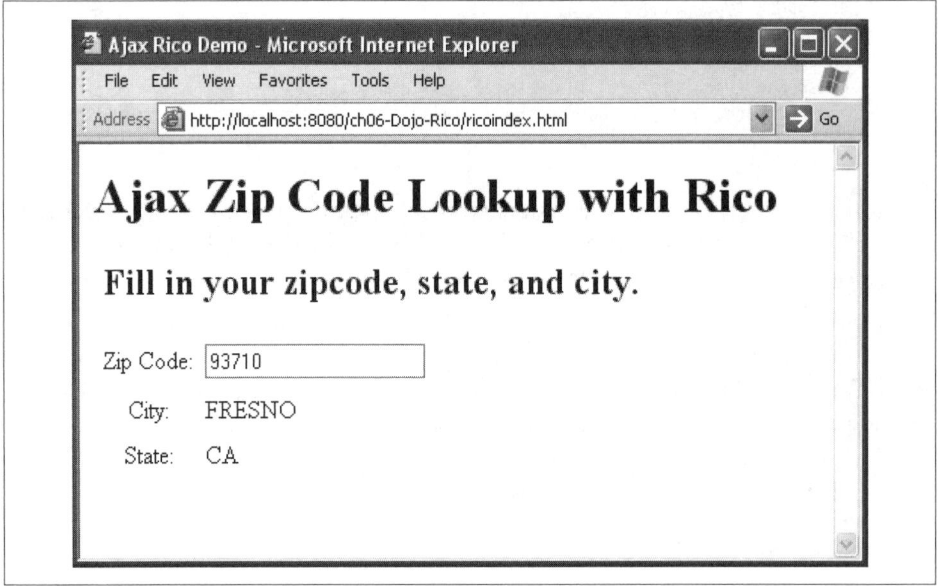


*Figure 6-3. Successful zip code lookup with Rico*

## Using Rico's Object Response Type

The Object Response Type allows the client JavaScript code to pull each element out of the XML response. It can then modify it or put it into the document as is.

To use the Object Response Type, we must register an object with the Rico `ajaxEngine`:

```
ajaxEngine.registerAjaxObject('locationUpdater', cityStateUpdater);
```

Now we need to create a `cityStateUpdater` object that has the method `ajaxUpdate( )`, as shown in Example 6-2.

*Example 6-2. Creating an object for registerAjaxObject()*

```
var CityStateUpdater = Class.create( );

CityStateUpdater.prototype = {
    initialize: function( ) {
    },
    ajaxUpdate: function(ajaxResponse) {
        this.setFields(ajaxResponse.childNodes[0]);
    },
    setFields: function(aState) {
        document.getElementById('stateDiv').innerHTML=aState.getAttribute('state');
        document.getElementById('cityDiv').innerHTML=aState.getAttribute('city');
    }
};

cityStateUpdater = new CityStateUpdater( );
```

We must then ensure that the XML response coming back from the server has the attribute `type="object"` and an `id` that matches the object set by `registerAjaxObject( )`. In this case, the `id` must be `locationUpdater`, and the data must be attributes in XML format. The XML response should look like this:

```
<ajax-response>
    <response type="object" id="locationUpdater">
        <location state="OH" city="NEWTON FALLS" />
    </response>
</ajax-response>
```

Here is the servlet code that produces the response:

```
public static String buildRicoObjectXML(HashMap map, String message) {
    StringBuffer ricoXML = new StringBuffer("<ajax-response>\r\n
           <response type=\"object\" id=\"locationUpdater\"><location ");
    String key = "";
    String value = "";
    // loop through all the map entries
    Iterator it = map.entrySet().iterator( );

    while (it.hasNext( )) {
        Map.Entry e = (Map.Entry) it.next( );
        value = (String) e.getValue( );
        key = (String) e.getKey( );
        ricoXML.append(key+"=\""+ value +"\" " );
    }
    ricoXML.append("/></response>\r\n</ajax-response>");
    return ricoXML.toString( );
}
```

If you missed how the data was inserted in the form, look back at the `setFields( )` function in Example 6-2. That function merely gets an element from the DOM and puts the value from the XML response into that element. In this method, you can extract a value from the XML response and modify it or implement some logic based on the value.

# Using DWR with Ajax

Direct Web Remoting (DWR) is an open source toolkit that's available from *http://getahead.ltd.uk/dwr*. It gives you everything you need to use Ajax in a Java web application. While DWR is not the only Ajax toolkit available for the Java platform, it is one of the most mature, and it offers a great deal of useful functionality.

DWR provides a set of server-side Java classes, including a servlet that runs the whole show, in one nice little file named *dwr.jar*. On the browser side, there's a JavaScript library that mirrors the server-side classes. The *dwr.xml* file provides the plumbing that connects the server-side classes with the JavaScript. That file resides with *web.xml* in the *WEB-INF* directory.

To demonstrate the DWR library, we'll create another zip code lookup page. We need only three classes: the connector class for the database, the Zipcode POJO class, and the ZipcodeManager class. To get started, download *dwr.jar* from *http://getahead.ltd.uk/dwr* and place it in the *WEB-INF/lib* directory of your application. DWR provides its own servlet, so our first task is to configure that servlet in *web.xml*:

```
<servlet>
    <servlet-name>dwr-invoker</servlet-name>
    <display-name>DWR Servlet</display-name>
    <servlet-class>uk.ltd.getahead.dwr.DWRServlet</servlet-class>
    <init-param>
        <param-name>debug</param-name>
        <param-value>true</param-value>
    </init-param>
</servlet>
<servlet-mapping>
    <servlet-name>dwr-invoker</servlet-name>
    <url-pattern>/dwr/*</url-pattern>
</servlet-mapping>
```

The *dwr.xml* file controls the mirroring between the Java objects on the server and the client-side JavaScript, as you can see in Example 6-3.

*Example 6-3. The control and plumbing for DWR stored in dwr.xml*

```
<!DOCTYPE dwr PUBLIC "-//GetAhead Limited//DTD Direct Web Remoting 1.0//EN"
    "http://www.getahead.ltd.uk/dwr/dwr10.dtd">
<dwr>
    <allow>
        <create creator="new" javascript="ZipcodeManager"
                class="com.oreilly.ajax.ZipcodeManager">
            <include method="getZipcode"/>
        </create>
        <convert converter="bean" match="com.oreilly.ajax.Zipcode">
            <param name="include" value="city,state,zipcode"/>
        </convert>
    </allow>
</dwr>
```

The `<convert>` tag tells JavaScript that there will be a `Zipcode` bean and that there will be support for `city`, `state`, and `zipcode` class variables that can be accessed following the JavaBean conventions (via `getCity( )`, `getState( )`, and `getZipcode( )`).

The `<create>` tag sets up the `ZipcodeManager` to have the JavaScript functions to support the `getZipcode( )` method. That way, we can later make a reference to `ZipcodeManager.getZipcode( )`. We are mirroring only one method here, but you will usually need to mirror multiple methods. In that case, each method must be listed in its own `<include>` tag. For example, if you wanted a `setZipcode( )` method, you would change the `<create>` portion of *dwr.xml* to look like this:

```
<create creator="new" javascript="ZipcodeManager"
        class="com.oreilly.ajax.ZipcodeManager">
    <include method="getZipcode"/>
```

```
    <include method="setZipcode"/>
</create>
```

Of course, com.oreilly.ajax.ZipcodeManager would have to have the setZipcode( ) method as well. We're not supporting that feature, though; our ZipcodeManager class (presented in Example 6-4) only has the getZipcode(String zip) method.

*Example 6-4. The ZipcodeManager class*

```
public class ZipcodeManager {

    static public Zipcode getZipcode(String zip) {
        Zipcode zipcode = null;
        Connection con = DatabaseConnector.getConnection( );
        String sqlString = "";
        zipcode = new Zipcode( );
        zipcode.setZipcode(zip); // put in original zip code

        try {
            sqlString = "SELECT CITY,STATE,ZIPCODE FROM ZIPCODES WHERE
                        ZIPCODE='"+zip+"';";
            Statement select = con.createStatement( );
            ResultSet result = select.executeQuery(sqlString);
            if (result.next( )) { // process results one row at a time
                zipcode.setCity(result.getString(1));
                zipcode.setState(result.getString(2));
                zipcode.setZipcode(result.getString(3));
            }

        } catch (Exception e) {
            System.out.println("exception in login"+e.getMessage( ));
        } finally {
            if (con != null) {
                try {
                    con.close( );
                } catch (SQLException e) {
                }
            }
        }
        return zipcode;
    }
}
```

Now we can reference the Java objects as if they existed in our JavaScript:

```
function retrieveCityState( ) {
    zip = document.getElementById("zipcode");

    ZipcodeManager.getZipcode(zip.value,populateData);
}

function populateData(zipcode) {
    document.getElementById('state').value=zipcode.state;
    document.getElementById('city').value=zipcode.city;
}
```

The Java method `ZipcodeManager.getZipcode(String zipcode)` from Example 6-4 is different from the JavaScript method `ZipcodeManager.getZipcode(String zipcode, function)` called by `retrieveCityState( )`. DWR mirrors the Java methods almost exactly, but with an added parameter to handle the callback. That extra parameter tacked onto the end is the callback function that handles the data returning from the Ajax request.

Since DWR handles the communications between the client and the server, there's a lot less JavaScript to write. Further, it's a lot easier to see what the application is doing.

So, how does the JavaScript application know about the mapping to our server-side Java classes and methods? The application's HTML must import three files: *dwr/engine.js*, *dwr/util.js*, and a third file that DWR generates at runtime. The name of this third file is given by *dwr.xml*'s `<create>` tag: the parameter `javascript="ZipcodeManager"` tells us to include *ZipcodeManager.js* in our HTML or JSP file. The *dwrindex.html* file is shown in Example 6-5.

*Example 6-5. dwrindex.html*

```
<!DOCTYPE html PUBLIC "-//W3C//DTD HTML 4.01 Transitional//EN">
<html>
<head>
    <title>AJAX DWR Zipcode Lookup</title>
    <script src='dwr/interface/ZipcodeManager.js'></script>
    <script src='dwr/engine.js'></script>
    <script src='dwr/util.js'></script>

    <script language="JavaScript" type="text/javascript">
    function retrieveCityState( ) {
        zip = document.getElementById("zipcode");

        ZipcodeManager.getZipcode(zip.value,populateData);
    }

    function populateData(zipcode) {
        document.getElementById('state').value=zipcode.state;
        document.getElementById('city').value=zipcode.city;
    }
    </script>
</head>
<body>
    <h1>AJAX ZIPCODES with DWR</h1>
    <table align="left" class="borderless">
        <tr>
            <td>Zip Code:</td>
            <td align="left">
                <input type="text" id="zipcode" name="zipcode"
                       onblur="retrieveCityState( )">
            </td>
        </tr>
```

*Example 6-5. dwrindex.html (continued)*

```
        <tr>
            <td>City:</td>
            <td align="left"><input type=text id="city"></td>
        </tr>
        <tr>
            <td>State:</td>
            <td align="left"><input type=text id="state"></td>
        </tr>
    </table>
</body>
</html>
```

Figure 6-4 shows what the zip code lookup application created with DWR looks like.

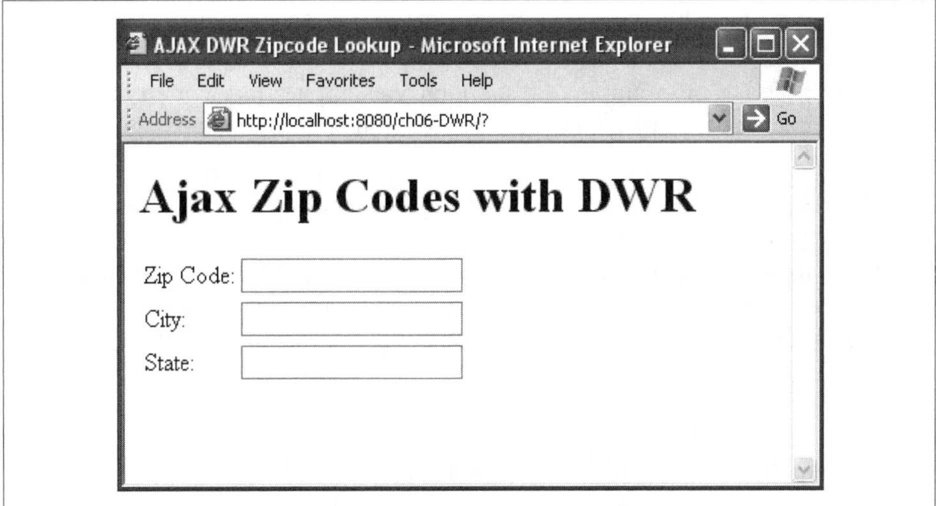


*Figure 6-4. Looking up zip codes with DWR*

DWR is one of the best Ajax frameworks for Java out there. This example barely touches on its features. For example, if you have to make several calls, DWR supports *call batching*, which allows the application to group the remote calls, storing them up and then sending them together in a single larger remote call.

DWR also has built-in security and JavaScript helper methods to make the display easier to manage. Check out DWR's home page for more information (*http://getahead.ltd.uk/dwr/documentation/*); because DWR has been around longer than many other Ajax frameworks, you'll find a lot of good documentation on it.

## Drag 'n' Drop with Scriptaculous and Prototype

Scriptaculous was written by Thomas Fuchs, a software developer from Austria. He writes: "Disappointed by current web application frameworks making no sense to me, I set out on a search for the perfect underpinnings of my web sites and web apps. I think I've found it." Scriptaculous can be used freely with the MIT license described on the Scriptaculous home page (*http://script.aculo.us*). You only need to include the copyright in the code that uses it.

You'll often find Scriptaculous used in conjunction with the Prototype library (*http://prototype.conio.net*) for communication with the server. We've seen Prototype before; it was one of the first Ajax frameworks and is used by many frameworks, including Rico.

Both Scriptaculous and Prototype are now part of the Ruby on Rails project, but that won't stop us from using them with Java; they are too rich to ignore. The Scriptaculous home page has an example of a shopping cart application written in PHP. To explore the power of Scriptaculous, let's build a drag and drop shopping cart of our own.

Our shopping cart will tie directly to a database. When the user clicks on a product image and drags it to the shopping cart, a JavaScript function will call the server to update the database, adding the new item to the user's cart. Then another function will query the database for the items in the shopping cart and update the cart on the web page. Figure 6-5 shows the look we're going for.

The shopping cart needs the following features:

- A signup page with a database to store the users
- A login page that authenticates against the database of users
- A products list generated from information in the database
- A shopping cart tied to the user that is persisted in the database
- A list of items in the shopping cart, also persisted to the database

As with previous examples, we will persist the information to a MySQL database. Here's how to set up the `USERS` table, which we'll use to store user account information. It's similar to the `USERS` table we used in Chapter 5, with two additional fields (`JOINED` and `LAST_LOGIN`):

```
DROP TABLE USERS;
CREATE TABLE USERS
(
    USER_ID int PRIMARY KEY auto_increment not null,
    USERNAME varchar(50),
    PASSWORD varchar(50),
    FIRST_NAME varchar(50),
    LAST_NAME varchar(50),
    EMAIL varchar(50),
```

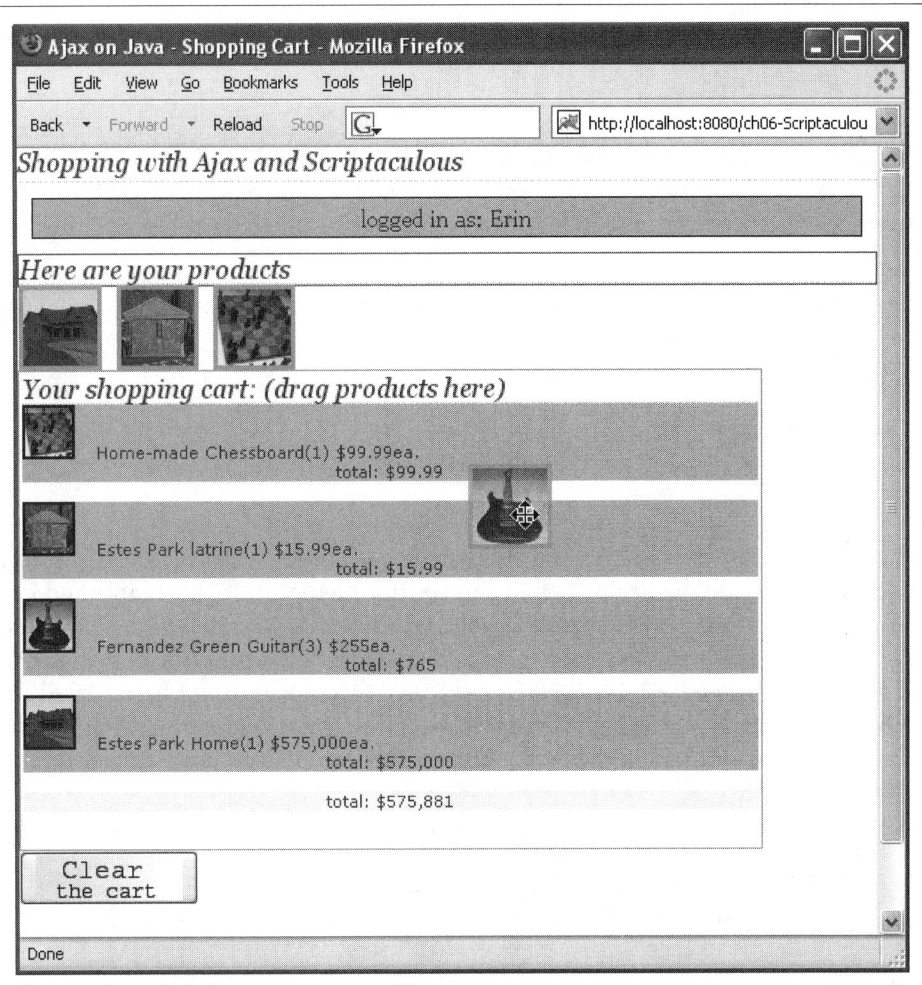


Figure 6-5. Scriptaculous drag and drop in action

```
        ADDRESS varchar(50),
        ZIPCODE varchar(10),
        CITY varchar(50),
        STATE varchar(2),
        JOINED date,
        LAST_LOGIN date
    );
```

While we are working on the database, we will need some other tables. After a user signs up and then signs in, he will need a shopping cart. Here's how to create the SHOPPING_CART table:

```
    CREATE TABLE SHOPPING_CART
    (
        CART_ID int PRIMARY KEY auto_increment not null,
```

```
    USER_ID int,
    START_DATE datetime,
    LAST_UPDATED datetime,
    ACTIVE tinyint
);
```

This table ties to the USERS table through the USER_ID field. It also gives us a START_DATE (datetime) field for when the shopping cart was created and a LAST_UPDATED (datetime) field to record how long it has been since something has been added to the cart.

Next, we need a table called ITEMS_IN_CART, which ties the products and the quantity of each item to the cart:

```
CREATE TABLE ITEMS_IN_CART
(
    ITEM_ID int,
    CART_ID int,
    COUNT int
);
```

Why don't we just use the SHOPPING_CART table and forget about the ITEMS_IN_CART table? We could add the fields ITEM_ID and COUNT to the SHOPPING_CART table and just add a new row to the SHOPPING_CART table for each new item selection. However, we'd still need a new row for every item added. That would result in a lot of duplicate information: the USER_ID, ACTIVE, and START_DATE fields would be repeated for every item in the cart. Having only one row for the shopping cart and linking the items to the shopping cart in their own table makes the database more efficient.

This is called *normalizing*; it adds flexibility and efficiency to the database design. For more information about database design, see *Java Database Best Practices*, by George Reese (O'Reilly). You'll find a discussion of normalization in Part I, Chapter 2, Section 2.3 of his book.

Now that we have the USERS, SHOPPING_CART, and ITEMS_IN_CART tables, we need a table to store the products that can be put into a shopping cart. This is the PRODUCTS table:

```
CREATE TABLE PRODUCTS
(
    PRODUCT_ID int PRIMARY KEY auto_increment not null,
    PRODUCT_NAME varchar(50),
    DESCRIPTION varchar(100),
    FILENAME varchar(100),
    PRICE decimal(9,2)
);
```

The FILENAME field contains the name of the image file that is used to display the product. So, the images need to be stored somewhere on the disk. In Chapter 8, we will use Struts to manage the products, but for now let's just hand-enter some to get started:

```
INSERT INTO PRODUCTS VALUES (1,'house','Estes Park Home2','house.png',575000.00);
INSERT INTO PRODUCTS VALUES (2,'latrines','Estes Park latrine',
                             'latrine.png','15.99');
INSERT INTO PRODUCTS VALUES (3,'chessboard','Home-made Chessboard',
                             'chessboard.png','99.99');
INSERT INTO PRODUCTS VALUES (4,'Guitar','Fernandez Green Guitar',
                             'guitar.png','255.00');
INSERT INTO PRODUCTS VALUES (5,'Tortoise','Cherry Box Turtle',
                             'cherry.png','19.99');
```

That completes the database setup, but the issue of where to put the images remains. I've included the images for these examples with the source distribution for the book, which is available from *http://www.oreilly.com/catalog/9780596101879*. Put the images in a subdirectory called *images* under the *war* directory. The images should be 100×100 pixels and in *.jpg*, *.png*, or *.gif* format.

Next, we will build the page that allows the user to sign up for the shopping cart application.

## The User Signup Application

The signup portion of our application won't really be any different from that of most other applications, except for the lack of any obvious submit/response activity. Thanks to Ajax, the submit/response is done in the background; as a result, this web application feels more like a desktop application.

The sequence diagram in Figure 6-6 shows how the application works. When a user signs up for the shopping cart system, a request is passed through `XMLHTTPRequest` to `AjaxSignupServlet`. The servlet creates a `User` object and calls `UserManager`. In turn, the `UserManager` makes a connection to the database and persists the user to the database.

When the application is first loaded, several variables and the initial screen view need to be initialized:

```
function init( ) {
    loginDiv = document.getElementById("loginDivId");
    signupDiv = document.getElementById("signupDivId");
    signupDiv.style.visibility ="hidden";
    shoppingCartDiv = document.getElementById("cart");
    loginmessageDiv = document.getElementById("loginmessage");
    shoppingCartDiv.style.visibility="hidden";
    productsdiv = document.getElementById("products");
    productsdiv.style.visibility="hidden";
    buttonsDiv = document.getElementById("buttonsDiv");
    buttonsDiv.style.visibility="hidden";
}
```

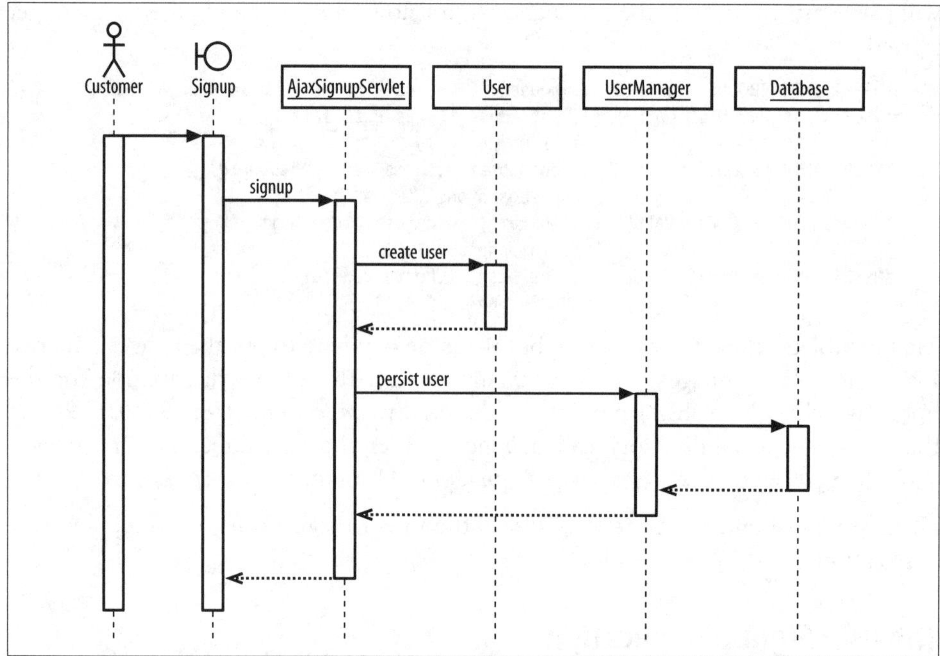


*Figure 6-6. Signup sequence diagram*

The `init()` function is called by `window.onload()`, which also initializes the key handler for the `loginDiv`. The `window.onload()` function (defined in *oreillyajaxdragndrop.js*) is automatically called whenever the page is loaded:

```
window.onload = function () {
    init();
    obj = document.getElementById("username");
    obj.focus();
    loginDiv.onkeydown = function (inEvent) {
        if (!inEvent) {
            inEvent = window.event;
        }
        keyDownHandler(inEvent);
    }
}
```

The "Sign up" button on the login screen (Figure 6-7) uses the `onClick` trigger to call the `signup()` JavaScript function. In this function, the signup div's visibility is set to `visible` and the login div's visibility is set to `hidden`:

```
function signup() {
    loginDiv.style.visibility="hidden";
    signupDiv.style.visibility="visible";
}
```

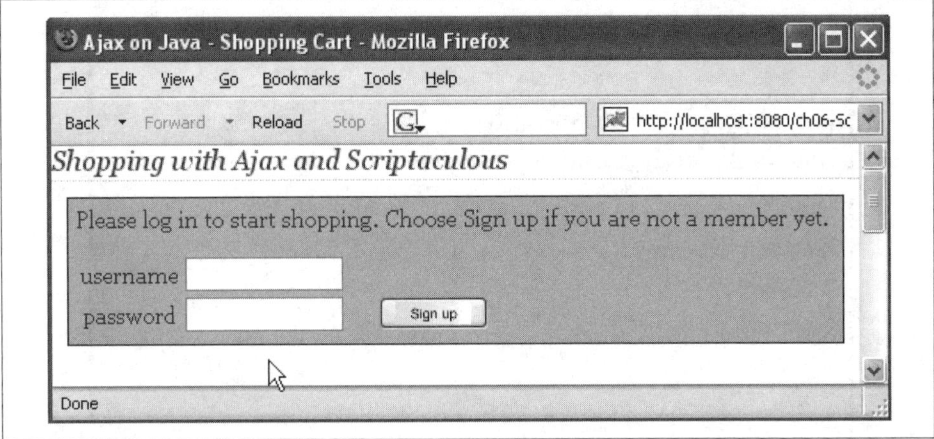


*Figure 6-7. The shopping cart login screen*

This technique (using dynamic styling to show and hide divs) gives the application a rich feel. It becomes much more responsive, because there's no need to load new pages for different stages of the application.

Once the login div has been hidden and the signup div is visible (Figure 6-8), the user can fill in the requested information and click the Signup button to send a request to `AjaxSignupServlet`.

It's important to understand that users are not moving between different web pages as they click from the login screen to the signup screen to the actual shopping screen. There's only one page in this application: *dragNdrop.html*. Rather than downloading a new page for each response, the application changes the screen by hiding and exposing different `<div>` tags. What we're doing is changing the behavior of a single page by modifying the document object model, which is the structure in which the browser represents the page. The whole page is downloaded and rendered once; all we do is tweak the DOM to show and hide different parts of it.

When a new user enters data and clicks the Signup button, a JavaScript trigger invokes the `addUser( )` JavaScript function. This function creates a new `Ajax.Request` object, which sends a request to the signup URL. That URL passes control to the `AjaxSignupServlet`, which adds the user to the database. The code for the `AjaxSignupServlet` is shown in Example 6-6.

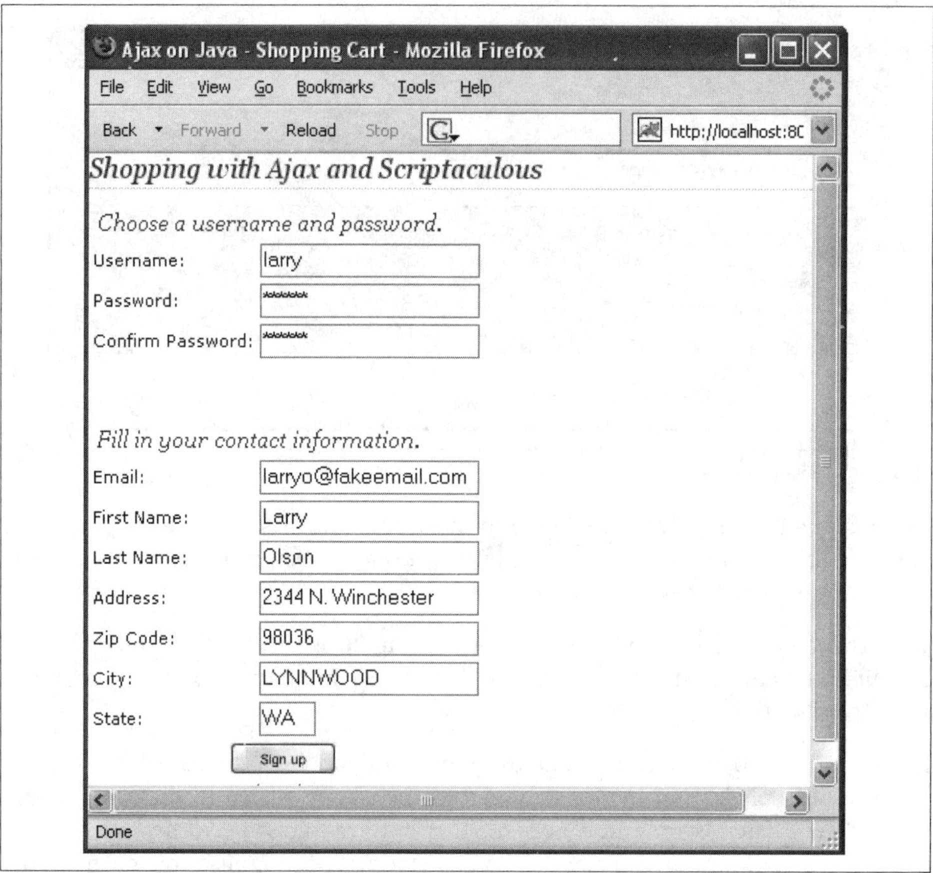


*Figure 6-8. The signup screen*

*Example 6-6. The AjaxSignupServlet*

```
public class AjaxSignupServlet extends HttpServlet {
    public void doGet(HttpServletRequest req, HttpServletResponse res)
            throws ServletException, IOException {
        ServletContext sc = getServletContext( );
        RequestDispatcher rd = null;
        User user = new User( );
        user.setUsername(req.getParameter("username"));
        user.setFirstName(req.getParameter("firstname"));
        user.setLastName(req.getParameter("lastname"));
        user.setEmail(req.getParameter("email"));
        user.setPassword(req.getParameter("password"));
        user.setAddress(req.getParameter("address"));
        user.setCity(req.getParameter("city"));
        user.setState(req.getParameter("state"));
        user.setZipCode(req.getParameter("zipcode"));
        if (UserManager.addUser(user)) {
            rd = sc.getRequestDispatcher("/confirmation.html");
```

*Example 6-6. The AjaxSignupServlet (continued)*

```
            rd.forward(req, res);
        }
        else {
            rd = sc.getRequestDispatcher("/failure.html");
            rd.forward(req, res);
        }
    }
}
```

## Using Prototype to Wrap XMLHttpRequest

The JavaScript code behind the Signup button is largely contained in the `addUser( )` function. This is one place where Prototype comes in handy: using Prototype's wrapper around `XMLHttpRequest` is easy. Example 6-7 shows a call to Prototype's `new Ajax.Request( )` constructor. First we pass in the target URL (in this case, simply `"signup"`). Then we pass in parameters that specify whether the call will be asynchronous (true), specify the HTTP type ("get"), and set the parameters to send in the request. The final two parameters, `onSuccess` and `onFailure`, are actually function definitions; they specify what happens after the request has been sent. `onFailure` determines what happens when an error occurs, whereas `onSuccess` sends the newly signed-up user to the login page—which is just the current page, so a reload isn't needed.

*Example 6-7. Invoking Ajax.Request*

```
function addUser( ) {
    var ajaxUsername = document.getElementById("ajax_username");
    var password = document.getElementById("confirmpassword");
    var ajax_password = document.getElementById("ajax_password");
    if (ajax_password.value != password.value) {
        alert("passwords don't match: "+password.value+
              " != "+ajax_password.value);
        return;
    }
    var firstName = document.getElementById("firstname");
    var lastName = document.getElementById("lastname");
    var email = document.getElementById("email");
    var address = document.getElementById("address");
    var city = document.getElementById("city");
    var state = document.getElementById("state");
    if (state.length > 2) {
        alert("State can only have 2 characters: "+
              state+" has more than 2 characters");
        return;
    }
    var zipcode = document.getElementById("zipcode");
    alert("username="+ajaxUsername.value+" password:"+password.value);
    parameterString = "username=" + escape(ajaxUsername.value)+
            "&password=" +escape(ajax_password.value)+
            "&firstname=" +escape(firstName.value)+
```

*Example 6-7. Invoking Ajax.Request (continued)*

```
            "&lastname=" +escape(lastName.value)+
            "&email="+escape(email.value)+
            "&address="+escape(address.value)+
            "&city="+escape(city.value)+
            "&state="+escape(state.value)+
            "&zipcode="+escape(zipcode.value);

    new Ajax.Request("signup", {
        asynchronous: true,
        method: "get",
        parameters: parameterString,
        onSuccess: function(request) {
            alert('signup successful, welcome '+
                  ajaxUsername.value+", please login");
            window.location.reload( false );
        },
        onFailure: function(request) {
            alert('failed to signup username');
        }
    });
}
```

Let's look again at the URL passed to the `Ajax.Request` constructor. The URL, `"signup"`, is mapped to the servlet that is waiting for the `XMLHTTPRequest`. Here's how we map that URL to the processing servlet in *web.xml*:

```
<servlet>
    <servlet-name>AjaxSignupServlet</servlet-name>
    <servlet-class>
        com.oreilly.ajax.servlet.AjaxSignupServlet
    </servlet-class>
    <load-on-startup>4</load-on-startup>
</servlet>
<servlet-mapping>
    <servlet-name>AjaxSignupServlet</servlet-name>
    <url-pattern>/signup</url-pattern>
</servlet-mapping>
```

## The User Login Functions

When the user logs in, a shopping cart is created and linked to the user by the `USER_ID` field in the `SHOPPING_CART` table. At this point, the user is ready to start shopping.

The login sequence diagram (Figure 6-9) is similar to the signup sequence diagram, with the following differences:

- The `AjaxLoginServlet` is called instead of the `AjaxSignupServlet`.
- The `UserManager` gets the user information but isn't responsible for persisting it.
- The `ShoppingCartManager` gets a shopping cart for the user.
- The user is persisted into the session.

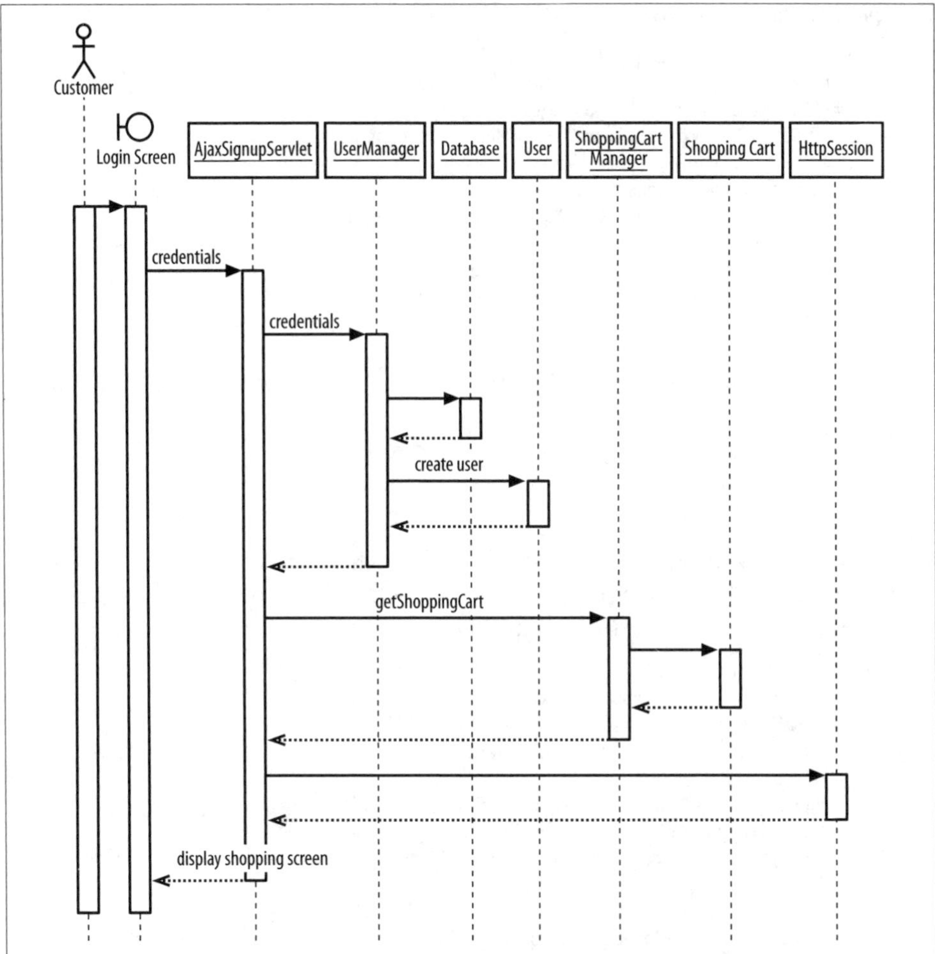


*Figure 6-9. Login sequence diagram*

When the user logs in to the shopping cart application, the login div is changed to display the message "logged in as: <username>" and the product list and shopping cart divs are set to `visible`. The product list div is populated with the products in the database's `PRODUCTS` table via the `ProductManager` class. To get a list of products in the shopping cart, the `AjaxLoginServlet` (shown in Example 6-8) calls `ShoppingCartManager:getCartContents( )`, which returns a JSON object.

*Example 6-8. The AjaxLoginServlet*

```
public class AjaxLoginServlet extends HttpServlet {
    public void doGet(HttpServletRequest req, HttpServletResponse res)
            throws ServletException, IOException {
        res.setContentType("text/xml");
        res.setHeader("Cache-Control", "no-cache");
```

*Example 6-8. The AjaxLoginServlet (continued)*

```
        String username = req.getParameter("username");
        String password = req.getParameter("password");
        if (username != null && password != null) {
            User user = UserManager.login(username,password);
            if (user!=null) {
                String responseString =
                        ShoppingCartManager.getJSONShoppingCart(user);
                HttpSession session = req.getSession( );
                session.setAttribute("user",user);
                res.getWriter( ).write(responseString);
            }
            else
                res.getWriter( ).write("fail");
        }
        else
            res.getWriter( ).write("fail");
    }
}
```

The JSON object is sent back to the browser, where it is parsed by the call to `updateCart(request)`. This method takes the JSON object out of the request and populates the shopping cart div with the items in the cart:

```
    function updateCart(req) {
        var jsonData = req.responseText;
        var myJSONObject = eval('(' + jsonData + ')');
        var cartdiv = document.getElementById("cart");
        // clear cart
        var output="<p> Your shopping cart: (drag products here) </p>";
        for(i=0;i<myJSONObject.cartcontents.length-1;i++) {
            output+='<div><img src="images/'+myJSONObject.cartcontents[i].filename+ '">
                    '+myJSONObject.cartcontents[i].description+
                    '('+myJSONObject.cartcontents[i].value+')$'+
                    myJSONObject.cartcontents[i].price+
                    'ea. <CENTER> total: $'+
                    myJSONObject.cartcontents[i].total+
                    '</CENTER></div><br />';
        }
        output+='<div height:32px; style="background-color:#FFFF99;
                margin-bottom:10px;">
                <CENTER> total: $'
                +myJSONObject.cartcontents[myJSONObject.cartcontents.length-1].total
                +'</CENTER></div><br />';
        cartdiv.innerHTML=output;
    }
```

Figure 6-10 shows what the application looks like at this point.

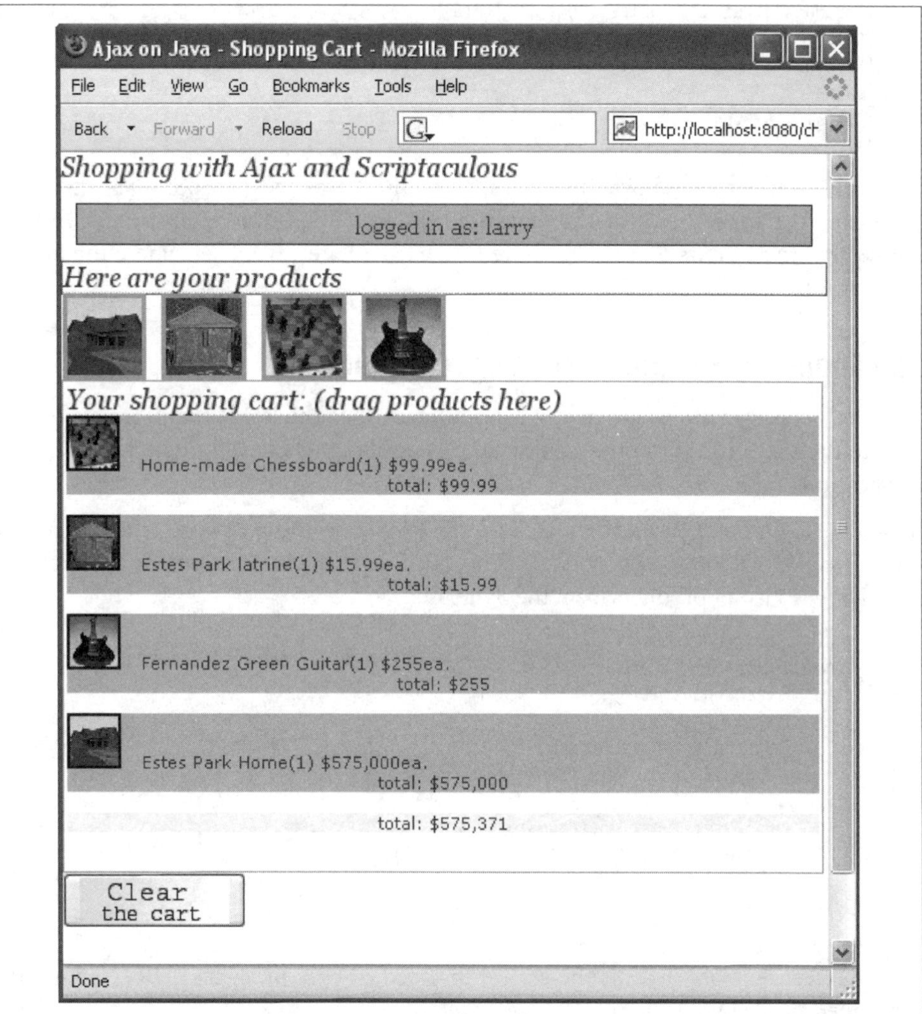


*Figure 6-10. Typical view of a user's shopping cart*

This view was built from a JSON array that lists the description, price, total price, and quantity of each item in the cart. The final element of the array represents the total price of all the items in the cart:

```
{"cartcontents":[
{"product":"chessboard","price":"99.99","total":"99.99","description":"Chessboard",
"value":"1"},
{"product":"latrine","price":"15.99","total":"47.97","description":"latrine",
"value":"3"},
```

```
{"product":"guitar","price":"99.99","total":"499.95","description":"guitar", "value":
"5"},
{"product":"house","price":"575,000","total":"575,000","description":"house",
"value":"1"},
{"total":"575,647.94"}
]}
```

It's fairly simple to see how the data in this object was used to populate the shopping cart: the value field for the guitar is 5 in the JSON object, and the web page shows that five guitars ("guitar(5)") are in the cart. Later, we'll see where the images come from.

## The Shopping Functions: Getting a Product List

Now let's see how the products div is populated. This div holds the products for the user to drag into the shopping cart div and is updated whenever a user logs in to the application.

When the login function finds a match for the username and password entered into the login screen, it calls getProductList( ). This JavaScript function creates an Ajax.Request object to get a list of products from the database:

```
function getProductList( ) {
    new Ajax.Request("products", {
        asynchronous: true,
        method: "get",
        onSuccess: function(request) {
            updateProductList(request);
        },
        onFailure: function(request) {
            alert('failed to get product list');
        }
    });
}
```

The Ajax.Request object calls the servlet mapped to the "products" URL. That URL is mapped to the ProductServlet by *web.xml*:

```
<servlet>
    <servlet-name>ProductServlet</servlet-name>
    <servlet-class>
        com.oreilly.ajax.servlet.ProductServlet
    </servlet-class>
    <load-on-startup>6</load-on-startup>
</servlet>
<servlet-mapping>
    <servlet-name>ProductServlet</servlet-name>
    <url-pattern>/products</url-pattern>
</servlet-mapping>
```

The ProductServlet, shown in Example 6-9, returns a JSON object that contains information about all the products that can be selected.

*Example 6-9. The ProductServlet*

```
public class ProductServlet extends HttpServlet {

    private static final long serialVersionUID = 1L;

    public void doGet(HttpServletRequest req, HttpServletResponse res)
            throws ServletException, IOException {

        res.setContentType("text/xml");
        res.setHeader("Cache-Control", "no-cache");

        String responseString = ProductManager.getJSONProducts( );
        if (responseString != null) {
            res.getWriter( ).write(responseString);
        }
        else
            res.getWriter( ).write("fail");
    }
}
```

The JSON object is actually constructed by a call to `ProductManager.getJSONProducts( )` (Example 6-10). This method builds the JSON object by manipulating a `StringBuffer`, but this could alternatively have been done using one of the JSON libraries discussed in the latter part of Chapter 4.

*Example 6-10. ProductManager.getJSONProducts()*

```
private static String getProducts( ) {
    Product product = new Product( );
    String title = "products";
    Connection con = DatabaseConnector.getConnection( );
    StringBuffer jsonString = new StringBuffer("\r\n{\"" + title + "\": [");
    String sqlString = "";

    try {
        sqlString = "SELECT * FROM PRODUCTS;";
        Statement select = con.createStatement( );
        ResultSet result = select.executeQuery(sqlString);
        while (result.next( )) {
            // process results one row at a time

            product.setProductName(result.getString("PRODUCT_NAME"));
            product.setDescription(result.getString("DESCRIPTION"));
            product.setFilename(result.getString("FILENAME"));
            product.setPrice(result.getFloat("PRICE"));
            product.setProductId(result.getInt("PRODUCT_ID"));
            jsonString.append("\r\n{\"description\":\"" +
                    product.getDescription( ) + "\",\"name\":\"" +
                    product.getProductName( ) + "\",\"filename\":\"" +
                    product.getFilename( ) + "\", \"price\":\"" +
                    product.getPrice( ) + "\"},");

        }
```

*Example 6-10. ProductManager.getJSONProducts() (continued)*

```
        int lastCharIndex = jsonString.length( );
        jsonString.deleteCharAt(lastCharIndex - 1);
        jsonString.append("\r\n]}");
    }
    catch(Exception e) {
        System.out.println("exception caught getting Product" +
                          sqlString + " " + e.getMessage( ));
    }
    finally {
        if (con != null) {
            try {
                con.close( );
            }
            catch(SQLException e) {
            }
        }
    }
    return jsonString.toString( );
}
```

Here's what the JSON document embedded in the response looks like:

```
{"products": [
{"description":"house","name":"house","filename":"images/house.png",
"price":"575000.0"},
{"description":"latrine","name":"latrine","filename":"images/latrine.png",
"price":"15.99"},
{"description":"Chessboard","name":"chessboard",
"filename":"images/chessboard.png","price":"99.99"},
{"description":"guitar","name":"guitar","filename":"images/guitar.png",
"price":"99.99"}
]}
```

For each product, there is a description, a product name, the filename for an image file, and a price. That information is necessary to build the product list.

The `onSuccess` parameter of `getProductList( )` is a function that transfers execution to `updateProductList( )` if the request is successful. In turn, `updateProductList( )` takes the JSON object from the request (the listing of the products that are available) and uses it to populate the product list div:

```
function updateProductList(req) {

    jsonData = req.responseText;
    var myJSONObject = eval('(' + jsonData + ')');
    // clear cart
    productsdiv.innerHTML="<p>Here are your products</p>";
    for(i=0;i<myJSONObject.products.length;i++) {
        productsdiv.innerHTML+='<img height="100px" alt='
                + myJSONObject.products[i].description
                + ' class="products" id="'
                + myJSONObject.products[i].name
                + '" name="'+ myJSONObject.products[i].name
                + '" src="'+ myJSONObject.products[i].filename+'"/>';
```

```
        }
        // I should be able to put the draggable in the above loop, but that
        // doesn't work so I had to do this in a separate loop. Strange, but true.
        for (i=0;i<myJSONObject.products.length;i++) {
            new Draggable(myJSONObject.products[i].name, {revert:true});
        }
        Droppables.add('cart', {
            onDrop:function(element) {
                addToCart(element.id);
            }
        });
    }
```

The result is that the application updates the product list whenever a user logs in. The `updateProductList()` function iterates through the products listed in the JSON object and creates an HTML string that holds the information about each product. For the guitar that's for sale, the string looks like this:

```
<img height="100px" alt="guitar" class="products" id="guitar"
     name="guitar" src="images/guitar.png"/>
```

The JavaScript assembles this image element from data in the JSON response. Among other things, the JSON object contains the image filename, which is inserted into the `<img>` element by `updateProductList()`.

Once we've created a sequence of `<img>` tags to display the product list, we make another pass through the JSON array. This loop sets up the drag-and-drop feature by calling `Draggable()` from the Scriptaculous library and passing in the IDs of each element on the HTML page:

```
new Draggable(myJSONObject.products[i].name, {revert:true})
```

For some reason, objects cannot be set to `Draggable` in the same loop that puts the images into the products div. If you think it's redundant to have two `for` loops with the same logic, I agree—it is redundant. However, as of Scriptaculous version 1.6.1, the draggable functionality will not work without this second loop.

The `products[i].name` reference refers to an element in the `products` array that is contained by the JSON object. The server built this array with a call to `JSONUtil.convertMapToProducts()` (which you'll see later, in Example 6-12).

Finally, we need to make the shopping cart accept draggable items. To enable dropping, we call `Droppables.add()` from the Scriptaculous library and pass it the ID of the shopping cart div, `'cart'`. Now the shopping cart div can accept draggable items. The second parameter, `onDrop`, specifies what to do when an item is dropped on the shopping cart. In this case, we call `addToCart()` with the ID of the element we want to add.

Each time the customer drags a product to the shopping cart, `addToCart()` is invoked. This function creates a new `Ajax.Request` object with the target URL of `"shoppingcart"`; in turn, this URL maps to the `ShoppingCartServlet`. The request makes a simple HTTP GET request, with the "item=" parameter string appended to the URL:

```
function addToCart(item) {
    parameterString = "item="+item;

    new Ajax.Request("shoppingcart", {
        asynchronous: true,
        method: "get",
        parameters: parameterString,
        onSuccess: function(request) {
            updateCart(request);
        },
        onFailure: function(request) {
            alert('failed to add item to cart');
        }
    });
}
```

The ShoppingCartServlet, shown in Example 6-11, then picks up the information in the parameter string and creates an entry in the ITEMS_IN_CART table. This entry includes the Shopping Cart ID and the Product ID. It packs the contents of the shopping cart into a JSON object and ships that back to the client.

*Example 6-11. The ShoppingCartServlet*

```
public class ShoppingCartServlet extends HttpServlet {
    public void doGet(HttpServletRequest req, HttpServletResponse res)
            throws ServletException, IOException {
        String responseString = "success";
        User user = (User) req.getSession( ).getAttribute("user");
        String item = req.getParameter("item");
        if (item != null) {
            HashMap shoppingCartMap = ShoppingCartManager.addToShoppingCart(
                    user, item);
            if (shoppingCartMap == null) {
                responseString = "fail";
            }
            else {
                responseString = JSONUtil.convertMapToProducts(shoppingCartMap,
                        "cartcontents");
            }
        }
        if (responseString != null) {
            System.out.println(responseString);
            res.setContentType("text/xml");
            res.setHeader("Cache-Control", "no-cache");
            res.getWriter( ).write(responseString);
        }
    }
}
```

The ShoppingCartServlet makes a call to convertMapToProducts( ) (Example 6-12), a method from the JSONUtil class that converts a Map to a JSON String that contains an array of products.

*Example 6-12. convertMapToProducts()*

```
public static String convertMapToProducts(HashMap map, String title) {
    StringBuffer returnJSON = new StringBuffer("\r\n{\"" + title + "\":[ ");
    String key = "";
    String value = "";
    // loop through all the map entries
    Iterator it = map.entrySet().iterator( );
    Product product = null;
    String totalCostFormatted="";

    DecimalFormat nf = new DecimalFormat("###,###.##");
    float itemTotalCost = 0.0F;
    float totalCost = 0.0F;
    while (it.hasNext( )) {
        Map.Entry e = (Map.Entry) it.next( );
        value = (String) e.getValue( ); // item quantity
        key = (String) e.getKey( );     // item id
        product = ProductManager.getProductById(key);
        if (value!=null) {
            // if the count is null,
            // don't care (not in shopping cart)
            int intValue = Integer.parseInt(value);
            itemTotalCost = intValue * product.getPrice( );
            totalCost += itemTotalCost;

            returnJSON.append("\r\n{\"product\":\"" + product.getProductName( ) +
                    "\",\"price\":\"" + nf.format(product.getPrice( )) +
                    "\",\"filename\":\"" + product.getFilename( ) +
                    "\",\"total\":\"" + nf.format(itemTotalCost) +
                    "\",\"description\":\"" + product.getDescription( ) +
                    "\", \"value\":\"" + value + "\"},");
        }
    }
    totalCostFormatted = nf.format(totalCost);

    returnJSON.append("\r\n{\"total\":\""+totalCostFormatted+"\"}");
    returnJSON.append("\r\n]}");

    return returnJSON.toString( );
}
```

The getProducts( ) function inserts the appropriate images from the PRODUCTS table into the product list div (Figure 6-11).

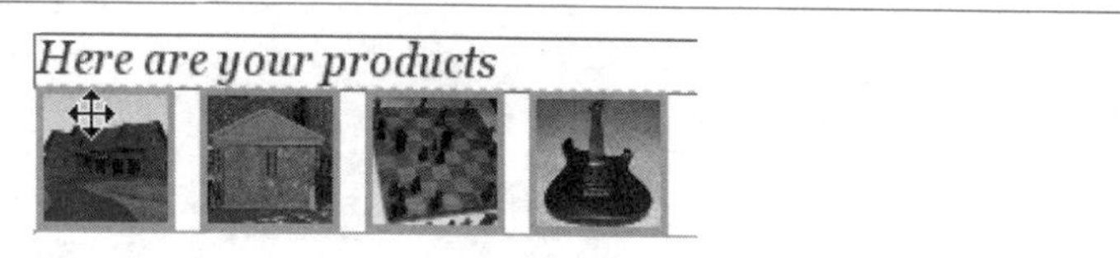


*Figure 6-11. The product list div*

The images are from the filesystem, but their paths are stored in the FILENAME field of the PRODUCTS table (Figure 6-12).

| PRODUCT_ID | PRODUCT_NAME | DESCRIPTION | FILENAME | PRICE |
|---|---|---|---|---|
| 1 | house | house | images/house.png | 575000.00 |
| 2 | latrine | latrine | images/latrine.png | 15.99 |
| 3 | chessboard | Chessboard | images/chessboard.png | 99.99 |
| 4 | guitar | guitar | images/guitar.png | 99.99 |

*Figure 6-12. The PRODUCTS table viewed in SQuirreL SQL*

Adding new products is easy: just add a new product image to the server's *images* directory, and then add an entry for it in the database's PRODUCTS table.

Now you have seen what it takes to build a complete application using one HTML page. This page makes heavy use of CSS formatting, *Scriptaculous.js*, and a JavaScript file with our own custom functions. The backend to the application consists of some simple Java servlets backed by a database. Is it a lot of work? Possibly—though probably not much more work than building a traditional shopping cart application. Will your customers be satisfied? Most definitely. By using Ajax and DOM rewriting, we've made an application that's much more responsive than most of the web applications available.

CHAPTER 7

# Ajax Tags

Writing Ajaxian code over and over can be tedious and error-prone. Although many libraries with a lot of reusable code are available, you may develop some custom features that you want to use repeatedly throughout your applications. In that case, you can encapsulate the functionality in a JSP tag for easy reuse. Using tag libraries will save you time and enhance the maintainability of your code. If you fix a bug in a tag library, you can easily propagate the change to all of your code: instead of rewriting the code in every application, merely drop your new library into the deploy directory.

## Creating a Tag Library

In the two previous chapters, we developed code that enabled us to look up city and state information based on a user-entered zip code. Now we'll explore how to add this feature to a tag library, encapsulating the details of the Ajax code. To start, we must define our tag. Tags are defined in Tag Library Definition (TLD) files. The names of these files end with the extension *.tld*; in this example, the TLD file will be called *ajax-oreilly.tld*.

### Writing a TLD

A TLD is written in XML and describes the attributes of each tag in the tag library. The parent tag is `<taglib>`; within that tag, you need a `<tag>` tag for each type of tag that the TLD defines. Our library will have only a single tag, but most libraries define many tags.

Each `<tag>` definition must have a `<name>` tag, which specifies the tag's name, and a `<tagclass>` tag. The `<tagclass>` tag specifies the tag handler class that handles the tag.

The `<bodycontent>` tag is used if the tag handler needs to read or modify the content of the body. The body is the content between the start and end of the tag. For example, if the `zipCode` tag had a body, it would be expressed like this:

```
<ajax:zipCode>
    Body
</ajax:zipCode>
```

The tag that is presented here will not have a body; therefore, we'll declare the body as empty in the *.tld* file.

There can be any number of attributes in a tag. Each attribute must have a `<name>` tag and a `<required>` tag. If the value of the `<required>` tag is `true`, that attribute must be present whenever the tag is used. For example, because all the attributes for the `zipCode` tag defined in the *oreillyAjax.tld* file presented in Example 7-1 have `<required>` set to `true`, all those attributes must be set when the `zipCode` tag is used or the taglib will throw an exception.

*Example 7-1. oreillyAjax.tld*

```
<?xml version="1.0" encoding="ISO-8859-1" ?>
<!DOCTYPE taglib
    PUBLIC "-//Sun Microsystems, Inc.//DTD JSP Tag Library 1.1//EN"
    "http://java.sun.com/j2ee/dtds/web-jsptaglibrary_1_1.dtd">

<taglib>
    <tlibversion>1.0</tlibversion>
    <jspversion>1.1</jspversion>
    <shortname>ajax</shortname>
    <info>adds ajax enabled tags to your jsp </info>
    <tag>
        <name>zipCode</name>
        <tagclass>com.oreilly.ajax.ZipCodeTag</tagclass>
        <bodycontent>empty</bodycontent>
        <attribute>
            <name>zipcodeId</name>
            <required>true</required>
        </attribute>
        <attribute>
            <name>stateId</name>
            <required>true</required>
        </attribute>
        <attribute>
            <name>cityId</name>
            <required>true</required>
        </attribute>
        <attribute>
            <name>url</name>
            <required>true</required>
            <rtexprvalue>true</rtexprvalue>
            <description>
                the url of the servlet that handles the request for city and state
                based on zip code
            </description>
        </attribute>
    </tag>
</taglib>
```

The `zipcodeId`, `stateId`, `cityId`, and `url` attributes are all required. The `zipcodeId` gets the HTML input element into which the user enters the zip code. The `stateId` and `cityId` attributes represent the IDs of the elements that this tag populates with the city and state. Finally, the `url` attribute specifies the URL of the servlet that the tag invokes. In our case, the tag will insert an Ajaxian JavaScript function into the web page. This function invokes the `zipcodes` URL, which must match the URL of a servlet defined in *web.xml*.

## Using the Tags in a JSP

Armed with a *.tld* file, we can now put a declaration referencing the tag library in a JSP and give it a handle. In this case, the handle is `ajax`, and it is defined by the `prefix` as follows:

```
<%@ taglib uri="/WEB-INF/oreillyAjax.tld" prefix="ajax" %>
```

Once we've assigned a handle to the library, we can use it to reference any tag the library contains. Here's how to use the `zipCode` tag in a JSP page:

```
<ajax:zipCode zipcodeId="zipcode" stateId="state" cityId="city" url="zipcodes" />
```

`ajax` is the handle; `zipCode` is the tag we're invoking. Again, note that all four attributes must be present. The `stateId` is the `id` of the input field for the state, the `cityId` is the `id` of the input field for the city, the `zipcodeId` is the `id` of the zip code input field, and the `url` is the URL of the servlet the tag invokes. The entire JSP file is shown in Example 7-2.

*Example 7-2. The custom <ajax:zipCode> tag in oreillyajaxtags.jsp*

```
<%@ page language="java" contentType="text/html" %>
<%@ taglib uri="/WEB-INF/oreillyAjax.tld" prefix="ajax" %>
<html>
<head>
    <h1>O'Reilly Ajax with Custom Tags</H1>
</head>
<body>
    Enter the zip code, then TAB.<br />
    The State and City fields will automatically populate.<br />
    <ajax:zipCode zipcodeId="zipcode" stateId="state" cityId="city"
                  url="zipcodes" />
    <table>
        <tr>
            <td> Zipcode: </td>
            <td> <input type="text" id="zipcode" /> </td>
        </tr>
        <tr>
            <td> City: </td>
            <td> <input type="text" id="city" /> </td>
        </tr>
        <tr>
            <td> State: </td>
            <td> <input type="text" id="state" /><br /> </td>
        </tr>
    </table>
</body>
</html>
```

See how each HTML `<input>` tag has an `id` that matches one of the attributes of the `zipCode` tag? The tag library uses those `id`s to populate the fields, so an Ajax request is sent when a user fills in the zip code field and the results that come back from the server are used to populate the city and state fields.

## Writing the TagSupport Class

To support the tag, we need a class that extends `javax.servlet.jsp.tagext.TagSupport`.* The `ZipCodeTag` class presented in Example 7-3 provides the support we need.

*Example 7-3. The ZipCodeTag class*

```
package com.oreilly.ajax;
import java.io.IOException;
import javax.servlet.jsp.tagext.TagSupport;
public class ZipCodeTag extends TagSupport {
    private String zipcodeId = "0";
    private String stateId = "";
    private String cityId = "";
    private String url = "";
    public int doStartTag( ) {
        try {
            this.pageContext.getOut( ).print(
                    JavaScriptCode.getZipCodeScript(stateId, cityId, zipcodeId,
                    url));
        }
        catch (IOException e) {
            System.out.println("couldn't write JavaScript to jsp"
                    + e.getMessage( ));
        }
        return SKIP_BODY;
    }
    public String getCityId( ) {
        return cityId;
    }
    public void setCityId(String city) {
        this.cityId = city;
    }
    public String getStateId( ) {
        return stateId;
    }
    public void setStateId(String state) {
        this.stateId = state;
    }
    public String getUrl( ) {
        return url;
    }
```

* The *.jar* file in which `TagSupport` is defined has changed over the years. It was originally in *servlet.jar*, which is the *.jar* file you should use for Tomcat 4. It's currently in *jsp-api.jar*; use this *.jar* file for Tomcat 5. If you're using another servlet engine, it's up to you to find the *.jar* file that contains `TagSupport`.

*Example 7-3. The ZipCodeTag class (continued)*

```
    public void setUrl(String url) {
        this.url = url;
    }
    public String getZipcodeId( ) {
        return zipcodeId;
    }
    public void setZipcodeId(String zipcodeId) {
        this.zipcodeId = zipcodeId;
    }
}
```

TagSupport provides the coupling between ZipCodeTag and the JSP. The set and get accessor methods are the key to this coupling; the set and get methods for each instance variable are used to pass in values from the JSP or, conversely, to write results back to the JSP. There must be set and get accessor methods for every attribute in the JSP tag (in the case of the zipCode tag, url, zipcodeId, stateId, and cityId).

Most tag classes also need to add some code to the HTML page the JSP produces. To do so, the tag class overrides one or more of the methods provided by the TagSupport class (usually doStartTag( ), doEndTag( ), or both). doStartTag( ) inserts code at the point where the start tag is inserted into the JSP. doEndTag( ) inserts code at the point where the tag is terminated. In this application, we don't expect anything to intervene between <zipCode> and </zipCode>, so the code inserted by doEndTag( ) would immediately follow the code coming from doStartTag( ). The zipCode tag really only needs to override one of these methods. In this case, doStartTag( ) was used, but it makes sense to override doEndTag( ) if the code logically should be inserted at the end of the tag block.

The following line from doStartTag( ) injects the code into the JSP:

```
    this.pageContext.getOut( ).print(
            JavaScriptCode.getZipCodeScript(stateId, cityId, zipcodeId,
            url));
```

pageContext.getOut.print( ) inserts the text of our JavaScript into the JSP page. To keep the JavaScript details out of the tag class itself, I created a JavaScriptCode class (shown in Example 7-4) that has a single method: getZipCodeScript( ). This method returns a String containing our JavaScript code.

*Example 7-4. The JavaScriptCode class*

```
package com.oreilly.ajax;

public class JavaScriptCode {
    public static String getZipCodeScript(String stateId, String cityId,
            String zipcodeId, String url) {
        StringBuffer sb = new StringBuffer( );
        sb.append("<script>    ");
```

*Example 7-4. The JavaScriptCode class (continued)*

```
        sb.append("function retrieveCityState( ) { ");
        sb.append("    var zip = document.getElementById('"+zipcodeId+"'");
        sb.append("    var url = '"+url+"?zip=' + escape(zip.value); ");
        sb.append("    if (window.XMLHttpRequest) { ");
        sb.append("        req = new XMLHttpRequest( ); ");
        sb.append("    } " );
        sb.append("    else if (window.ActiveXObject) { ");
        sb.append("        req = new ActiveXObject('Microsoft.XMLHTTP'); ");
        sb.append("    } ");
        sb.append("    req.open('Get',url,true); ");
        sb.append("    req.onreadystatechange = callbackCityState; ");
        sb.append("    alert ('sending request to '+url);");
        sb.append("    req.send(null);");
        sb.append("}");
        sb.append("function populateCityState( ) {");
        sb.append("    var jsonData = req.responseText;");
        sb.append("    var myJSONObject = eval('(' + jsonData + ')');");
        sb.append("    var city = document.getElementById('"+cityId+"');");
        sb.append("    city.value=myJSONObject.location.city;");
        sb.append("    var state = document.getElementById('"+stateId+"');");
        sb.append("    state.value=myJSONObject.location.state;");
        sb.append("}");
        sb.append("function callbackCityState( ) { ");
        sb.append("    if (req.readyState==4) { ");
        sb.append("        if (req.status == 200) { ");
        sb.append("            populateCityState( );");
        sb.append("        }");
        sb.append("    }");
        sb.append("}");
        sb.append("</script> ");
        return sb.toString( );
    }
}
```

This is not the neatest or most flexible way to get the JavaScript text, though it is the fastest in some cases. Keeping the JavaScript in a file is a more flexible alternative to hard-coding the JavaScript into a class; it's slower because the application has to read the file at runtime, but it does allow you to debug the JavaScript without recompiling after each change.

Example 7-5, which gives another version of the `doStartTag( )` method, shows how to retrieve the JavaScript from a file.

*Example 7-5. ZipCodeTag::getJavaScript() retrieves JavaScript from a file*

```
private String getJavaScript( ) {
    if (javaScript != null) {
        return javaScript;
    }
    else {
        String tempString = "";
        String outString = "";
```

*Example 7-5. ZipCodeTag::getJavaScript() retrieves JavaScript from a file (continued)*

```
        try {

            InputStream is = getClass( ).getResourceAsStream("oreillyajaxtags.js");
            BufferedReader br = new BufferedReader(new InputStreamReader(is));

            while ((tempString = br.readLine( )) != null) {
                outString += tempString;
            }

            outString = outString.replaceAll("stateId", stateId);
            outString = outString.replaceAll("cityId", cityId);
            outString = outString.replaceAll("zipcodeId", zipcodeId);
            outString = outString.replaceAll("urlName", url);
            br.close( );
            is.close( );
            javaScript = outString;

        } catch (IOException e) {
            System.out.println("couldn't get JavaScript from oreillyajaxtags.js"
                               + e.getMessage( ));
        }
    }
    return javaScript;
}
```

The doStartTag( ) method can then simply call getJavaScript( ) to get the JavaScript String. A call to pageContext.getOut().print( ) will put the JavaScript into the place where the tag occurs in the JSP:

```
public int doStartTag( ) {
    try {
        pageContext.getOut().print(getJavaScript( ));
    } catch (IOException e) {
        System.out.println("couldn't write JavaScript to jsp" + e.getMessage( ));
    }
    return SKIP_BODY;
}
```

The preceding code assumes that the JavaScript file is in the same directory as the ZipCodeTag class. It is simpler to keep the JavaScript code in the same directory as the class using it because it is not used anywhere else and both files stay within a *.jar* file. (See the *build.xml* file in Example 7-7 to see how the *.jar* file can be built.)

As mentioned earlier, the body is the portion of code between the start tag and the end tag. In this case there is no body, and either EVAL_BODY_INCLUDE or SKIP_BODY can be returned. EVAL_BODY_INCLUDE is returned to indicate that the body is to be evaluated and then included in the page at the location of the tag; SKIP_BODY is returned to indicate that if there is a body, it should be neither evaluated nor included. In this case, because the tag does not have a body, it is more accurate to return SKIP_BODY.

Now, in order to add flexibility to the tag, the ids of the input text fields are passed into the tag handler:

```
<ajax:zipCode zipcodeId="zipcode" stateId="state" cityId="city" url="zipcodes" />
<table>
    <tr>
        <td> Zipcode: </td>
        <td> <input type="text" id="zipcode" onblur="retrieveCityState( )"/> </td>
    </tr>
```

The input field for the zip code, for example, has an id of zipcode. That id is passed into the tag as a parameter: zipcodeId="zipcode".

Later, when the tag handler processes the tag, the ids are put into the JavaScript with the following code:

```
outString = outString.replaceAll("stateId", stateId);
outString = outString.replaceAll("cityId", cityId);
outString = outString.replaceAll("zipcodeId", zipcodeId);
outString = outString.replaceAll("urlName", url);
```

Let's face it: debugging JavaScript is not easy. There are some debugging tools available, such as Venkman and the JavaScript debugger for Mozilla, but these tools have trouble with code embedded in Java Strings. The file approach allows you to debug the JavaScript before you use it in the tag library; then, when the code is ready for prime time, you can just put the JavaScript file in the *.jar* file and load it with an InputStream, as shown in Example 7-5.

## Writing the Support Servlet

The tag library needs the URL of a service to satisfy its request. In this example, that service is provided by a servlet named AjaxZipCodesServlet, but you may want to use some other kind of service—nothing requires you to stick with Java. The AjaxZipCodesServlet servlet (shown in Example 7-6) returns the city and state for a given zip code. The tag library uses this information to populate the city and state fields in a form.

*Example 7-6. The AjaxZipCodesServlet*

```
package com.oreilly.ajax.servlet;

import java.io.IOException;
import java.sql.Connection;
import java.sql.ResultSet;
import java.sql.SQLException;
import java.sql.Statement;
import java.util.HashMap;

import javax.servlet.ServletException;
import javax.servlet.http.HttpServlet;
import javax.servlet.http.HttpServletRequest;
import javax.servlet.http.HttpServletResponse;
```

*Example 7-6. The AjaxZipCodesServlet (continued)*

```
import com.oreilly.ajax.DatabaseConnector;
import com.oreilly.ajax.JSONUtil;

public class AjaxZipCodesServlet extends HttpServlet {
    public void doGet(HttpServletRequest req, HttpServletResponse res)
            throws ServletException, IOException {
        String responseString = null;

        String zipCode = req.getParameter("zip");
        if (zipCode != null) {
            HashMap location = getCityState(zipCode);
            responseString = JSONUtil.buildJSON(location, "location");
        }
        if (responseString != null) {
            res.setContentType("text/xml");
            res.setHeader("Cache-Control", "no-cache");
            res.getWriter( ).write(responseString);
        } else {
            // if key comes back as a null, return a question mark
            res.setContentType("text/xml");
            res.setHeader("Cache-Control", "no-cache");
            res.getWriter( ).write("?");
        }
    }

    private HashMap getCityState(String zipCode) {
        Connection con = DatabaseConnector.getConnection( );
        HashMap cityStateMap = new HashMap( );
        cityStateMap.put("zip", "zipCode");
        String queryString = "";
        try {
            queryString = "SELECT CITY, STATE FROM ZIPCODES where ZIPCODE="
                    + zipCode + ";";
            Statement select = con.createStatement( );
            ResultSet result = select.executeQuery(queryString);

            while (result.next( )) { // process results one row at a time
                String city;
                String state;

                city = result.getString("CITY");
                if (result.wasNull( )) {
                    city = "";
                }
                cityStateMap.put("city", city);
                state = result.getString("state");
                if (result.wasNull( )) {
                    state = "";
                }
                cityStateMap.put("state", state);
            }
        } catch (Exception e) {
```

*Example 7-6. The AjaxZipCodesServlet (continued)*

```
            System.out.println("exception caught getting city/state:"
                                +queryString + " " + e.getMessage( ));
        } finally {
            if (con != null) {
                try {
                    con.close( );
                } catch (SQLException e) {
                }
            }
        }
        return cityStateMap;
    }
}
```

This is the same servlet that we used in previous examples to get the city and state from a zip code.

## Using Ant to Put It All Together

The *build.xml* file for this project (presented in Example 7-7) builds the tag library's class files, packages the class files and support files in *ajax-ora.jar*, and deploys them to the web server. It assumes that the environment variable `TOMCAT_HOME` is set properly, as discussed in Chapter 1. If you are using another web server, you will need to change `webapp.dir` to match the directory where your server's web applications are deployed. The `jarit` target builds the *.jar* file for the tag library.

*Example 7-7. build.xml for the custom Ajax tag library*

```
<?xml version="1.0"?>
<project name="AJAX on Java LAB8" default="compile" basedir=".">

    <property environment="env"/>
    <property name="src.dir" value="src"/>
    <property name="war.dir" value="war"/>
    <property name="db.dir" value="db"/>
    <property name="lib.dir" value="${war.dir}/WEB-INF/lib"/>
    <property name="class.dir" value="${war.dir}/WEB-INF/classes"/>
    <property name="tomcat.common" value="${env.TOMCAT_HOME}/common/lib"/>
    <property name="webapp.dir" value="${env.TOMCAT_HOME}/webapps/ajax-JSPTag"/>

    <path id="ajax.class.path">
        <fileset dir="${lib.dir}">
            <include name="*.jar"/>
        </fileset>
        <fileset dir="${tomcat.common}">
            <include name="*.jar"/>
        </fileset>
    </path>

    <target name="init">
        <mkdir dir="${class.dir}"/>
```

*Example 7-7. build.xml for the custom Ajax tag library (continued)*

```
    </target>
    <target name="jarit">
        <jar destfile="${lib.dir}/ajax-ora.jar"
             basedir="${class.dir}"
             excludes="**/Test.class"
        />
    </target>
    <target name="compile" depends="init"
            description="Compiles all source code.">
        <javac srcdir="${src.dir}" destdir="${class.dir}" debug="on"
               classpathref="ajax.class.path"/>
    </target>
    <target name="clean" description="Erases contents of classes dir">
        <delete dir="${class.dir}"/>
    </target>
    <target name="deploy" depends="compile,jarit"
            description="Copies the jar, servlet, etc to destination dir">
        <copy todir="${webapp.dir}">
            <fileset dir="${war.dir}">
                <exclude name="**/*.class"/>
            </fileset>
            <fileset dir="${war.dir}">
                <include name="**/*Servlet.class"/>
            </fileset>
        </copy>
    </target>
</project>
```

The *web.xml* file for the project is shown in Example 7-8. Again, notice that the `<url-pattern>` in the `<servlet-mapping>` is `/zipcodes`. This must match the URL value in the taglib so that when the tag makes an Ajax call to that URL, it will find a servlet waiting to handle the request.

*Example 7-8. The servlet configuration file, web.xml*

```
<web-app>
    <servlet>
        <servlet-name>AjaxZipCodesServlet</servlet-name>
        <servlet-class>
            com.oreilly.ajax.servlet.AjaxZipCodesServlet
        </servlet-class>
        <load-on-startup>1</load-on-startup>
    </servlet>
    <servlet-mapping>
        <servlet-name>AjaxZipCodesServlet</servlet-name>
        <url-pattern>/zipcodes</url-pattern>
    </servlet-mapping>
    <!-- taglibs -->
    <taglib>
        <taglib-uri>/WEB-INF/oreillyAjax.tld</taglib-uri>
        <taglib-location>/WEB-INF/oreillyAjax.tld</taglib-location>
    </taglib>
```

*Example 7-8. The servlet configuration file, web.xml (continued)*

```
    <!-- The Welcome File List -->
    <welcome-file-list>
        <welcome-file>oreillyajaxtags.jsp</welcome-file>
    </welcome-file-list>
</web-app>
```

# Third-Party Tag Libraries

Now you know how to create a tag library that encapsulates your own Ajaxian features. But what about third-party tag libraries? Do such libraries exist?

Yes, they do. In the rest of this chapter, we're going to look at three: AjaxTags, Ajax-Anywhere, and JavaWebParts.* Being able to create your own tag library is valuable, but relying on someone else's expertise and experience can be even better.

## AjaxTags

AjaxTags is a SourceForge project (*http://ajaxtags.sourceforge.net*) that allows you to use Ajax with minimal effort. It consists of a set of JSP tags that tie into Ajax functionality. You don't need to write JavaScript to use these tags. If you want to use some tested JavaScript and reduce your development time, AjaxTags might be the library you're looking for.

AjaxTags 1.2 currently provides 10 tags, which are listed in Table 7-1. More tags may be available by the time you read this book.

*Table 7-1. AjaxTags tags*

| Tag name | Description |
|---|---|
| Autocomplete | Displays a list of entries that match the text entered into the autocomplete field. (I've called this a "suggestion" field elsewhere in this book.) |
| Callout | Displays a pop-up balloon anchored to an HTML element. |
| HTML Content Replace | Connects a content area to an HTML element's `onclick` event. |
| Portlet | Adds a portlet to the JSP page. |
| Select/Dropdown | Populates a select field based on the selection in another select field. |
| Tab Panel | Sets up tabs with their respective Ajax-enabled content. |
| Toggle | Toggles the value of a hidden field (`true`/`false`) while simultaneously switching the source of an image field. |
| Update Field | Updates the values of one or more form fields based on the text entered in another field. |
| Area and Anchor | Shows how to Ajax-enable any area of a page. |
| Ajax DisplayTag | Shows how to Ajax-enable `DisplayTag`. |

* Note that AjaxTags and JavaWebParts started out with the same name, AjaxTags. This can be a source of confusion.

One of the most interesting tags in the library is the Tab Panel tag, which is used to set up tabs in an application that displays the contents of some tables. Let's see what it takes to use that tag. Figure 7-1 shows the application we're heading toward.

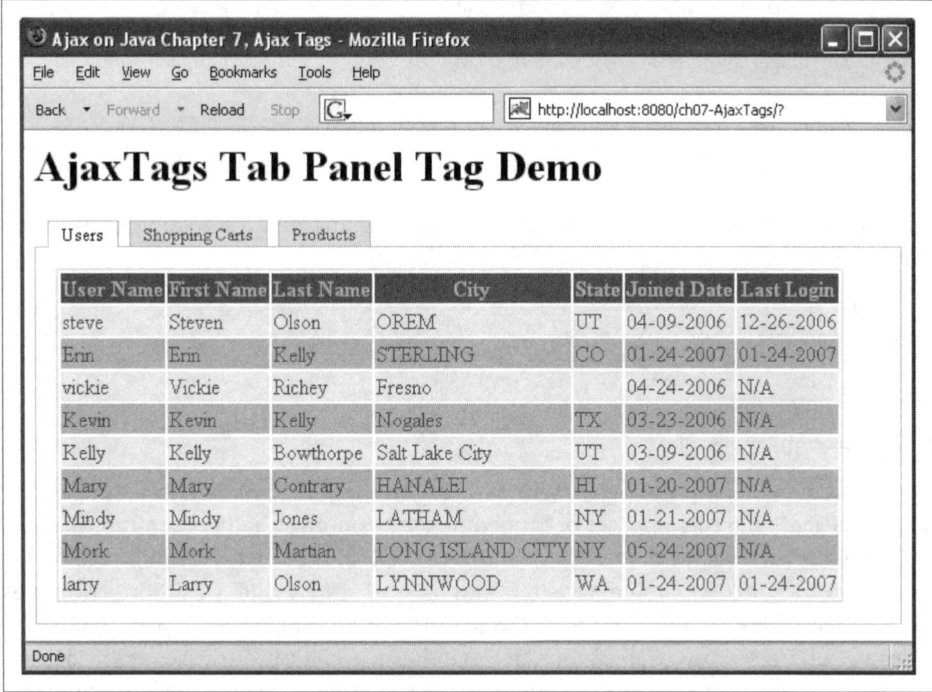


| User Name | First Name | Last Name | City | State | Joined Date | Last Login |
|---|---|---|---|---|---|---|
| steve | Steven | Olson | OREM | UT | 04-09-2006 | 12-26-2006 |
| Erin | Erin | Kelly | STERLING | CO | 01-24-2007 | 01-24-2007 |
| vickie | Vickie | Richey | Fresno | | 04-24-2006 | N/A |
| Kevin | Kevin | Kelly | Nogales | TX | 03-23-2006 | N/A |
| Kelly | Kelly | Bowthorpe | Salt Lake City | UT | 03-09-2006 | N/A |
| Mary | Mary | Contrary | HANALEI | HI | 01-20-2007 | N/A |
| Mindy | Mindy | Jones | LATHAM | NY | 01-21-2007 | N/A |
| Mork | Mork | Martian | LONG ISLAND CITY | NY | 05-24-2007 | N/A |
| larry | Larry | Olson | LYNNWOOD | WA | 01-24-2007 | 01-24-2007 |

*Figure 7-1. The Tab Panel tag displaying user information from the database*

When you click on a tab, the browser requests the data to populate the tab. Clicking on the Shopping Carts tab displays all the items currently in the shopping cart, and clicking on the Products tab displays all the products in the database.

### Getting and installing AjaxTags

To get started, go to *http://ajaxtags.sourceforge.net*, locate the current version of AjaxTags in the Downloads section, and download it. The AjaxTags project will probably come as a zipped archive for Windows and a tar archive for Linux. Uncompress the archive, find the *ajaxtags.jar* file, and copy it into your *WEB-INF/lib* directory. The *.jar* file will probably be in the *dist* directory and should be named *ajaxtags* with the version appended to it (e.g., *ajaxtags-1.2-beta2.jar*).

When you're running Tomcat 5.5 with AjaxTags 1.2, Tomcat may throw several exceptions because of missing classes. One of the missing classes, `ExpressionEvaluatorManagerl`, is found in *standard-1.1.2.jar*.

Another missing class is `org.apache.commons.lang.StringUtils`, which at the time of this writing is found in *commons-lang-2.1.jar*. You can get the latest version of that *.jar* file from *http://jakarta.apache.org/commons/lang*.

To avoid those exceptions, place both *.jar* files in the *WEB-INF/lib* directory.

Next, copy *ajaxtags.tld* into the *WEB-INF* directory and add the taglib definition to the *web.xml* definition file in *WEB-INF*, as follows:

```
<taglib>
    <uri>http://ajaxtags.org/tags/ajax</uri>
    <location>/WEB-INF/ajaxtags.tld</location>
</taglib>
```

### Using the <tabPanel> tag

To use a tab panel, put the `<ajax:tabPanel>` tag in the JSP, as shown in Example 7-9. The `<tabPanel>` tag sets up a set of tabbed panels. You must define each tab that you would like your page to display within the `<ajax:tabPanel>` with an `<ajax:tab>` tag. The `<ajax:tab>` takes `caption`, `baseUrl`, and `parameters` attributes as input. The tabs display the labels defined by their `caption` attributes. The `baseUrl` parameter provides the address of the web service that handles the call (in our case, `/tabcontent`), and you can use the `parameters` parameter to set the request parameter for a tab. You can also select one tag in the set to be the default; to do so, set `defaultTab="true"`.

*Example 7-9. index.jsp uses AjaxTags to produce a tab panel*

```
<%@ page language="java" %>
<%@ taglib uri="http://ajaxtags.org/tags/ajax" prefix="ajax" %>
<html>
<head>
    <meta http-equiv="Content-Type" content="text/html; charset=ISO-8859-1" />
    <title>AJAX JSP Tag Library Examples</title>

    <script type="text/javascript" src="<%=request.getContextPath( )%>/js/ajaxtags-
            1.2/prototype-1.4.0.js"></script>
    <script type="text/javascript" src="<%=request.getContextPath( )%>/js/ajaxtags-
            1.2/scriptaculous.js"></script>
    <script type="text/javascript" src="<%=request.getContextPath( )%>/js/ajaxtags-
            1.2/overlibmws.js"></script>
    <script type="text/javascript" src="<%=request.getContextPath( )%>/js/ajaxtags-
            1.2/ajaxtags.js"></script>

    <link rel="stylesheet" type="text/css" href="css/ajaxtags-sample.css" />
    <style>
        Table.Product {border: solid 2px; border-color:#CCFF66;}
        TD.Product{background-color:#CCCCFF;border: solid 2px; color:#000099}
```

*Example 7-9. index.jsp uses AjaxTags to produce a tab panel (continued)*

```
        TH.Product{background-color:#000099; color:#CCCCFF}

        Table.User {border: solid 2px; border-color:#CCFF66;}
        TR.UserDark {background-color:#CCCCFF;border: solid 2px; color:#6666CC}
        TR.UserLight {background-color:#CCFFFF;border: solid 2px; color:#6666CC}
        TH.User {background-color:#6666CC; color:#CCCCFF}

        Table.Cart {border: solid 2px; border-color:#339966;}
        TR.CartLight {background-color:#CCCCFF;border: solid 2px; color:#336666}
        TR.CartDark {background-color:#33FF99;border: solid 2px; color:#336666}
        TH.Cart {background-color:#336666; color:#CCCCFF}
    </style>
</head>

<body>
    <h1>AjaxTags Tab Panel Tag Demo</h1>
    <div>

    <ajax:tabPanel panelStyleId="tabPanel"
                   contentStyleId="tabContent"
                   panelStyleClass="tabPanel"
                   contentStyleClass="tabContent"
                   currentStyleClass="ajaxCurrentTab">
        <ajax:tab caption="Users"
                  baseUrl="${pageContext.request.contextPath}/tabcontent?tab=Users"
                  defaultTab="true"/>
        <ajax:tab caption="Shopping Carts"
                  baseUrl="${pageContext.request.contextPath}/tabcontent"
                  parameters="tab=Carts"/>
        <ajax:tab caption="Products"
                  baseUrl="${pageContext.request.contextPath}/tabcontent"
                  parameters="tab=Products"/>
    </ajax:tabPanel>

    </div>
</body>
</html>
```

Notice that the Users tab does not have a `parameters` attribute. That is to illustrate that the `parameters` attribute is not required and that the tab's request parameters can be passed in the `baseUrl` attribute, as in `/tabcontent?tab=Users`.

In addition to including the tag library *ajaxtags.tld* and the two JavaScript library files *prototype-1.4.0.js* and *ajaxtags.js*, the *index.jsp* page links to an important support file, *ajaxtags-sample.css*. The CSS support file comes with the AjaxTags demo application. The tabs rely heavily upon these support files. To get them, go to *http://ajaxtags.sourceforge.net/index.html* and download the Demo War files. The CSS files will be in the *web/css* directory. (You can customize these files later if you like; the downloadable versions just provide a starting point to get your applications working.)

### Writing the servlet code

Once you've created the JSP for your tabbed panel, you need a servlet to respond to the Ajax requests generated by the tabs. The response should be an HTML-formatted string to fill the div for each tag. We'll call our servlet `TabContentServlet`.

The `TabContentServlet` must return text for the tab that has been selected. This servlet must extend `BaseAjaxServlet` and override the `getXMLContent( )` method. (`BaseAjaxServlet` is provided by the AjaxTags project and can be found in its JAR file.)

The servlet pulls the parameter `tab` from the request and uses it to see which tab is requesting content. For this application, a simple `if/else` block will suffice for the controller. The `TabContentServlet` code is shown in Example 7-10.

*Example 7-10. The TabContentServlet*

```
package com.oreilly.ajax.servlet;

import javax.servlet.http.HttpServletRequest;
import javax.servlet.http.HttpServletResponse;

import org.ajaxtags.servlets.BaseAjaxServlet;

import com.oreilly.ajax.ProductManager;
import com.oreilly.ajax.ShoppingCartManager;
import com.oreilly.ajax.UserManager;

public class TabContentServlet extends BaseAjaxServlet {

    public String getXmlContent(HttpServletRequest request,
            HttpServletResponse response) throws Exception {
        String tab = request.getParameter("tab");
        String returnString =
                "<H1>Tab parameter is null, please make sure you pass it in the
                request.</H1>";
        if (tab == null) {
            return (returnString);
        }
        if (tab.equals("Users")) {
            returnString = UserManager.getUsersView( );
        }
        else if (tab.equalsIgnoreCase("Products")) {
            returnString = ProductManager.getProductsView( );
        }
        else if (tab.equalsIgnoreCase("Carts")) {
            returnString = ShoppingCartManager.getShoppingCartView( );
        }
        return (returnString);
    }
}
```

The value for the tab parameter was set up in our JSP, as part of the request URL. For example, the Users tab includes the tab=Users pair at the end of the URL:

```
<ajax:tab caption="Users"
          baseUrl="${pageContext.request.contextPath}/tabcontent?tab=Users"
          defaultTab="true"/>
```

### Displaying data in the tabs

The next step is to pass formatted data back to the tab for display. I feel squeamish about returning a formatted HTML string from the model, which should not have to deal with formatting issues. For this application, however, it is the best course. The Tab Panel tag in the AjaxTags library expects the contents of the tabs to be returned as formatted HTML. The alternative is to return the data in a format that JavaScript can parse, but that would add a lot of complexity. If you are writing a more sophisticated application and must separate the model from the formatting details, you can simply return the object as an XML or JSON string and either parse and format the details in JavaScript or switch to Struts and use the *bean.tld* that Struts provides.

Example 7-11 presents the method that returns the HTML for the Users tab. The HTML is simple because most of the heavy-duty formatting is handled by the CSS. Therefore, getUsersView( ) only needs to generate the <table>, <td>, <tr>, and <th> tags. The properties are limited to CSS class names, which allows you to manipulate much of the formatting from the CSS file.

*Example 7-11. Excerpt from UserManager.java*

```
static public String getUsersView( ) {
    Connection con = DatabaseConnector.getConnection( );
    String sqlString = "";
    String userclass = "";
    int index = 0;
    SimpleDateFormat sf = new SimpleDateFormat("MM-dd-yyyy");
    StringBuffer htmlStringBuffer = new StringBuffer("<table class=\"User\">");
            htmlStringBuffer.append("\n<tr><th class=\"User\">User Name</th>");
            htmlStringBuffer.append("\n<th class=\"User\">First Name</th>");
            htmlStringBuffer.append("\n<th class=\"User\">Last Name</th>");
            htmlStringBuffer.append("\n<th class=\"User\">City</th>");
            htmlStringBuffer.append("\n<th class=\"User\">State</th>");
            htmlStringBuffer.append("\n<th class=\"User\">Joined Date</th>");
            htmlStringBuffer.append("\n<th class=\"User\">Last Login</th></tr>");
    try {
        sqlString = "select * from USERS";
        Statement select = con.createStatement( );
        ResultSet result = select.executeQuery(sqlString);
        Date tempDate = null;
        while (result.next( )) { // process results one row at a time
            if (index++ % 2 == 0)
                userclass = "UserLight";
            else
                userclass = "UserDark";
```

*Example 7-11. Excerpt from UserManager.java (continued)*

```
                htmlStringBuffer.append("\n<tr class=\""+userclass+"\">");
                htmlStringBuffer.append("\n<td class=\"User\">"
                        +result.getString("USERNAME")+"</td>");
                htmlStringBuffer.append("\n<td class=\"User\">"
                        +result.getString("FIRST_NAME")+"</td>");
                htmlStringBuffer.append("\n<td class=\"User\">"
                        +result.getString("LAST_NAME")+"</td>");
                htmlStringBuffer.append("\n<td class=\"User\">"
                        +result.getString("CITY")+"</td>");
                htmlStringBuffer.append("\n<td class=\"User\">"
                        +result.getString("STATE")+"</td>");
                tempDate = result.getDate("JOINED");
                if (tempDate != null)
                    htmlStringBuffer.append("\n<td class=\"User\">"
                            +sf.format(tempDate)+"</td>");
                else
                    htmlStringBuffer.append("\n<td class=\"User\">N/A</td>");

                tempDate = result.getDate("LAST_LOGIN");
                if (tempDate != null)
                    htmlStringBuffer.append("\n<td class=\"User\">"
                            +sf.format(tempDate)+"</td>");
                else
                    htmlStringBuffer.append("\n<td class=\"User\">N/A</td>");

                htmlStringBuffer.append("</tr>");
            }
        }
        catch (Exception e) {
            System.out.println("exception caught getting USERS"
                             + sqlString + " " + e.getMessage( ));
        }
        finally {
            if (con != null) {
                try {
                    con.close( );
                }
                catch (SQLException e) {
                }
            }
        }
        return htmlStringBuffer.toString( );
    }
```

`getUsersView( )` establishes a connection with the database and performs a query to get the information about the users; the results are then parsed and formatted into an HTML string. The class property of each HTML element is given a different name, so you can control most of the formatting in an external CSS file, without touching the Java code. This makes for as clean a separation as possible when using the AjaxTags library.

Data for the other tabs is managed with similar methods. The view for the Shopping Cart tab is managed with a call to `getShoppingCartView( )`, as shown in Example 7-12.

*Example 7-12. The getShoppingCartView() method of ShoppingCartManager*

```
static public String getShoppingCartView( ) {
    Connection con = DatabaseConnector.getConnection( );
    String sqlString = "";
    String cartclass = "";
    SimpleDateFormat sf = new SimpleDateFormat("MM-dd-yyyy");
    StringBuffer htmlStringBuffer = new StringBuffer("<table class=\"Cart\">");
    htmlStringBuffer.append("\n<tr><th class=\"Cart\">User Name</th>");
    htmlStringBuffer.append("\n<th class=\"Cart\">Start Date</th>");
    htmlStringBuffer.append("\n<th class=\"Cart\">Last Updated</th>");
    htmlStringBuffer.append("\n<th class=\"Cart\">Active </th></tr>");
    try {
        sqlString = "select  u.USERNAME," + "sc.START_DATE," + "sc.LAST_UPDATED,"
                + "sc.ACTIVE " + "from SHOPPING_CART sc," + "USERS u "
                + "where sc.USER_ID=u.USER_ID;";

        Statement select = con.createStatement( );
        ResultSet result = select.executeQuery(sqlString);
        int index = 0;
        while (result.next( )) { // process results one row at a time
            if (index++ % 2 == 0)
                cartclass = "CartLight";
            else
                cartclass = "CartDark";
            htmlStringBuffer.append("\n<tr class=\"" + cartclass + "\">");
            htmlStringBuffer.append("\n<td class=\"" + cartclass + "\">"
                    + result.getString("USERNAME") + "</td>");
            htmlStringBuffer.append("\n<td class=\"" + cartclass + "\">"
                    + sf.format(result.getDate("START_DATE")) + "</td>");
            htmlStringBuffer.append("\n<td class=\"" + cartclass + "\">"
                    + sf.format(result.getDate("LAST_UPDATED")) + "</td>");
            if (result.getBoolean("ACTIVE")) {
                htmlStringBuffer.append("\n<td class=\"" + cartclass
                        + "\">true</td>");
            }
            else {
                htmlStringBuffer.append("\n<td class=\"" + cartclass
                        + "\">false</td>");
            }
            htmlStringBuffer.append("</tr>");
        }
    }
    catch (Exception e) {
        System.out.println("exception caught getting Shopping Cart"
                + sqlString + " " + e.getMessage( ));
    }
    finally {
        if (con != null) {
```

*Example 7-12. The getShoppingCartView() method of ShoppingCartManager (continued)*

```
            try {
                con.close( );
            }
            catch (SQLException e) {
            }
        }
    }
    return htmlStringBuffer.toString( );
}
```

Except for the query, this method is similar to `getUsersView( )`. Both methods use an index value in the `while` loop to tag every other row with a different CSS class. This allows you to make the contents of the tabbed panel more readable by giving alternate rows different looks. The most common way to do this is to give every other row a gray background:

```
if (index++ % 2 == 0)
    cartclass = "CartLight";
else
    cartclass = "CartDark";
```

The `getProductsView( )` method, presented in Example 7-13, gets product information from the database and sends it to the Products tab as an HTML string.

*Example 7-13. The getProductsView() method*

```
static public String getProductsView( ) {
    Connection con = DatabaseConnector.getConnection( );
    String sqlString = "";
    StringBuffer htmlStringBuffer = new StringBuffer(
            "<table class=\"Product\">");
    htmlStringBuffer.append("\n<tr><th class=\"Product\">Product Name</th>");
    htmlStringBuffer.append("\n<th class=\"Product\">Description</th>");
    htmlStringBuffer.append("\n<th class=\"Product\">Filename</th>");
    htmlStringBuffer.append("\n<th class=\"Product\">Price </th></tr>");
    try {
        sqlString = "select * from PRODUCTS";
        Statement select = con.createStatement( );
        ResultSet result = select.executeQuery(sqlString);
        Date tempDate = null;
        while (result.next( )) { // process results one row at a time
            htmlStringBuffer.append("\n<tr>");
            htmlStringBuffer.append("\n<td class=\"Product\">"
                    + result.getString("PRODUCT_NAME") + "</td>");
            htmlStringBuffer.append("\n<td class=\"Product\">"
                    + result.getString("DESCRIPTION") + "</td>");
            htmlStringBuffer.append("\n<td class=\"Product\">"
                    + result.getString("FILENAME") + "</td>");
            htmlStringBuffer.append("\n<td class=\"Product\">"
                    + result.getString("PRICE") + "</td>");

            htmlStringBuffer.append("</tr>");
```

*Example 7-13. The getProductsView() method (continued)*

```
        }
    }
    catch (Exception e) {
        System.out.println("exception caught getting PRODUCTS" + sqlString + " "
                + e.getMessage( ));
    }
    finally {
        if (con != null) {
            try {
                con.close( );
            }
            catch (SQLException e) {
            }
        }
    }
    return htmlStringBuffer.toString( );
}
```

There's nothing particularly new or notable here; this method is similar to `getUsersView( )` and `getShoppingCartView( )`. We've dispensed with using alternating CSS tags, though, so you can't change the background color of every other row to make the tab's contents more readable.

The CSS code for this example was embedded in the JSP, but it should eventually be put into another file, especially if the application is going to see a production environment:

```
<style>
    Table.Product {border: solid 2px; border-color:#CCFF66;}
    TD.Product{background-color:#CCCCFF;border: solid 2px; color:#000099}
    TH.Product{background-color:#000099; color:#CCCCFF}

    Table.User {border: solid 2px; border-color:#CCFF66;}
    TR.UserDark {background-color:#CCCCFF;border: solid 2px; color:#6666CC}
    TR.UserLight {background-color:#CCFFFF;border: solid 2px; color:#6666CC}
    TH.User {background-color:#6666CC; color:#CCCCFF}

    Table.Cart {border: solid 2px; border-color:#339966;}
    TR.CartLight {background-color:#CCCCFF;border: solid 2px; color:#336666}
    TR.CartDark {background-color:#33FF99;border: solid 2px; color:#336666}
    TH.Cart {background-color:#336666; color:#CCCCFF}
</style>
```

The `CartLight` and `CartDark` values for `Table.Cart` are not used because the Java code does not tag anything with those classes.

The final step is to add the definition of `TabContentServlet` to the *web.xml* file:

```
<servlet>
    <servlet-name>tabcontent</servlet-name>
    <servlet-class>com.oreilly.ajax.servlet.TabContentServlet</servlet-class>
    <load-on-startup>1</load-on-startup>
```

```
    </servlet>
    <servlet-mapping>
        <servlet-name>tabcontent</servlet-name>
        <url-pattern>/tabcontent </url-pattern>
    </servlet-mapping>
```

After you implement this demo, try changing the data in the database and then switching through the tabs to see how each panel is updated. One great thing about using Ajax in an application like this is that real-time updates occur as you shift through the tabs, without any browser caching issues.

## JavaWebParts

JavaWebParts is a large library comprised of many separate components. See the documentation at *http://javawebparts.sourceforge.net* for the latest information on JavaWebParts. The documentation is very sparse, but it gives you an idea of what's available. The SourceForge forum is also useful; Frank Zametti, one of the core developers of the Ajax-enabled tags, is active in answering questions about using those tags.

No JavaScript programming is required to use the JavaWebParts library. You simply insert the tags you need into a JSP and then write the server-side support for those tags in Java. If you're not a fan of JavaScript, this approach has obvious advantages, but the drawback is that you are limited to the tags that have been implemented.

Table 7-2 summarizes the JavaWebParts components. Note that there are many different kinds of components available, not just components implementing Ajax features. They're all worth investigating.

*Table 7-2. JavaWebParts components*

| Component | Description |
|---|---|
| Filter | Servlet filters |
| Listener | Context and session listeners |
| Misc | Components that don't fit in the other categories |
| Taglib | AjaxTags and other tag libraries |
| Servlet | Servlets |
| Request | Components that deal with `HTTPRequest` |
| Response | Components that deal with `HTTPResponse` |
| Session | Components that deal with `HTTPSession` |
| Context | Servlet context components |

Rather than providing a library of Ajax-enabled components, JavaWebParts takes a more general approach. Instead of a specific tag with a specific name, you place a generic tag, `<ajax:event>`, after the HTML element that you want to trigger an Ajax event. Then you connect up that event in a configuration file, which is normally called *ajax_config.xml*.

To demonstrate how to use JavaWebParts, we'll look at an application that uses Ajax to populate one select field based on the selection in another select field. Figure 7-2 shows the application we're working toward.

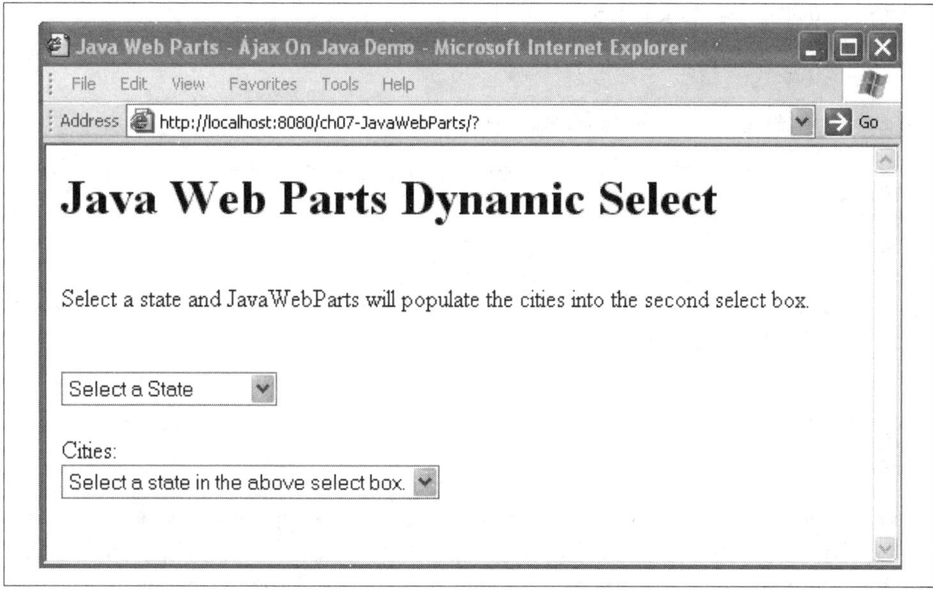


*Figure 7-2. Populating one select field based on the selection in another*

The JSP for this application sets up the select fields so that when the user selects a state, a request is sent to the server, which returns a list of cities in that state. That list is used to fill a `<div>`, which in turn populates the "Cities:" select field. It starts with a taglib directive that loads the JavaWebParts tag library. The JSP uses only two Ajax-specific tags: `<ajax:event>`, which follows the state selection box, and `<ajax:enable />`. Other than that, as you can see in Example 7-14, the JSP contains no extra code to indicate that this is an Ajax-enabled web page.

*Example 7-14. index.jsp*

```
<%@ taglib prefix="ajax" uri="javawebparts/taglib/ajaxtags" %>
<html>
<head>
    <title>
        Java Web Parts - Ajax on Java demo
    </title>
</head>
<body>
    <h1>
        Java Web Parts Dynamic Select
    </h1>
    <br />
    Select a state and JavaWebParts will populate the cities into the second
    select box.
```

*Example 7-14. index.jsp (continued)*

```
    <br />
    <form name="StateSelectForm">
        <br />
        <select name="stateSelected">
            <option value="" selected="selected">Select a State</option>
            <option value="AL">Alabama</option>
            ...
            <option value="WY">Wyoming</option>
        </select>
        <ajax:event ajaxRef="StateSelectForm/stateSelectionChange" />
    </form>

    Cities:
    <div id="cities">
        <select name="citySelected">
            <option>Select a state in the above select box.</option>
        </select>
    </div>
    <ajax:enable />
</body>
</html>
```

The `<ajax:enable />` tag injects the JavaScript that will support the Ajax calls to the server. To see what code `<ajax:enable />` produces, load the page in your browser and look at its source. You should see something similar to the following:

```
<script>
var calls = new Array( );
var pendingResponseCount = 0;
var shouldDebugAjax = false;
var assureUnique = 1;

function ajaxRequestSender(form, target, qs, dom, resHandler, resHandlerParam,
        method, async, mungedRef, timerObj, ajaxRef) {
...
}
function onResponseStateChange(callKey) {
...
}

function createXMLHttpRequest( ) {
    var xmlHttpRequest;
    if (window.XMLHttpRequest) {
        return new XMLHttpRequest( );
    } else if (window.ActiveXObject) {
        return new ActiveXObject('Microsoft.XMLHTTP')
    }
}
</script>
```

The *ajax_config.xml* file contains the information to set up the tags that are used in the JSP. The ajaxRef attribute of the <form> tag specifies the name given to the form in the JSP (in this case, "StateSelectForm"):

```
<ajaxConfig>
    <form ajaxRef="StateSelectForm">
        <element ajaxRef="stateSelectionChange">
            <event type="onchange">
                <requestHandler type="std:QueryString" method="get">
                    <target>JWPSelectServlet</target>
                    <parameter>state=stateSelected</parameter>
                </requestHandler>
                <responseHandler type="std:InnerHTML">
                    <parameter>cities</parameter>
                </responseHandler>
            </event>
        </element>
    </form>
</ajaxConfig>
```

Within the form, <ajax:event> tags determine which elements trigger Ajax events; within the configuration file, the <element> tag with its ajaxRef attribute specifies the element whose events we're mapping (in this case, the stateSelectionChange element within the StateSelectForm). The <ajax:event> tag in the form has an ajaxRef attribute of "StateSelectForm/stateSelectionChange". Back in the configuration file, the type attribute of the <event> tag specifies what kind of events we're looking for (here, onchange events). So, putting it all together, we're looking for onchange events coming from the stateSelectionChange element within the StateSelectForm.

The next two elements within the <event> tag specify what to do with these events when they arrive. The <requestHandler> tag connects the Ajax request to a handler (in this case, our servlet). This tag also specifies that the JSP will make a "get" request to the JWPSelectServlet, which is the <servlet-mapping> configured in *web.xml*.

In order to pass data back to the servlet, we need to pass request parameters. The <parameter> tag defines those parameters. In this case, we're passing a key/value pair in a GET request. The name of the key is state; its value is from the element in the JSP with the id stateSelected.

Finally, the <responseHandler> tag sets up the JSP to handle the response from the servlet. The servlet sends HTML text, which is inserted into the JSP element with an id of cities using the innerHTML method. The cities parameter is wrapped in the <parameter> tag.

The *web.xml* file (shown in Example 7-15) must include the <context-param> tag, which sets the ajaxTagsConfig file to */WEB-INF/ajax_config.xml*. *web.xml* also configures a listener for incoming events (the AjaxInit class) and the servlet that processes the events, and returns the data back to the client (JWPSelectServlet).

*Example 7-15. The web.xml file that sets up JavaWebParts*

```
<?xml version="1.0" encoding="ISO-8859-1"?>
<!DOCTYPE web-app PUBLIC  "-//Sun Microsystems, Inc.//DTD Web Application 2.3//EN"
    "http://java.sun.com/dtd/web-app_2_3.dtd">
<web-app>
    <context-param>
        <param-name>ajaxTagsConfig</param-name>
        <param-value>/WEB-INF/ajax_config.xml</param-value>
    </context-param>
    <listener>
        <listener-class>javawebparts.taglib.ajaxtags.AjaxInit</listener-class>
    </listener>
    <servlet>
        <servlet-name>JWPSelectServlet</servlet-name>
        <servlet-class>com.oreilly.ajax.servlet.JWPSelectServlet</servlet-class>
    </servlet>
    <servlet-mapping>
        <servlet-name>JWPSelectServlet</servlet-name>
        <url-pattern>/JWPSelectServlet</url-pattern>
    </servlet-mapping>
</web-app>
```

We've now connected the listener and the configuration file and configured the servlet that will send the data back to the JavaWebParts tags. The code for this servlet is presented in Example 7-16.

*Example 7-16. The JWPSelectServlet*

```
public class JWPSelectServlet extends HttpServlet {

    public void doGet(HttpServletRequest req, HttpServletResponse res)
            throws ServletException, IOException {
        doPost(req, res);
    }

    public void doPost(HttpServletRequest req, HttpServletResponse res)
            throws ServletException, IOException {
        String state = (String) req.getParameter("state");
        if (state != null) {
            res.setContentType("text/xml");
            res.setHeader("Cache-Control", "no-cache");
            res.getWriter( ).write(getCities(state));
        }
    }

    private String getCities(String state) {
        Connection con = DatabaseConnector.getConnection( );
        StringBuffer sb = new StringBuffer("<select name=\"citySelected\">");
        try {
            Statement statement = con.createStatement( );
            String sqlString = "SELECT DISTINCT CITY FROM ZIPCODES WHERE STATE='"
                    + state + "' ORDER BY CITY;";
            ResultSet resultSet = statement.executeQuery(sqlString);
            while (resultSet.next( )) {
```

*Example 7-16. The JWPSelectServlet (continued)*

```
                sb.append("<option>" + resultSet.getString(1) + "</option>\n");
            }
        }
        catch (Exception e) {
            System.out.println("exception caught getting cities for " + state);
        }
        finally {
            sb.append("</select> <ajax:event
                     ajaxRef=\"CitySelectForm/citySelectionChange\"/>");
            if (con != null) {
                try {
                    con.close( );
                }
                catch (SQLException e) {
                }
            }
        }
        return sb.toString( );
    }
}
```

The servlet builds a list of cities for the selected state, wraps each city name with an `<option>` tag, and then sends the results back to the form, where they are placed in the element specified by the *ajax_config* file.

I tried to make this application fancier by taking the list of cities and applying an event on the drop-down list. My plan was to select a city and return all of the states that have a city with the same name. However, JavaWebParts doesn't seem to have a way to enable a derived select field to trigger yet another Ajax event.

AjaxAnywhere does have support for applying an event on a dynamically displayed select element. I'll show how to do that in the next section.

JavaWebParts provides many tags and features that you can add to your applications. Its design is relatively flexible; rather than providing components with fixed functions, it provides capabilities that you can integrate into your applications. Its main disadvantage is that there is limited documentation, and you must live with the way the features work unless you are willing to fix and contribute to the project. JavaWebParts is an active project that's constantly undergoing revision and improvement; I suspect it will continue to evolve into a valuable addition to the Ajax toolkit.

## AjaxAnywhere

The AjaxAnywhere project has been available on SourceForge since September 2005. It provides a browser-independent JavaScript API for sending data to a server via `XMLHttpRequest`. Once data has been sent to the server, AjaxAnywhere uses the response to update "zones" in your web application with the returned data. A zone can be any HTML element that can take an `id`, such as a `<div>`.

To start, visit the home page of AjaxAnywhere at *http://ajaxanywhere.sourceforge.net*, look at the documentation, and download the library (a *.jar* file).

The server-side application calls the static method `AAUtils.addZonesToRefresh()` to configure which zones are to be updated. This method is usually called in a servlet or JSP. The servlet sends data back to the JSP containing the zone or zones to be updated; a filter intercepts the response and converts it to XML that contains only the HTML needed to update the client. The client receives the XML and updates the zone or zones selected for refresh.

In this section, we'll look at an application that contains two select elements, the first of which is populated with a list of states (Figure 7-3). After the user clicks on a state, the second select area populates with a list of the cities in that state. Then, if the user clicks on one of the cities, the third area populates with a listing of all the states in which a city by that name is found. The code for the application will illustrate how to look up an item and then execute a reverse lookup on the result. I wanted to demonstrate this capability of AjaxAnywhere—specifically, the ability to dynamically insert Ajax triggers—because it is not currently supported by JavaWebParts.

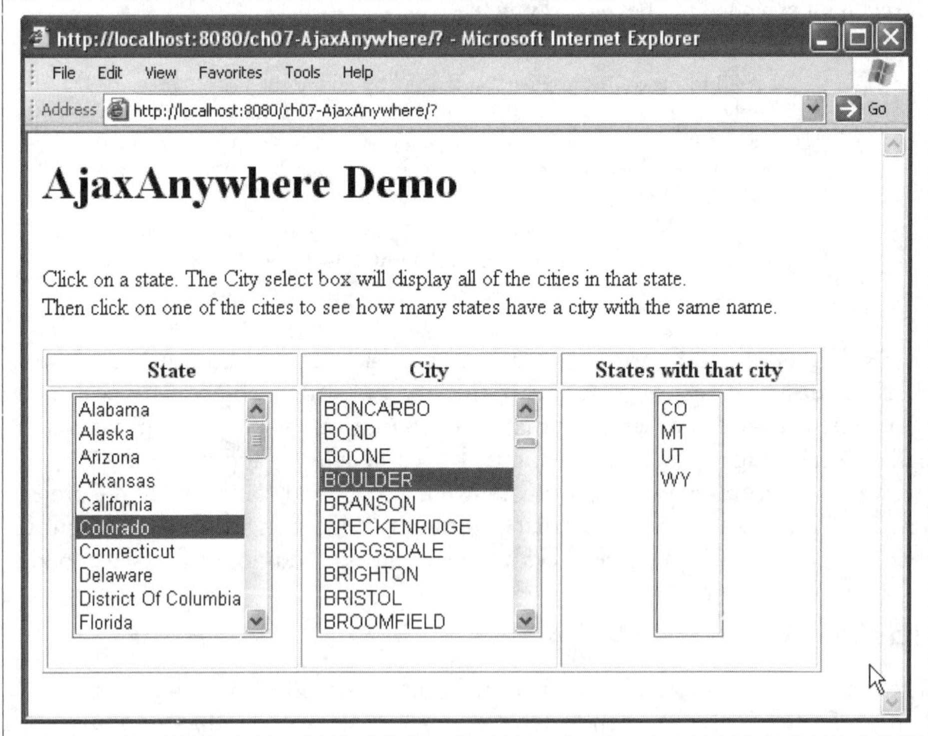


*Figure 7-3. AjaxAnywhere Demo—select a state, then a city*

When the user clicks one of the states in the State list, the browser sends a call to the `AjaxAnywhereSupportServlet`. The servlet determines which field has been sent by calling `request.getParameter( )`. The appropriate zone is configured with a call to `AAUtils.addZonesToRefresh( )`, and the data needed for that zone is stored as an object in the session. With this data, the browser displays a list of cities that are in the selected state in the second select field. After the user selects a city, the browser displays a list of all the states in which a city with that name is found in the box on the right.

So far, we've said that the servlet handling the request stores the data needed to update a zone in the session. How does that update happen? To do the refresh, we can use either Java in a JSP, or the AjaxAnywhere JavaScript API. For this example, we'll use Java code in the JSP.

### Enabling AjaxAnywhere in the JSP

The AjaxAnywhere implementation in *index.jsp* is presented in Example 7-17.

*Example 7-17. AjaxAnywhere implementation in index.jsp*

```
<%@ page pageEncoding="UTF-8" import="java.util.*" %>
<%@ taglib uri="http://ajaxanywhere.sourceforge.net/" prefix="aa" %>
<%
    ArrayList cityList = (ArrayList)session.getAttribute("cityList");
    ArrayList stateList = (ArrayList)session.getAttribute("stateList");
%>
<script src="aa.js"></script>
<script>ajaxAnywhere.formName = "main";</script>

<h1> AjaxAnywhere Demo </h1><br />
<div>
Click on a state. The City select box will display all of the cities in that
state.<br /> Then click on one of the cities to see how many states have a city
with the same name.
</div>
<br />

<form method="POST" ACTION="AjaxAnywhereSupport" name="main">
<table border = "1">
    <tr>
        <th width="30%">State</th>
        <th width="30%">City</th>
        <th width="30%">States with that city</th>
    </tr>
    <tr>
        <td align="center" valign="top">
            <select size="10" name="state"
                    onchange="ajaxAnywhere.submitAJAX('function=state');">
                <option value="AL">
                    Alabama
                </option>
```

*Example 7-17. AjaxAnywhere implementation in index.jsp (continued)*

```
                <option value="AK">
                    Alaska
                </option>
                .
                .
                .
                <option value="WI">
                    Wisconsin
                </option>
                <option value="WY">
                    Wyoming
                </option>
            </select>
        </td>
        <td align="center" valign="top">
            <aa:zone name="citiesList">
            <select size="10" name="city"
                    onchange="ajaxAnywhere.submitAJAX('function=city')">
                <%
                    String cityName = "";
                    StringBuffer sb = new StringBuffer( );
                    if (cityList != null) {
                        Iterator it = cityList.iterator( );
                        while (it.hasNext( )) {
                            cityName = (String)it.next( );
                            sb.append("<option value=\""+cityName+"\">"
                                      +cityName+"</option> \n");
                        }
                        out.println(sb.toString( ));
                    }
                    else
                        out.println("<option></option>");
                %>
            </select>
            </aa:zone>
        </td>
        <td  align="center" valign="top">
            <aa:zone name="stateswcityList">
            <select size="10" name="statewcity" >
                <%
                    String stateName = "";
                    StringBuffer sb2 = new StringBuffer( );
                    if (stateList != null) {
                        Iterator it = stateList.iterator( );
                        while (it.hasNext( )) {
                            stateName = (String)it.next( );
                            sb2.append("<option value=\""+stateName+"\">"
                                       +stateName+"</option> \n");
                        }
                        out.println(sb2.toString( ));
                    }
```

*Example 7-17. AjaxAnywhere implementation in index.jsp (continued)*

```
                    else
                        out.println("<option></option>");
                %>
            </select>
            </aa:zone>
        </td>
    </tr>
</table>
</form>
```

The first bit of code pulls a couple of `ArrayList` objects (the `cityList` and `stateList`) from the session. The first time through, these `ArrayLists` will be `null`; eventually, they will be used to populate the different select fields.

We then import the AjaxAnywhere JavaScript library, *aa.js*:

```
<script src="aa.js"></script>
```

This library provides support for the AjaxAnywhere tag library, including the `submitAJAX( )` function. Next, we initialize the variable `ajaxAnywhere.formName` with the name of the form that will be submitted by the call to `submitAjax( )`:

```
<script>ajaxAnywhere.formName = "main";</script>
```

Then we set the JavaScript onchange trigger to call `submitAJAX('function=state')`:

```
<select size="10" name="state"
        onchange="ajaxAnywhere.submitAJAX('function=state');">
```

Now when the selection is changed, AjaxAnywhere submits the form via `XMLHttpRequest`, passing in the request parameter `function=state`. So, an `XMLHttpRequest` is generated whenever the user selects a state.

Further down in the JSP there is another call to `submitAjax( )`, this time with the parameter `'function=city'`:

```
<select size="10" name="city"
        onchange="ajaxAnywhere.submitAJAX('function=city')">
```

This call generates the `XMLHttpRequest` when the user selects a city.

### Refresh zones

To understand AjaxAnywhere, you must understand the concept of refresh zones. A refresh zone is contained between `<aa:zone>` and `</aa:zone>` tags and contains the area that AjaxAnywhere will update when the AjaxAnywhere servlet sends back its response. (Configuring this servlet will be discussed in more detail later.)

When the servlet sends back the response to a `submitAjax( )` call, the Java code inside the `<aa:zone>` tag that is targeted for refresh is executed. (Note that this is the only time we've seen Java code, rather than JavaScript, used to update HTML components.) So, in this case, the servlet calls `AAUtils.addZonesToRefresh( )`, specifying that it wants to refresh the citiesList zone. When the response comes back, the Java code on lines 50–64 populates the city selection box with options taken from an ArrayList that was stored in the session.

Similar code on lines 71–85 populates the list of states on the right side of the window after the user selects a city. Again, this code executes only when the servlet has called AAUtils.addZonesToRefresh( ) to target the stateswcityList zone for refresh.

### Writing support for AjaxAnywhere

Now that we've looked at the JSP that creates the HTML the browser renders, let's look at the AjaxAnywhereSupportServlet. This servlet must be written by the developer to support AjaxAnywhere for a specific application; it is not part of the AjaxAnywhere package.

The AjaxAnywhereSupportServlet (Example 7-18) handles the XMLHttpRequests sent by the browser. First, the servlet verifies that the requests have come from an AjaxAnywhere application by calling AAUtils.isAjaxRequest( ). If this method returns true, the servlet goes on with the rest of the processing. If it isn't dealing with an AjaxAnywhere request, there's clearly no point in dealing with zones and the rest of the AjaxAnywhere mechanism.

*Example 7-18. The AjaxAnywhereSupportServlet*

```
public class AjaxAnywhereSupportServlet extends HttpServlet {
    private static final long serialVersionUID = 1L;

    public void doGet(HttpServletRequest req, HttpServletResponse res)
            throws ServletException, IOException {
        doPost(req, res);
    }

    public void doPost(HttpServletRequest req, HttpServletResponse res)
            throws ServletException, IOException {
        String state = req.getParameter("state");
        String city = req.getParameter("city");
        String function = req.getParameter("function");

        if (AAUtils.isAjaxRequest(req)) {
            HttpSession session = req.getSession( );
            if (function.equals("city")) {
                AAUtils.addZonesToRefresh(req, "stateswcityList");
                session.setAttribute("stateList", getStates(city));
            }
            else if (function.equals("state")) {
                AAUtils.addZonesToRefresh(req, "citiesList");
                session.setAttribute("cityList", getCities(state));
            }
        }
```

*Example 7-18. The AjaxAnywhereSupportServlet (continued)*

```
        String url = "/index.jsp";
        ServletContext sc = getServletContext( );
        RequestDispatcher rd = sc.getRequestDispatcher(url);
        rd.forward(req, res);
    }

}
```

If the call to `AAUtils.isAjaxRequest( )` returns `true`, the servlet decides whether to update the list of states or the list of cities, depending on the value of the `function` parameter that `submitAjax( )` added to the request URL. If the value of the `function` parameter is `"city"`, we're being asked for a list of states that match the city included in the request. In this case, the servlet first calls `AAUtils.addZonesToRefresh( )` to say that it is updating the `stateswcityList` zone. It then calls the `getStates( )` method, which returns an `ArrayList` of states that contain a city of the given name. This list is then added to the session, under the `stateList` attribute. The logic is similar if a list of cities is requested (i.e., if the value of the `function` parameter is `"state"`): the servlet states that it wants to update the `citiesList` zone and calls `getCities( )` to find the list of cities in the given state, and then this `ArrayList` is added to the session under the `cityList` attribute.

Why not just check for a `null` value in either the `city` or the `state`? That seems logical, but doing so would constitute an error. If you look back at the JSP code in Example 7-17, you will see that both zones are in the same form. That means that the request will always have a `state` and a `city` parameter. This makes it difficult to use those parameters as a way to determine which one was actually passed in fresh.

Once all the hard work is done, the servlet gets the `ServletContext`, uses the context to get the `RequestDispatcher`, and then uses the `RequestDispatcher` to send the response back to *index.jsp*.

The `AjaxAnywhereSupportServlet` has two other methods that help it get the data for the cities and states. The `getCities( )` method, presented in Example 7-19, returns a collection of strings containing all the cities for a given state.

*Example 7-19. The getCities() method*

```
private Collection getCities(String state) {
    ArrayList cityList = new ArrayList( );
    Connection con = DatabaseConnector.getConnection( );
    try {
        Statement statement = con.createStatement( );
        String sqlString =
                "SELECT DISTINCT CITY FROM ZIPCODES WHERE STATE='" + state
                + "' ORDER BY CITY;";
```

*Example 7-19. The getCities() method (continued)*

```
        ResultSet resultSet = statement.executeQuery(sqlString);
        while (resultSet.next( )) {
            cityList.add(resultSet.getString(1));
        }
    }
    catch(Exception e) {
        System.out.println("exception caught getting cities for " + state);
    }
    finally {
        if (con != null) {
            try {
                con.close( );
            }
            catch(SQLException e) {
            }
        }
    }
    return cityList;
}
```

The other method that AjaxAnywhereSupportServlet needs is getStates( ), presented in Example 7-20, which returns a collection of strings containing the names of all the states in which a city with the given name is found.

*Example 7-20. The getStates() method*

```
private Collection getStates(String city) {
    ArrayList stateList = new ArrayList( );
    Connection con = DatabaseConnector.getConnection( );
    try {
        Statement statement = con.createStatement( );
        String sqlString = "SELECT DISTINCT STATE FROM ZIPCODES where CITY='"
                + city + "' ORDER BY STATE;";
        ResultSet resultSet = statement.executeQuery(sqlString);
        while (resultSet.next( )) {
            stateList.add(resultSet.getString(1));
        }
    }
    catch(Exception e) {
        System.out.println("exception caught getting states from zipcodes table");
    }
    finally {
        if (con != null) {
            try {
                con.close( );
            }
            catch(SQLException e) {
            }
        }
    }
    return stateList;
}
```

### The AjaxAnywhere filter

The last thing we need to do before we can get the application up and running is to configure the AjaxAnywhere filter. This filter formats the code coming from the servlet to trigger zone updates. When I first began writing this section, I neglected to add a filter mapping for the servlet, and it took me a while to figure out why the application was not working. The lesson to be learned is to make sure that you have the filter mapping configured correctly in *web.xml*!

The *web.xml* file in Example 7-21 contains examples of the different filter mappings that can be used for AjaxAnywhere. The only filter mapping that is actually needed is the one that maps AjaxAnywhere to `/AjaxAnywhereSupport`; the others have been left in for illustrative purposes.

*Example 7-21. web.xml with servlet and filter mappings for AjaxAnywhere*

```
<!DOCTYPE web-app PUBLIC
    "-//Sun Microsystems, Inc.//DTD Web Application 2.3//EN"
    "http://java.sun.com/dtd/web-app_2_3.dtd">
<web-app>
    <servlet>
        <servlet-name>AjaxAnywhereSupportServlet</servlet-name>
        <servlet-class>
            com.oreilly.ajax.servlet.AjaxAnywhereSupportServlet
        </servlet-class>
    </servlet>
    <servlet-mapping>
        <servlet-name>AjaxAnywhereSupportServlet</servlet-name>
        <url-pattern>/AjaxAnywhereSupport</url-pattern>
    </servlet-mapping>
    <filter>
        <filter-name>AjaxAnywhere</filter-name>
        <filter-class>org.ajaxanywhere.AAFilter</filter-class>
    </filter>
    <filter-mapping>
        <filter-name>AjaxAnywhere</filter-name>
        <url-pattern>/AjaxAnywhereSupport</url-pattern>
    </filter-mapping>
    <filter-mapping>
        <filter-name>AjaxAnywhere</filter-name>
        <url-pattern>*.jsp</url-pattern>
    </filter-mapping>
    <filter-mapping>
        <filter-name>AjaxAnywhere</filter-name>
        <url-pattern>*.do</url-pattern> <!-- default Struts mapping -->
    </filter-mapping>
    <filter-mapping>
        <filter-name>AjaxAnywhere</filter-name>
        <url-pattern>*.htm</url-pattern> <!-- other frameworks mapping-->
    </filter-mapping>
    <welcome-file-list>
        <welcome-file>index.jsp</welcome-file>
    </welcome-file-list>
</web-app>
```

The AjaxAnywhere tag library is a very flexible tool for building sophisticated Ajaxian applications. Don't expect to find ready-made Ajax applications in this library, but do expect to find some very useful ways to add Ajax to an existing or new application, with hardly any knowledge of JavaScript.

## Which Tag Library Should I Use?

Good question. I've tried to cover the major Ajax tag libraries here. None is a clear winner; each has its place.

If you find a component like the Tab Panel in AjaxTags to be useful, use AjaxTags in your project. If you find a component in JavaWebParts to be useful in your code, use JavaWebParts. If you don't need a specific component, but want to have the freedom of writing Ajax-enabled code without JavaScript, try using AjaxAnywhere. The bottom line is to use whatever benefits your project the most. Now that you have seen what each tag library can do, you are in a position to choose wisely.

And of course, if you want to reuse your code as tags and you can't find a tag library that works for you, you can always write your own tag library. But if you do this, try to contribute the result to one of the existing projects so our programming community can benefit. The Java community needs more collaboration, fewer libraries, and more features in each library. Then we can spend less time learning the various libraries and more time implementing their features in our code.

CHAPTER 8

# Ajax on Struts

Struts is one of the most mature and widely used Model-View-Controller (MVC) frameworks for Java web applications, so it's natural to ask the question, "How do you add Ajax features to Struts applications?" And, as you'd expect, there are several good answers. In this chapter, we'll investigate two approaches: using Struts-Layout, which implements some Ajax features, and using the DWR library (introduced in Chapter 6) within Struts applications.

This chapter isn't a tutorial on or introduction to Struts. If you want to learn more about Struts, some good sources are *Programming Jakarta Struts*, by Chuck Cavaness, and *Jakarta Struts Cookbook*, by Bill Siggelkow (both published by O'Reilly). It's also worth looking at the documentation at *http://struts.apache.org*.

## Struts-Layout

Struts-Layout (*http://struts.application-servers.com*) is a custom tag library that provides a number of ready-made Struts components. The most notable for our purposes is the suggestion field. Although Struts-Layout has other tags (for panels, input fields, tables, treeviews, sortable lists, data grids, pop-ups, calendars, and more), the suggestion field is the only one that's Ajax-enabled, and it's such a nice implementation that it's worth discussing. The other tags in the Struts-Layout library are worth investigating, too, but I'll leave that up to you. Its creators claim that Struts-Layout enables you to create web pages without knowing HTML. That's a bit extreme, but they have done a good job of encapsulating powerful features into a tag library.

Figure 8-1 shows a simple application that uses the Struts-Layout suggestion field. It's easy to see the power of the Struts-Layout tags even in this simple example. The view is created with only four Struts-Layout tags: `<layout:html>`, `<layout:form>`, `<layout:suggest>`, and `<layout:submit>` (more about these tags later). You don't need to write any JavaScript to create a suggestion field, and only minimal HTML is required.

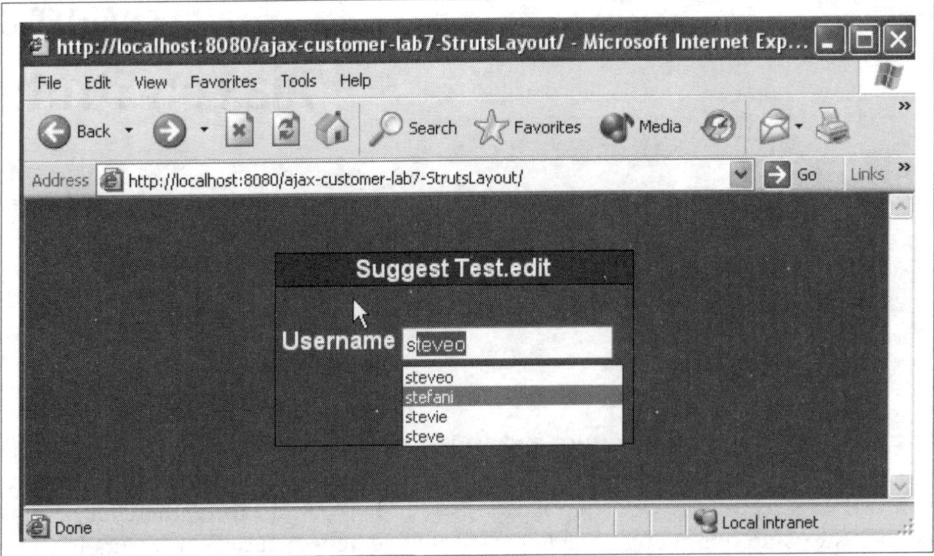


*Figure 8-1. A Struts-Layout suggestion field*

Most of the work involved in getting a Struts-Layout application running is in the configuration. Setting up the application to run on the server can take a little work, so let's step through it now.

## Installing Struts-Layout

First, you'll need to download and install the Struts-Layout library. Download the library from *http://struts.application-servers.com/download.html*. After unpacking the *.zip* file, locate the tag library *struts-layout.tld* and the *.jar* file *struts-layout.jar*; you'll find these in the directory *src/library*. You'll also need numerous support files, which are located in the */resources* directory. For the current release of Struts-Layout, move the images in */resources/images* into */resources/config*. Then copy that entire *config* directory into the root of your web application. Put *struts-layout.jar* in your application's *WEB-INF/lib* directory, and put *struts-layout.tld* in *WEB-INF*. Figure 8-2 shows how your development environment and *WAR* file should be organized.

A lot of support files need to be in the right place before Struts-Layout will work properly, so if you have trouble, refer to this diagram. The version of Struts-Layout (version 1.2) that I used for this application did not have all the files in the correct directories, and I had to move some files around to get it to work.

## Writing the Struts-Layout JSP

It's simply amazing how such a small bit of code in the JSP can create a suggestion field for an application.

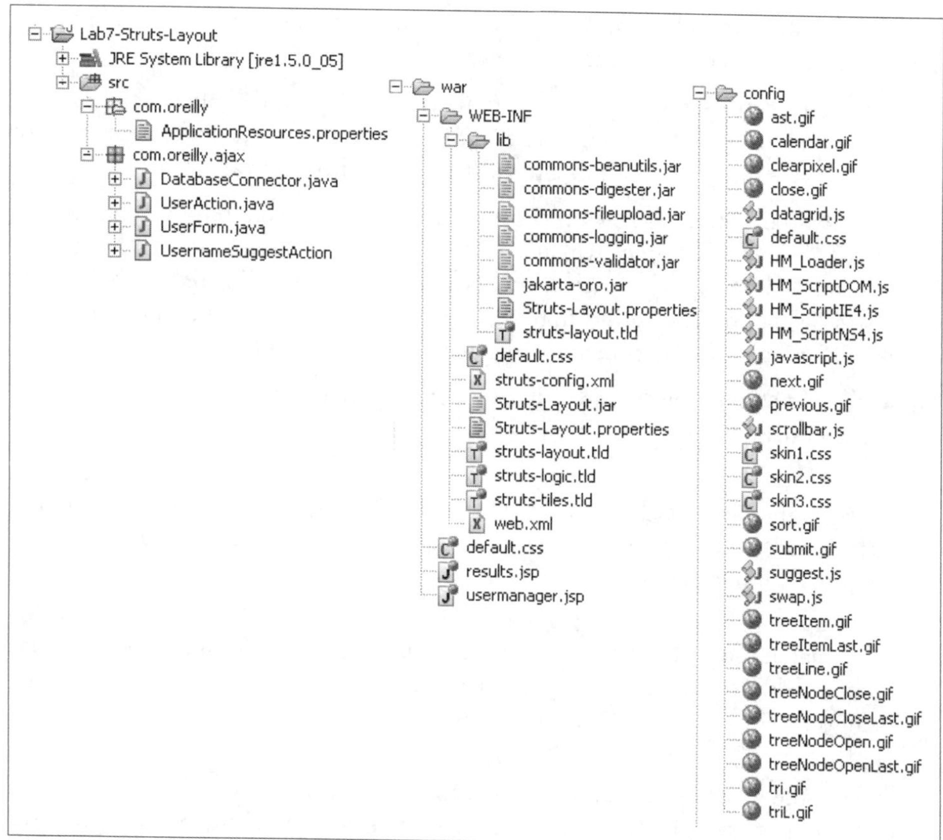


*Figure 8-2. The Struts-Layout directories and files*

The JSP begins with a `<taglib>` directive (Example 8-1). This directive specifies the location of the tag library (*/WEB-INF/struts-layout.tld*) and assigns the `layout` prefix to the tags defined in the *struts-layout.tld* file. (I've used the prefix `layout` to stay consistent with the suggested use of the tag library, but the prefix is arbitrary; you can use anything, provided it isn't used elsewhere in your application, although it's a good idea to stick with a prefix that's related to the library's purpose.)

*Example 8-1. usermanager.jsp created with Struts-Layout tags*

```
<%@ taglib uri="/WEB-INF/struts-layout.tld" prefix="layout" %>
<link href="default.css" media="screen" rel="Stylesheet" type="text/css" />
<layout:html>
    <layout:form action="useraction.do" styleClass="FORM" key="Suggest Test">
        <layout:suggest name="username" suggestAction="/getSuggestionList"
                        property="username" key="Username" styleId="myTextField"
                        value="" suggestCount="8" />
        <layout:submit />
    </layout:form>
</layout:html>
```

Early in the JSP, we link to *default.css*, a stylesheet provided by Struts-Layout that gives us the colors and alignment that we need to create the suggestion field.

`<layout:html>` defines the HTML area that will be displayed. When using Struts-Layout, avoid using any HTML in the JSP. Don't substitute an `<HTML>` tag for `<layout:html>`—the `<layout:html>` and `<HTML>` tags are not equivalent.

Next, the `<layout:form>` tag sets up the form and the Struts action to which the form submits. This line also defines which CSS class the form will use, as well as the title that is displayed on top of the select box (known as the *key*). Figure 8-1 shows how the key is displayed. The action that the `<layout:form>` sets is `useraction.do`; we'll define this action in the later section "The Struts Configuration."

The `<layout:suggest>` tag declares the Ajax-enabled suggestion field. It's a complicated tag, with a number of parameters:

`name`
: Specifies the bean used to get the suggestion field's properties; in this case, the "username" bean. The bean must be in the current scope (`pageContext`, request, session, or application scope).

`suggestAction`
: Must match the path for the web service that returns the list of data for the suggestion field. Its value, `"/getSuggestionList"`, is defined in *struts-config.xml* (see Example 8-5).

`property`
: Defines the name of the parameter that the form passes to the Struts action. The form in our case is *UserForm.java* (Example 8-3); it contains the property `username`, which must match the `property` parameter in the `<layout:suggest>` tag.

`key`
: Specifies the label that will be displayed for the field; this label ("Username") is visible in Figure 8-1.

`styleId`
: Sets up the CSS style for the suggestion field. If you use the `styleId` attribute, you need to include a Cascading Style Sheet and set up a style that matches the `styleId` in the `<layout:suggest>` tag.

`value`
: Sets the suggestion field's initial value. We want to start out with the field empty, so the value for this attribute is the empty string (`""`). The `value` parameter is required, so we cannot omit it. If you put a string in the value field, you will see that string when the form comes up.

`suggestCount`
: Specifies the maximum number of suggestions that are displayed at any given time. In our case, the maximum is eight. If there are more than eight matches, a scrollbar appears to allow the user to scroll through the matches.

There are many fields in the <layout:suggest> definition that are not listed in the Struts-Layout documentation, and some of these are critical. If you find that you need more information about any tag in Struts-Layout, open the *struts-layout.tld* file in a text editor and search for the name of the tag you're interested in (for example, the `suggest` tag); all the attributes of that tag are wrapped in <attribute> tags. Since Ajax is relatively new, you should expect libraries like Struts-Layout to change, and you'll frequently find that the documentation isn't up-to-date. When you're in this situation, always check the *.tld* file: that will give you the clues you need.

That's it for the tags! They are very compact and deceptively powerful; just one tag, <layout:suggest>, encapsulates all of the client functionality that required many lines when we coded it by hand in Chapter 5.

Name this JSP *usermanager.jsp* and copy it into the root of your web application context (the *war* directory).

Now it's time to do some configuration in *web.xml*. The Struts package (*struts.jar*) includes a special servlet called the `ActionServlet`. This servlet reads a configuration file; the name of this configuration file is specified as the `config` parameter in *web.xml*. In most cases, the name of the configuration file should be */WEB-INF/struts-config.xml*. The *web.xml* file showing the setup for Struts and the Struts-Layout tag file is presented in Example 8-2.

*Example 8-2. web.xml*

```
<web-app>
    <servlet>
        <servlet-name>action</servlet-name>
        <servlet-class>org.apache.struts.action.ActionServlet</servlet-class>
        <init-param>
            <param-name>application</param-name>
            <param-value>ApplicationResources</param-value>
        </init-param>
        <init-param>
            <param-name>config</param-name>
            <param-value>/WEB-INF/struts-config.xml</param-value>
        </init-param>
        <init-param>
            <param-name>debug</param-name>
            <param-value>3</param-value>
        </init-param>
        <init-param>
            <param-name>detail</param-name>
            <param-value>3</param-value>
        </init-param>
        <load-on-startup>1</load-on-startup>
    </servlet>
    <!-- Action Servlet Mapping -->
```

*Example 8-2. web.xml (continued)*

```
    <servlet-mapping>
        <servlet-name>action</servlet-name>
        <url-pattern>*.do</url-pattern>
    </servlet-mapping>
    <!-- The Welcome File List -->
    <welcome-file-list>
        <welcome-file>usermanager.jsp</welcome-file>
    </welcome-file-list>
    <!-- taglibs -->
    <taglib>
        <taglib-uri>/WEB-INF/struts-layout.tld</taglib-uri>
        <taglib-location>/WEB-INF/struts-layout.tld</taglib-location>
    </taglib>
</web-app>
```

This is a fairly typical *web.xml* file for a Struts application. It configures a single servlet, the Struts `ActionServlet`, and specifies the location of *struts-layout.tld*. It also sets the name of the Struts configuration file, *struts-config.xml*. This file controls which Struts actions the Struts application will use.

The last piece of configuration in *web.xml* is the setup of the Struts-Layout tag library. That's handled by the `<taglib>` tag toward the end of the file; it defines the layout tags that are used in the JSPs.

Later, you'll see how *struts-config.xml* sets the actions, forms, and tiles (views) to set up the Struts application.

## Struts Action Forms

A typical JSP application connects a JSP to a servlet through a call to `HTTPGet( )` or `HTTPPost( )`. Then the servlet gets any information it needs through a call to the request object (usually via `request.getParameter("paramname")`).

Struts introduces the concept of an action form to make a cleaner interface between the client and the server, avoiding all the `request.getParameter( )` calls on the server. An `action form` is a Struts class that encapsulates the parameters passed from the client to the server. The form you use in your application extends the `org.apache.struts.action.ActionForm` class, and each parameter that you post to the server is represented in the action form.

An *action form* is a Java bean that stores data for the view. Basically, that means that the form has private properties and public getter and setter methods for each property.

The data in the form is set by actions that are invoked before the JSP uses it. The JSP typically populates itself by calling tag libraries with the `property` field set to the field name of the form. For example, to access the `lastName` property of the form, a JSP could include the `<layout:write>` tag and pass the `property` field with the `property="lastName"` attribute. Look at *results.jsp* to see the exact syntax used to get the `lastName`.

So, instead of calling `request.getParameter("paramname")`, you can get the form from the action by calling `UserForm userForm = (UserForm)form`. The form is passed into the `ActionServlet`, so all you have to do is cast it to the `UserForm` class. At this point you can get the parameters from the form by using a get method: `String username = userForm.getUsername( )`.

Example 8-3 presents the `UserForm` that stores the data for the view, with its getters and setters: it's a plain old Java bean with accessor methods for `username`, `firstName`, and `lastName`.

*Example 8-3. The UserForm*

```
public class UserForm extends ActionForm {
    private String username;
    private String firstName;
    private String lastName;

    public String getFirstName( ) {
        return firstName;
    }
    public void setFirstName(String firstName) {
        this.firstName = firstName;
    }
    public String getLastName( ) {
        return lastName;
    }
    public void setLastName(String lastName) {
        this.lastName = lastName;
    }
    public String getUsername( ) {
        return username;
    }
    public void setUsername(String username) {
        this.username = username;
    }
    public void reset(ActionMapping mapping, HttpServletRequest request) {
        this.username = "";
        this.lastName = "";
        this.firstName = "";
    }
}
```

## What's an Action, and What Happened to My Servlet?

The familiar Java servlet is now represented by a Struts action. When writing Struts applications, instead of writing servlets, you write actions. Think of servlets as having been deprecated in favor of the Struts `Action` class. The `UserAction` class extends the Struts `Action` class, and instead of putting redirection code in the servlet, the program flow is controlled by *struts-config.xml*. The Struts action connects the business logic to the view.

Example 8-4 shows the code for the UserAction. Notice how the execute( ) method gets the UserForm, reads the username from the UserForm, calls a private method to gather information from the database, and then sets other values in the UserForm to be passed on to the next part of the application. The next part of the application is accessed by the call to mapping.findForward("success"), which forwards the user to the "success" tile. That tile is defined as *results.jsp* in the *struts-config.xml* file, which we'll look at in the next section.

*Example 8-4. The Struts action, UserAction.java*

```
public class UserAction extends Action {
    public ActionForward execute(ActionMapping mapping,
            ActionForm form,
            HttpServletRequest request,
            HttpServletResponse response) {
        String username = ((UserForm)form).getUsername( );
        HashMap userInfoMap = getUserInfo(username);
        String firstName =(String)userInfoMap.get("firstName");
        String lastName =(String)userInfoMap.get("lastName");
        ((UserForm)form).setFirstName(firstName);
        ((UserForm)form).setLastName(lastName);
        return mapping.findForward("success");
    }
    private HashMap getUserInfo(String username) {
        HashMap hashMap = null;
        Connection con = DatabaseConnector.getConnection( );
        try {
            Statement statement = con.createStatement( );
            String sqlString = "select FIRST_NAME,LAST_NAME from USERS where
                    USERNAME='"+username+"';";
            ResultSet resultSet = statement.executeQuery(sqlString);
            if (resultSet.next( )) {
                hashMap = new HashMap( );
                hashMap.put("firstName",resultSet.getString(1));
                hashMap.put("lastName",resultSet.getString(2));
            }
        }
        catch (Exception e) {
            System.out.println("exception caught getting usernames");
        }
        finally {
            if (con != null) {
                try {
                    con.close( );
                }
                catch (SQLException e) {
                }
            }
        }
        return hashMap;
    }
}
```

## The Struts Configuration

Now, on to the *struts-config.xml* file. Struts is an implementation of an MVC framework, where the model (the application data) is represented by your own objects (typically Java beans), the view is implemented by JSPs, and the actions, as configured by *struts-config.xml*, form the controller. The Struts `Form` objects carry information between the `Views` and the `Actions`. *Tile* is Struts lingo for the view, which is usually an HTML or JSP page.

The Struts configuration file, *struts-config.xml*, is presented in Example 8-5.

*Example 8-5. struts-config.xml*

```
<?xml version="1.0" encoding="UTF-8"?>
<!DOCTYPE struts-config PUBLIC
    "-//Apache Software Foundation//DTD Struts Configuration 1.1//EN"
    "http://jakarta.apache.org/struts/dtds/struts-config_1_1.dtd">
<struts-config>
    <data-sources />
    <form-beans>
        <form-bean name="userForm"
                   type="com.oreilly.ajax.UserForm" />
    </form-beans>
    <global-exceptions />
    <global-forwards />
    <action-mappings>
        <action path="/useraction"
                type="com.oreilly.ajax.UserAction"
                name="userForm"
                input="/usermanager.jsp">
            <forward name="success" path = "/results.jsp" />
            <forward name="failure" path="/usermanager.jsp" />
        </action>
        <action path="/getSuggestionList"
                type="com.oreilly.ajax.UsernameSuggestAction">
        </action>
    </action-mappings>
    <controller bufferSize="4096" debug="0" />
    <message-resources parameter="com.oreilly.ApplicationResources" />
</struts-config>
```

The `<form-beans>` tag tells the Struts application that when `userForm` is referenced, it should satisfy that reference with an instance of `com.oreilly.ajax.UserForm` (the Struts form that we developed earlier). `userForm` is nothing more than an alias for `com.oreilly.ajax.UserForm`.

`userForm` is referenced in *results.jsp* (Example 8-6), which displays information about the selected item. When a user is selected from the suggestion field in *usermanager.jsp*, control is passed to the `UserName` action and information about the selected user is stored in the `UserForm`. Next, control passes to *results.jsp*, which displays the results stored in the `UserForm` to the user.

*Example 8-6. results.jsp*

```
<%@ taglib uri="/WEB-INF/struts-layout.tld" prefix="layout" %>
<link href="default.css" media="screen" rel="Stylesheet" type="text/css" />
<layout:html>
Results:
    <layout:row>
        <layout:column>
            Username
        </layout:column>
        <layout:column>
            <layout:write name="userForm" property="username" />
        </layout:column>
   </layout:row>
   <layout:row>
        <layout:column>
            First Name:
        </layout:column>
        <layout:column>
            <layout:write name="userForm" property="firstName" />
        </layout:column>
   </layout:row>
   <layout:row>
        <layout:column>
            Last Name:
        </layout:column>
        <layout:column>
            <layout:write name="userForm" property="lastName" />
        </layout:column>
   </layout:row>
</layout:html>
```

The JSP retrieves the `userForm` with the `<layout:write>` tag. Once again, this JSP doesn't require any HTML; the Struts-Layout tag library takes care of all that for us. You can mix HTML tags with the `layout:` tags to give you more control over the page's appearance, but don't forget about the CSS file if you want more control over the look of the page.

Figure 8-3 shows the results page displaying information about the selected user.

## Where Does the Data Come From?

The data behind this application comes from the MySQL database that we have been using throughout this book. The application uses the `USERS` table in the `AJAX` database we created in Chapter 5. It also uses the `DatabaseConnector` class from Chapter 5 (see Example 8-7).

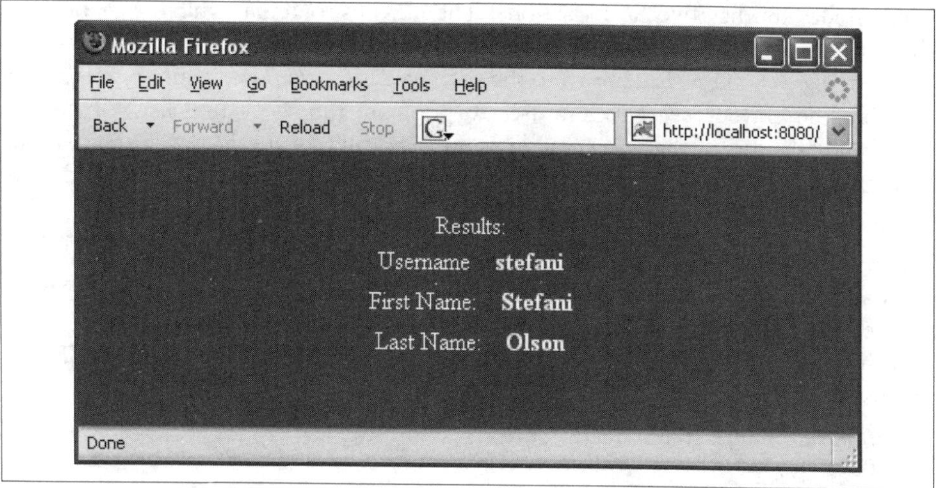


*Figure 8-3. The results JSP*

*Example 8-7. The DatabaseConnector class*

```
package com.oreilly.ajax;

import java.sql.Connection;
import java.sql.DriverManager;

public class DatabaseConnector {
    public static Connection getConnection( ) {
        Connection con = null;
        String driver = "com.mysql.jdbc.Driver";
        try {
            Class.forName(driver).newInstance( );
        } catch (Exception e) {
            System.out.println("Failed to load mySQL driver.");
            return null;
        }
        try {
            con = DriverManagergetConnection(
                    "jdbc:mysql:///AJAX?user=ajax&password=polygon");
        } catch (Exception e) {
            e.printStackTrace( );
        }
        return con;
    }
}
```

This application has two Struts actions. The class UserAction, which is mapped to the path */useraction*, supports the selection of the username. The other action, UsernameSuggestAction, is mapped to the path */getSuggestionList*; it supports the Ajax call that the <layout:suggest> tag uses to populate the suggestion list. Obviously, you could take this further: you could use an Ajax call to send the data to UserAction and then populate the form with other information, based on the username. I'll leave that as an exercise for the reader.

When the form is submitted, Struts invokes the UserAction action, which pulls the username out of the Struts form (UserForm) and then calls getUserInfo( ). In turn, getUserInfo( ) queries the database for the first name and last name of the selected user. Then the form values for lastName and firstName are set for the next JSP that will use it:

```
((UserForm)form).setFirstName(firstName);
((UserForm)form).setLastName(lastName);
```

When *results.jsp* is invoked again, the UserForm object will be ready with the data for the username field.

## Populating the Suggestion List

The UsernameSuggestAction class handles the Ajax call behind the <layout:suggest> tag. This class must extend fr.improve.struts.taglib.layout.suggest.SuggestAction and implement a method that returns a Collection. The contents of the Collection are used as the suggestions in the <layout:suggest> field; that list of suggestions should be an ArrayList of Strings.

The method used to get the Collection is set via the suggestAction parameter of the <layout:suggest> tag. Back in our *usermanager.jsp* file, we set this parameter to "/getSuggestionList", which matches the method name in UsernameSuggestAction (Example 8-8).

*Example 8-8. The UsernameSuggestAction class*

```
public class UsernameSuggestAction extends SuggestAction {
    public Collection getSuggestionList(HttpServletRequest in_request,
            String in_word) {
        Collection usernames = getUserSuggestions( );
        ArrayList suggestions = new ArrayList( );

        if (in_word != null && in_word.length( ) > 0) {
            Iterator iter = usernames.iterator( );

            while(iter.hasNext( )) {
                String currentWord = (String) iter.next( );

                if (currentWord.toLowerCase().startsWith(in_word.toLowerCase( )))
                    suggestions.add(currentWord);
```

*Example 8-8. The UsernameSuggestAction class (continued)*

```
            }
        }

        return suggestions;
    }
    private static Collection getUserSuggestions( ) {

        ArrayList arrayList = null;
        Connection con = DatabaseConnector.getConnection( );
        try {
            Statement statement = con.createStatement( );

            String sqlString = "select username from users;";
            ResultSet resultSet = statement.executeQuery(sqlString);
            arrayList = new ArrayList( );
            while (resultSet.next( )) {
                arrayList.add(resultSet.getString(1));
            }
        }
        catch (Exception e) {
            System.out.println("exception caught getting usernames");
        }
        finally {
            if (con != null) {
                try {
                    con.close( );
                }
                catch (SQLException e) {
                }
            }
        }
        return arrayList;
    }
}
```

In most cases, the values in the suggestion list should come from a data store. This example is no exception: the list is populated with a call to the private method `getUserSuggestions( )`. The `getSuggestionList( )` method is adapted from the demo example for `<layout:suggest>` on the Struts-Layout web site.

## Struts-Layout Is Cool Because...

Setting up a suggestion field using the Struts-Layout package is incredibly easy. This is one of the few frameworks that use Ajax without requiring any Ajax-specific coding: we didn't have to write any JavaScript at all. Unfortunately, it currently has only one Ajax-enabled tag, but I'm sure Struts-Layout will add more Ajax functionality in the future. Keep checking in, because this framework has a lot of potential.

## Adding Ajax to Struts with DWR

There is really nothing special about adding Ajax support to a Struts application. Once you understand how to add Ajax support to a regular application, you'll find that adding it to a Struts application follows the same rules: you have a JSP that either calls an Ajax library such as Prototype or DWR or contains your own implementations of Ajax features written in JavaScript. Using an established library such as DWR is more efficient than writing your own Ajaxian code, because it will already have been tested against many browsers and should support browsers that you haven't even tried.

In Chapter 6, we used Scriptaculous to build a shopping application, but that application lacked a way to add new products. Now we'll explore how to use Struts and DWR to add new products to the PRODUCTS table in the database.

Figure 8-4 shows what the application's product management page will look like after the coding in this section is implemented.

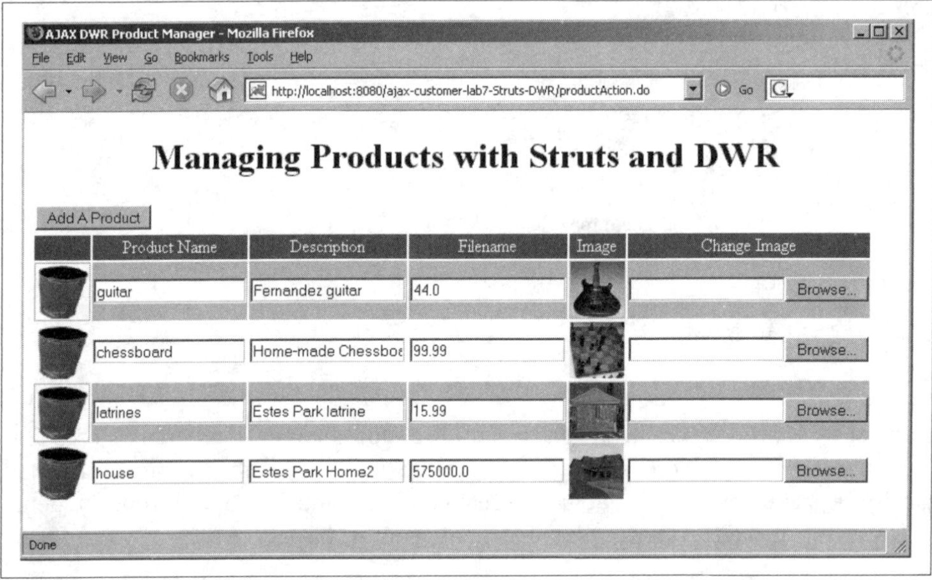


*Figure 8-4. The initial view of the Product Manager*

The DWR framework introduced in Chapter 6 is well suited to working with Struts, and because it automatically generates much of the JavaScript that is needed for Ajax, using DWR minimizes the amount of JavaScript that you need to write.

Let's look back at the database tables we used for the shopping cart example in Chapter 6. The tables are shown in Figure 8-5.

| users | |
|---|---|
| PK | USER ID |
| | USERNAME<br>PASSWORD<br>FIRST_NAME<br>LAST_NAME<br>EMAIL<br>ADDRESS<br>ZIPCODE<br>CITY<br>STATE<br>JOINED<br>LAST_LOGIN |

| products | |
|---|---|
| PK | PRODUCT ID |
| | PRODUCT_NAME<br>DESCRIPTION<br>FILENAME<br>PRICE |

| shopping_cart | |
|---|---|
| PK | CART ID |
| | USER_ID<br>START_DATE<br>LAST_UPDATED<br>ACTIVE |

| items_in_cart | |
|---|---|
| | |
| | ITEM_ID<br>CART_ID<br>COUNT |

| zipcodes | |
|---|---|
| **PK** | **ZIPCODE** |
| | CITY<br>STATE |

*Figure 8-5. The shopping cart database tables*

Figure 8-5 was generated using the MySQL ODBC driver. Notice that the table names are lowercase (e.g., `products`). That's how tables appear when you use MySQL on Microsoft Windows: the table names revert to lowercase, and the column references in the queries are not case-sensitive.

We have written support for all but the `PRODUCTS` table. In order to add a product to this table, we currently have to add a row manually and then copy the product's picture (a PNG file) to the correct directory. This application will make it easier to add or modify products.

There is no real difference between a Struts application and a standard servlet/JSP application when using Ajax techniques. In both cases, the JavaScript in the JSP calls methods in the model. Struts actions can answer the Ajax calls, but using Struts actions is only suggested, not required. In this application, Struts actions will not answer the Ajax calls; we'll use DWR to tie the `ProductManager` directly to the JavaScript calls.

The JSP for this application lists the existing products while allowing the user to add products to the database. A div wraps the product list; this div is dynamically updated each time a new product is added.

Figure 8-6 shows the sequence of events that adds a product to the database. The Product Manager makes a call through the browser to the `ProductManager` application. The browser issues a request to get the image path, which is the path (on the server) where the images are stored. Next, the browser issues a call to the DWR layer, requesting the product list. DWR marshals the request to an instance of the Java `ProductManager` class, which returns the list.

The next part of the sequence is a `Create`, `Update`, or `Delete` command, depending upon what the user needs to do next. Each of those commands is passed to the `ProductManager` through the DWR library.

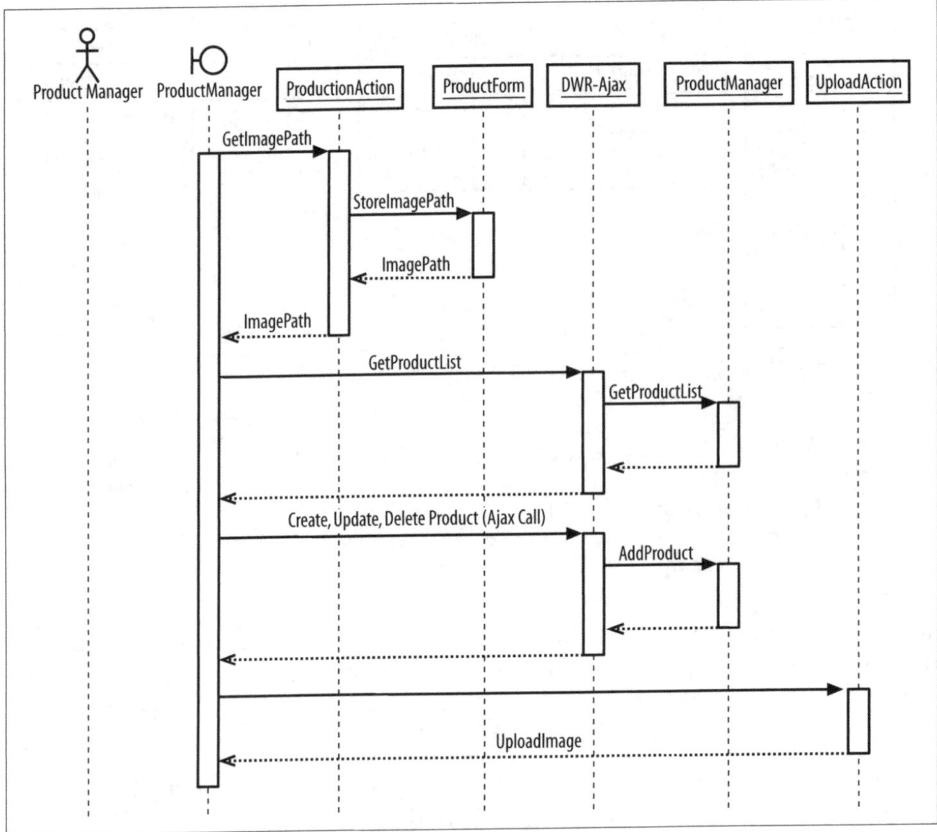


*Figure 8-6. The Product Manager Struts Ajax application*

The last command is `UploadImage`. This is not an Ajax call, because of security limitations; JavaScript isn't allowed to access files on the user's filesystem, so to put new images on the server, the JSP calls the Struts `UploadAction`.

## Uploading Files

Struts is only used to initialize the locations of the image files and to upload the product images. The Struts form that passes the image data to `UploadAction` is called `UploadForm` (Example 8-9). This form uses a special Struts class called `FormFile`, which allows a Struts form to hold a file. The file can later be manipulated by the corresponding action (in our case, `UploadAction`).

*Example 8-9. UploadForm.java*

```
import org.apache.struts.action.*;
import org.apache.struts.upload.FormFile;
```

*Example 8-9. UploadForm.java (continued)*

```
public class UploadForm extends ActionForm {
    private FormFile uploadFile;
    private int productId;
    public int getProductId( ) {
        return productId;
    }
    public void setProductId(int productId) {
        this.productId = productId;
    }
    public FormFile getUploadFile( ) {
        return uploadFile;
    }
    public void setUploadFile(FormFile uploadFile) {
        this.uploadFile = uploadFile;
    }
}
```

`UploadForm` is a simple Java bean that transfers data between the HTML form and the `UploadAction` (Example 8-10), which does the work. Again, `UploadAction` can't use Ajax because JavaScript does not have access to the filesystem. We have to use the `<input type="file" />` tag in the JSP and let the HTML tag do the work of browsing for a file.

*Example 8-10. The UploadAction*

```
public class UploadAction extends Action {
    static String productsDirectory = null;
    private String getFilePath( ) throws FileNotFoundException, IOException {
    String resourceFilepath = this.getServlet().getServletContext( ).getRealPath(
            "/shopping.properties");
    Properties configs = new Properties( );
    configs.load(new FileInputStream(resourceFilepath));
    String dir = this.getServlet().getServletContext( ).getRealPath("")+
            "/"+configs.getProperty("products.directory");
    return dir;
}

public ActionForward execute(
        ActionMapping mapping,
        ActionForm form,
        HttpServletRequest request,
        HttpServletResponse response) throws Exception {
    UploadForm myForm = (UploadForm)form;
    int productId = myForm.getProductId( );

    // process the FormFile
    FormFile myFile = myForm.getUploadFile( );
    String fileName = myFile.getFileName( );
    byte[] fileData = myFile.getFileData( );

    FileOutputStream out = new FileOutputStream(getFilePath( )+"/"+fileName);
```

*Example 8-10. The UploadAction (continued)*

```
        out.write(fileData);
        out.close( );
        ProductManager.updateProductById(productId,"FILENAME",fileName);

        return mapping.findForward("success");
    }
```

Although we can't use Ajax to upload the image, this drawback is hardly noticeable in light of all the other features that use Ajax. For example, one of the most common tasks that a product manager would perform would be to change a product's price. This is really easy using Ajax: simply editing the `PRICE` field and then moving to another field fires the `JavaScript:onchange` event and updates the database.

## Creating the JSP

Now that we've written our actions, let's dig into the fun stuff.

The *productmanager.jsp* page (Example 8-11) starts by including several JavaScript files, only one of which we're responsible for writing (*oreillyProductManager.js*). The next file, *dwr/interface/ProductManager.js*, is generated automatically by DWR; the remaining two files are DWR's support libraries (*engine.js* and *util.js*).

*Example 8-11. productmanager.jsp*

```
<html>
<head>
    <title>AJAX DWR Product Manager</title>
    <script src='scripts/oreillyProductManager.js'></script>
    <script src='dwr/interface/ProductManager.js'></script>
    <script src='dwr/engine.js'></script>
    <script src='dwr/util.js'></script>
    <style type="text/css">
        .productlist {border:1; border-color:#cccccc;}
    </style>
</head>
<body onload='populateData( )'>
    <div>
        <h1><center>Managing Products with Struts and DWR</center></h1>
        <table>
            <tr>
                <td>
                    <input type="button" value="Add A Product" name="name"
                           onclick="newProduct( )" />
                </td>
            </tr>
        </table>
    </div>
    <div id="products" class="productlist"></div>
</body>
</html>
```

The function populateData() is called the first time the page is loaded. There is a button (Add A Product) for adding a new product, and there is a <div> (id="products") that we'll populate with the product list.

## Writing the DWR Configuration File

Now for the DWR configuration file, *dwr.xml* (Example 8-12). It's so simple that it's actually exciting. (When was the last time you were excited by a configuration file?) The JavaScript that DWR generates is defined within the <allow> tag. The <create> tag defines the name of the JavaScript file to be generated (*ProductManager.js*) and included in the JSP; this file is linked to the actual Java class that responds to the Ajax requests.

*Example 8-12. The DWR configuration file, dwr.xml*

```
<dwr>
    <allow>
        <create creator="new" javascript="ProductManager"
                class="com.oreilly.ajax.ProductManager">
            <include method="getProduct"/>
            <include method="addProduct"/>
            <include method="getJSONProducts"/>
            <include method="updateProductById"/>
            <include method="deleteRow"/>
        </create>
        <convert converter="bean" match="com.oreilly.ajax.Product">
            <param name="include" value="productName,description,filename,price"/>
        </convert>
    </allow>
</dwr>
```

The <create> tag defines the JavaScript support for a given Java class. In this case, DWR creates a JavaScript ProductManager object that supports the ProductManager class (com.oreilly.ajax.ProductManager).

The <include> tags define the Java methods that are supported by JavaScript generated by DWR.

The <convert> tag builds a JavaScript bean from com.oreilly.ajax.Product with the values passed in through the <param> tag. This allows the application to retrieve data from DWR and display it in the browser.

## Displaying the Products in the Browser

We still have to write some JavaScript to populate the div in *productmanager.jsp*. That JavaScript code is included toward the top of *productmanager.jsp* in a file called *oreillyProductManager.js*.

The most complex part of the JavaScript is the loop that populates the product table. If the product table is appended directly to the div's `innerHTML`, the table won't work correctly in some browsers. A safer, browser-independent way to populate the div is to build a separate string that contains all the HTML for the table. After the table has been built, you can then set `innerHTML` to the string with one JavaScript statement. That's what happens in the `updateProductList()` function, as you can see in Example 8-13.

*Example 8-13. oreillyProductManager.js*

```
function newProduct() {
    ProductManager.addProduct(populateData)
}
function populateData() {
    ProductManager.getJSONProducts(updateProductList);
}
function updateProductList(jsonData) {
    var myJSONObject = eval('(' + jsonData + ')');
    productsdiv = document.getElementById('products');
    var output = "<table id='myTable' class='tableWrapper'>"+
                 "<tbody id='myTbody'><tr><td class='trh'> </td>"+
                 "<td class='trh'>Product Name</td>"+
                 "<td class='trh'>Description</td>"+
                 "<td class='trh'>Price</td>"+
                 "<td class='trh'>Image</td>"+
                 "<td class='trh'>Change Image</td></tr>";
    for (i=0;i<myJSONObject.products.length;i++) {
        output += "<tr class='tr" + (i%2) + "'>";
        output += "<td class='col2'>"+"<input type='image' width='50'
                  height='50' src='images/garbagecan.png'"+
                  " value=\""+myJSONObject.products[i].id +
                  "\" onclick='deleteRow(this.value);' /></td>";
        output += "<td class='col0'><input type=\"text\" value=\""+
                  myJSONObject.products[i].name +
                  "\" id=\"name_"+myJSONObject.products[i].id +
                  "\" onchange=\"updateProductById("+myJSONObject.products[i].id+
                  ",\'PRODUCT_NAME\',this.value)\" /> </td>";
        output += "<td class='col1'><input type=\"text\" value=\""
                  + myJSONObject.products[i].description +
                  "\" id=\"description_"+myJSONObject.products[i].id +
                  "\" onchange=\"updateProductById("+myJSONObject.products[i].id
                  +",\'DESCRIPTION\',this.value)\" /> </td>";
        output += "<td class='col2'><input type=\"text\" value=\"" +
                  myJSONObject.products[i].price +
                  "\" id=\"price_"+myJSONObject.products[i].id +
                  "\" onchange=\"updateProductById("+myJSONObject.products[i].id
                  +",\'PRICE\',this.value)\" /> </td>";
        output += "<td class='col2'><img width='50' height='50' src='"
                  +myJSONObject.products[i].imagepath+"' /></td>";
        output += "<td class='col3'>"
                  +"<form name='theuploadform' method='post'
                  action='uploadAction.do'" +" enctype='multipart/form-data' >"
```

*Example 8-13. oreillyProductManager.js (continued)*

```
                +"<input id='uploadFile' type='file' name='uploadFile'
                value='change'"+" onchange='submit( )'></input>"
                +"<input type='hidden' value='"+myJSONObject.products[i].id
                +"' name='productId' /></form></td>";
    }
    output += "</tbody></table>";
    alert (output);
    productsdiv.innerHTML = output;
}
function isNumber(allegedNumber) {
    var numberRegExp = /(^\d+$)|(^\d+\.\d+$)/
    if (numberRegExp.test(allegedNumber)) {
        return true
    }
    else {
        return false;
    }
}
function deleteRow(rowId) {
    ProductManager.deleteRow(rowId,populateData);
}
function updateProductById(id,column,newValue) {
    if (column == 'PRICE') {
        if (isNumber(newValue)) {
            ProductManager.updateProductById(id,column,newValue,populateData);
        }
        else {
            alert(newValue+' is not a number. Price must be a number.');
        }
    }
    else {
        ProductManager.updateProductById(id,column,newValue,populateData);
    }
}
function uploadFile(formdata) {
    filename = formdata.form.filename.value;
    alert('uploading file'+filename);
    formdata.form.submit( );
}
```

The `populateData( )` method is certainly the most complicated. It builds the table that contains the current product list, which is used to fill in the empty div in the JSP. The product list is full of JavaScript triggers that call the Ajax DWR functions and use Ajax to communicate with the servlets. The `for` loop in `populateData( )` connects all of the list's fields to JavaScript triggers: for example, the garbage can (`<input type='image'...>`) is attached to the `onclick` event, which calls the `deleteRow( )` function, and the Product Name field and many of the other fields are attached to the onchange event trigger, which calls `updateProductById( )`. These functions (`deleteRow( )`, `updateProductById( )`, and so on) each perform some operation via Ajax. In turn, DWR delegates the Ajax operation to a method in the server's ProductManager class. The JavaScript arranges for populateData( ) to be called when the Ajax operation has completed.

The servlet generates the image filenames (<img src=...>) from data in the database. Look back at the PRODUCTS table in Figure 8-5. The FILENAME field contains the name of the image file for a product.

## Viewing the DWR-Generated JavaScript

The heart of this application is the ProductManager Java class, which we'll discuss shortly. This class is mapped to JavaScript functions through *dwr.xml*. The archive, *dwr.jar*, holds the key to how the files get mapped. If you want to see the JavaScript that DWR creates, you can append the JavaScript file path that DWR uses to the root URL of your application. We've already seen that DWR is generating the file *dwr/interface/ProductManager.js*. If you take that file URL and append it to the application's root URL, you get *http://localhost:8080/ajax-customer-lab7-Struts-DWR/dwr/interface/ProductManager.jsp*. When you browse to that URL, you will see the JavaScript that DWR produces in the browser window (Example 8-14).

*Example 8-14. JavaScript code produced by DWR*

```
function ProductManager( ) {
}
ProductManager.getProduct = function(p0, callback) {
    DWREngine._execute('/ajax-customer-lab7-Struts-DWR/dwr',
            'ProductManager',
            'getProduct',
            p0, callback);
}
ProductManager.getJSONProducts = function(callback) {
    DWREngine._execute('/ajax-customer-lab7-Struts-DWR/dwr',
            'ProductManager',
            'getJSONProducts',
            callback);
}
ProductManager.updateProductById = function(p0, p1, p2, callback) {
    DWREngine._execute('/ajax-customer-lab7-Struts-DWR/dwr',
            'ProductManager',
            'updateProductById',
            p0, p1, p2, callback);
}
ProductManager.deleteRow = function(p0, callback) {
    DWREngine._execute('/ajax-customer-lab7-Struts-DWR/dwr',
            'ProductManager', 'deleteRow', p0, callback);
}
ProductManager.addProduct = function(callback) {
    DWREngine._execute('/ajax-customer-lab7-Struts-DWR/dwr',
            'ProductManager', 'addProduct', callback);
}
```

The DWR code won't be formatted this nicely (with linefeeds and such), but it will still give you an idea of what is going on behind the scenes. This is where DWR puts the JavaScript functions that support the calls defined in *dwr.xml*.

It's important to understand how DWR maps JavaScript calls into Java method calls on the `ProductManager` class. For example, our JavaScript calls a method like this:

```
ProductManager.deleteRow(rowId, populateData)
```

That method corresponds to the following JavaScript function:

```
ProductManager.deleteRow = function(p0, callback)
```

However, the `deleteRow( )` function in the Java `ProductManager` class has only a single argument:

```
static public boolean deleteRow(String productID)
```

Consequently, DWR adds an argument to each Java method exposed to the JSP. That additional argument is the name of a JavaScript callback method that's called when the Ajax operation has completed. In this example, we use that callback to call `populateData( )`, which performs its own Ajax operation: it gets the current product list from the server and (as its callback) invokes `updateProductList( )` to redisplay the list.

## Writing the ProductManager Class

In this application, the only class we need in order to support our Ajax functionality is `ProductManager` (Example 8-15). The methods we need in *ProductManager.jsp* are mapped in *dwr.xml* and defined in *ProductManager.java*. The `ProductManager` class is fairly big, but it contains everything we need to manage the products. There is a method to change product information (`updateProductById( )`) and a method to delete a product (`deleteRow( )`); there is also a method to add a product (`addProduct( )`) and a method to return all products formatted in a JSON string (`getJSONProducts( )`).

*Example 8-15. The ProductManager Java class*

```
public class ProductManager {
    static public String imagePath;
    public static String getImagePath( ) {
        return imagePath;
    }
    public static void setImagePath(String imagePath) {
        ProductManager.imagePath = imagePath;
    }
    static public Product getProduct(String productName) {
        Product product = new Product( );
        Connection con = DatabaseConnector.getConnection( );
        String sqlString = "";
        try {
            sqlString = "SELECT * FROM PRODUCTS WHERE PRODUCT_NAME='" + productName
                    + "';";
            Statement select = con.createStatement( );
            ResultSet result = select.executeQuery(sqlString);
```

*Example 8-15. The ProductManager Java class (continued)*

```
            if (result.next()) { // process results one row at a time
                product.setProductName(result.getString("PRODUCT_NAME"));
                product.setDescription(result.getString("DESCRIPTION"));
                product.setFilename(result.getString("FILENAME"));
                product.setPrice(result.getFloat("PRICE"));
                product.setProductId(result.getInt("PRODUCT_ID"));
            }
        }
        catch(Exception e) {
            System.out.println("exception caught getting Product" + sqlString + " "
                    + e.getMessage());
        }
        finally {
            if (con != null) {
                try {
                    con.close();
                }
                catch(SQLException e) {
                }
            }
        }
        return product;
    }
    static public boolean updateProductById(int id, String column,
            String newValue) {
        boolean result = false;
        String sqlString = "UPDATE PRODUCTS SET "+column+ " = '"+newValue
                +"' WHERE PRODUCT_ID='" + id + "';";
        Connection con = DatabaseConnector.getConnection();
        try {
            Statement select = con.createStatement();
            result = select.execute(sqlString);
        }
        catch(Exception e) {
            System.out.println("exception caught updating Product"
                    + sqlString + " " + e.getMessage());
        }
        finally {
            if (con != null) {
                try {
                    con.close();
                }
                catch(SQLException e) {
                }
            }
        }
        return result;
    }
    static public Product getProductById(String productID) {
        Product product = new Product();
        Connection con = DatabaseConnector.getConnection();
        String sqlString = "";
```

*Example 8-15. The ProductManager Java class (continued)*

```
        try {
            sqlString = "SELECT * FROM PRODUCTS WHERE PRODUCT_ID='" + productID
                    + "';";
            Statement select = con.createStatement( );
            ResultSet result = select.executeQuery(sqlString);

            if (result.next( )) { // process results one row at a time
                product.setProductName(result.getString("PRODUCT_NAME"));
                product.setDescription(result.getString("DESCRIPTION"));
                product.setFilename(result.getString("FILENAME"));
                product.setPrice(result.getFloat("PRICE"));
                product.setProductId(result.getInt("PRODUCT_ID"));
            }
        }
        catch(Exception e) {
            System.out.println("exception caught getting Product" + sqlString + " "
                    + e.getMessage( ));
        }
        finally {
            if (con != null) {
                try {
                    con.close( );
                }
                catch(SQLException e) {
                }
            }
        }
        return product;
    }
    static public boolean deleteRow(String productID) {
        Product product = new Product( );
        Connection con = DatabaseConnector.getConnection( );
        String sqlString = "";
        boolean result = false;
        try {
            sqlString = "DELETE FROM PRODUCTS WHERE PRODUCT_ID='" + productID
                    + "';";
            Statement select = con.createStatement( );
            result = select.execute(sqlString);
        }
        catch(Exception e) {
            System.out.println("exception caught deleteing Product" + sqlString
                    + " " + e.getMessage( ));
        }
        finally {
            if (con != null) {
                try {
                    con.close( );
                }
                catch(SQLException e) {
                }
            }
```

*Example 8-15. The ProductManager Java class (continued)*

```
        }
        return result;
    }
    public static String addProduct( ) {
        Connection con = DatabaseConnector.getConnection( );
        try {
            PreparedStatement ps = con.prepareStatement(
                    "INSERT INTO PRODUCTS (PRODUCT_NAME) values(?)");
            ps.setString(1,"New Product");
            ps.executeUpdate( );
        }
        catch(Exception e) {
            System.out.println("exception caught inserting New Product into product
                            table");
        }
        finally {
            if (con != null) {
                try {
                    con.close( );
                }
                catch(SQLException e) {
                }
            }
        }
        return getJSONProducts( );
    }
    public static String getJSONProducts( ) {
        return getProducts( );
    }

    public static String getProducts( ) {
        Product product = new Product( );
        String title = "products";
        Connection con = DatabaseConnector.getConnection( );
        StringBuffer jsonString = new StringBuffer("\r\n{\"" + title + "\": [");
        String sqlString = "";

        try {
            sqlString = "SELECT * FROM PRODUCTS ORDER BY PRODUCT_ID DESC;";
            Statement select = con.createStatement( );
            ResultSet result = select.executeQuery(sqlString);
            while (result.next( ))  { // process results one row at a time

                product.setProductName(result.getString("PRODUCT_NAME"));
                product.setDescription(result.getString("DESCRIPTION"));
                product.setFilename(result.getString("FILENAME"));
                product.setPrice(result.getFloat("PRICE"));
                product.setProductId(result.getInt("PRODUCT_ID"));
                jsonString.append("\r\n{\"description\":\"" +
                                 product.getDescription( ) +
                                 "\",\"name\":\"" + product.getProductName( ) +
```

*Example 8-15. The ProductManager Java class (continued)*

```
                                  "\",\"filename\":\"" + product.getFilename( ) +
                                  "\", \"price\":\"" + product.getPrice( ) +
                                  "\", \"id\":\"" + product.getProductId( ) +
                                  "\",\"imagepath\":\"" + imagePath +"/" +
                                  product.getFilename( ) + "\"},");

            }
            int lastCharIndex = jsonString.length( );
            jsonString.deleteCharAt(lastCharIndex - 1);
            jsonString.append("\r\n]}");
        }
        catch(Exception e) {
            System.out.println("exception caught getting Product" + sqlString + " "
                    + e.getMessage( ));
        }
        finally {
            if (con != null) {
                try {
                    con.close( );
                }
                catch(SQLException e) {
                }
            }
        }
        return jsonString.toString( );
    }
}
```

Look back at the *dwr.xml* configuration file in Example 8-12 and examine the methods listed in the `<include>` tags (nested in the `<create>` tag). Each method that is exposed to the JSP file is exposed through an `<include>` tag. For example, to expose the `ProductManager`'s `addProduct( )` method to the JSP, we added the `<include method="addProduct"/>` element within the `<create>` tag.

So, now that all the machinery is in place and wired together, how does it work? Our JSP is almost empty. Although it displays a list of products, nothing in the page looks like it's capable of displaying that list: instead of a table or a list, there's just an empty div with the ID `products` and the CSS class `productList`. So, how do we get the list of products to work with? The JSP calls the JavaScript function `populateData( )` (defined in *oreillyProductManager.js*) when it is loaded; that function delegates the call to `ProductManager.getJSONProducts( )` and arranges for our JavaScript function `updateProductList( )` to be called when the data returns. In turn, this is one of the methods mapped to the `ProductManager` by *dwr.xml*, via the automatically generated JavaScript file. Our `ProductManager` class implements `getJSONProducts( )`; it gets the current product list from the database, marshals it as a JSON object, and returns it to the browser, which passes it to `updateProductList( )`.

So, there's a lot going on behind the scenes. Let's look a bit further and see what happens when a user clicks on the delete icon (the trash can). It shouldn't be any surprise that `updateProductList( )` contains code to create a cell with a trash can image in each row of the product table. This cell is tied to the `deleteRow( )` function, which is called when the `onclick` event occurs. In turn, DWR maps `deleteRow( )` (in the generated JavaScript file) to the `deleteRow( )` method in `ProductManager`. The generated JavaScript also arranges for `populateData( )` to be called when the deletion has been processed, and as we've seen, `populateData( )` retrieves the current list of products and displays them.

## DWR Is Cool Because...

DWR connects straight to your Java classes. You don't need to write any of the supporting JavaScript that you normally need when connecting server-side Java to a JSP. This is essentially what we need to do when we are writing Ajax applications on Java.

DWR doesn't have any fancy widgets, but that's not what it's all about. The widgets are left to other libraries or the developer.

# Ajax with Struts: What Have We Learned Here?

Adding Ajax to Struts applications can enhance the usability of your applications. You can either write your own JavaScript to support the Ajax calls or use a library like DWR or Struts-Layout. If you are using your own JavaScript, map your Ajax calls to Struts actions instead of servlets.

Another good way to add Ajax to your Struts applications is by taking advantage of existing JSP tag libraries that support Ajax, or writing your own. Any of the JSP tag libraries discussed in Chapter 7 will work in the Struts environment. Pick the ones that have the functionality you need for your application, and leverage the work of others.

CHAPTER 9

# JavaServer Faces and Ajax

JavaServer Faces (JSF) is a user interface framework that runs on a Java application server and renders a user interface to a client. The most popular client is a web browser running on a desktop computer, but JSF is not limited to web applications. Although it is a complex technology—learning JSF isn't a trivial task—once you've learned it, you will be able to build many web applications faster. If you are unfamiliar with JSF, you can learn it by reading the JavaServer Faces Specification, Sun's tutorial (*http://java.sun.com/j2ee/1.4/docs/tutorial/doc/JSFIntro.html*), or one of the reference books written on the subject. Hans Bergsten, one of the spec's contributors, has written an excellent introduction and reference called *JavaServer Faces* (O'Reilly). I learned JavaServer Faces using that book and Sun's JSF tutorial (which is actually part of the J2EE tutorial) as my primary tools.

JavaServer Faces provides a clean separation between the business logic and presentation layers. It establishes a one-to-one mapping between HTTP requests and components. This mapping allows a finer-grained model for a web application than a typical JSP application can provide. With JSF, there is a lifecycle for communication between the web page and the Java beans that makes up the backend. There are listeners that listen for events and renderers that create a view for display to the user. Writing a JSF application is not unlike writing a Swing application—and it's radically different from writing a typical web application.

There are several ways to use Ajax with JavaServer Faces:

- Use an external service to handle the `XMLHttpRequest`. This strategy avoids the JSF lifecycle.
- Use a custom JSF component to render the JavaScript and process the Ajax `XMLHttpRequests`. In this case, the request is processed through the JSF lifecycle, just like any other JSF request.
- Use an external lifecycle to handle the Ajax requests.

This chapter presents one way to add Ajax to a JSF application: using a custom JSF component. We will process the Ajax request through the JSF lifecycle.

## The JSF Lifecycle

To work within the JSF lifecycle, an application makes an `XMLHTTPRequest` to a URL that has a JavaServer Faces servlet listening. The JSF request-processing lifecycle consists of the following phases:

*Restore view*
: The view is restored from the request data or the data saved on the server.

*Apply request values*
: The components in the view save their values in the request.

*Process validations*
: The components validate the new values coming from the request.

*Update model values*
: Model properties are updated. The model properties are bound to the components by value bindings.

*Invoke application*
: Event listeners call external methods to process the updated data.

*Render response*
: A response is sent to answer the original request.

*Process events*
: Any events that occurred during the previous phase are handled.

Figure 9-1 shows how a request moves through these phases. It's a simple high-level view of the JavaServer Faces lifecycle, but it illustrates the basic principle. The lifecycle begins with the Restore View phase and finishes with the Render Response phase, but a JSF request does not have to go through every phase of the lifecycle. Each Process Events phase gives the application a chance to handle any events (for example, validation failures) that occurred during the previous phase.

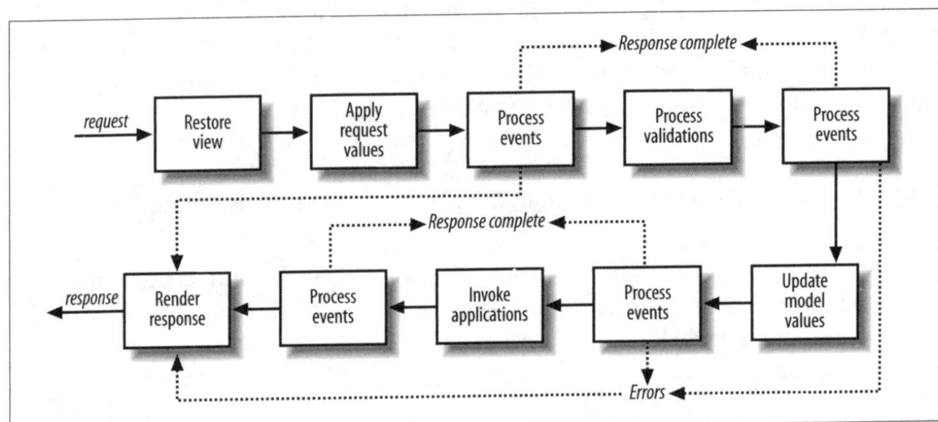


*Figure 9-1. The JavaServer Faces lifecycle*

## Writing a Custom JSF Component

*Using JavaServer Faces Technology with AJAX*, by Greg Murray et al. (*https://bpcatalog.dev.java.net/nonav/ajax/jsf-ajax/index.html*) describes the three ways to use Ajax with a JavaServer Faces component:

- Use a listener to service the backend request.
- Use a servlet in your JSF application to service the Ajax request.
- Use a servlet outside of JSF to service the backend request.

In earlier chapters, we used servlets to service the backend requests. This time, we'll use a listener; our custom JSF component will be entirely encapsulated in the JSF lifecycle. To keep things simple, we'll stick with the same example used in the previous chapters: we'll use Ajax to populate city and state fields in an HTML form based on a user-entered zip code. Figure 9-2 shows where we're headed.

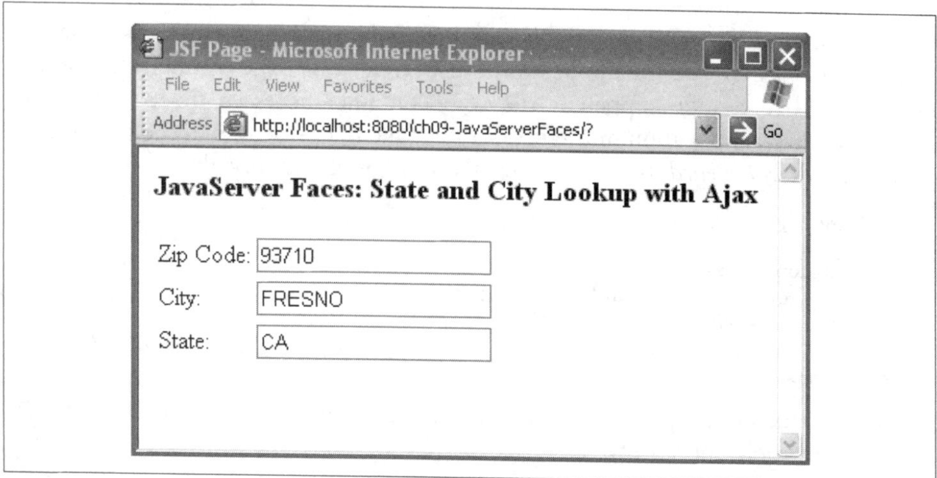


*Figure 9-2. Zip code lookup with JSF and Ajax*

We could simply add a custom JSP tag to a JSF view and write a servlet to service the Ajax request. This is a quick way to inject Ajax into a JSF application; it's not fundamentally different from the techniques we've already covered. But if you want to use the JSF framework, you need to write a custom component.

## Writing the JSP Page for the JSF Application

The JSP page for this application (Example 9-1) uses JSF's core and HTML tag libraries. In addition to these libraries, we'll develop a new Ajax tag library in this chapter. Our library will contain only one tag: `zipCode`.

*Example 9-1. The view for the JSF application: index.jsp*

```
<%@ taglib uri="http://java.sun.com/jsf/core" prefix="f" %>
<%@ taglib uri="http://java.sun.com/jsf/html" prefix="h" %>
<%@ taglib uri="http://ajax.oreilly.com/jsf/ajax" prefix="ajax" %>
<html>
<f:view>
    <head>
        <title>JSF Page</title>
    </head>
    <body>
        <h:form>
            <h3>JavaServer Faces: State and City Lookup with Ajax</h3>
            <ajax:zipCode zipcodeId="zipcode" stateId="state" cityId="city"
                          url="zipcodes" />
        </h:form>
    </body>
</f:view>
</html>
```

The web application can't access this JSP directly by including a `<welcome>` element in the *web.xml* file. The JSF application must render this page through the JSF lifecycle, and that cannot happen if the web container accesses the page directly. Instead, the web application must access a JSP page that forwards to the JSF application. That JSP is *forward.jsp*. Here's how it's configured in *web.xml*:

```
<web-app>
...
    <welcome-file-list>
        <welcome-file>forward.jsp</welcome-file>
    </welcome-file-list>
...
</web-app>
```

*forward.jsp* (Example 9-2) uses a `<jsp:forward>` tag to *index.faces* to render *index.jsp* from the JSF application lifecycle.

*Example 9-2. forward.jsp*

```
<%@ page language="java" pageEncoding="UTF-8" %>
<jsp:forward page="/index.faces" />
<html>
    this page should forward to the application
</html>
```

It may seem odd that the page forwards to *index.faces* rather than to *index.jsp* itself, but that's how it works. The JSF application references each page with a *.faces* extension; the JavaServer Faces servlet, `javax.faces.webapp.FacesServlet`, strips off the *.faces* extension and loads the JSP file with the *.jsp* extension.

## Configuring JSF: web.xml and faces-config.xml

The configuration resource file is unique to JavaServer Faces. As you can see in Example 9-3, *web.xml* defines the `javax.faces.CONFIG_FILES` parameter to point to *faces-config.xml*. *web.xml* also configures the `FacesServlet` that runs the JSF environment, setting it to intercept any URL with a *.faces* extension.

*Example 9-3. web.xml*

```
<?xml version="1.0" encoding="UTF-8"?>
<web-app xmlns="http://java.sun.com/xml/ns/j2ee"
        xmlns:xsi="http://www.w3.org/2001/XMLSchema-instance" version="2.4"
        xsi:schemaLocation="http://java.sun.com/xml/ns/j2ee
        http://java.sun.com/xml/ns/j2ee/web-app_2_4.xsd">
    <context-param>
        <param-name>javax.faces.CONFIG_FILES</param-name>
        <param-value>/WEB-INF/faces-config.xml</param-value>
    </context-param>
    <servlet>
        <servlet-name>Faces Servlet</servlet-name>
        <servlet-class>javax.faces.webapp.FacesServlet</servlet-class>
        <load-on-startup>0</load-on-startup>
    </servlet>
    <servlet-mapping>
        <servlet-name>Faces Servlet</servlet-name>
        <url-pattern>*.faces</url-pattern>
    </servlet-mapping>
    <welcome-file-list>
        <welcome-file>forward.jsp</welcome-file>
    </welcome-file-list>
</web-app>
```

The *faces-config.xml* file controls much of the behavior of the JSF application. It configures the JSF lifecycle, any beans that will be used in the lifecycle, the renderers that will be used, and so on. Here is a list of elements that can be used in *faces-config.xml*:

`<application>`
: Declares the pluggable classes for the JSF application.

`<component>`
: Declares the class for a component type.

`<converter>`
: Declares the class that implements the converter.

`<description>`
: Contains the element description, which is used in some development tools.

`<display-name>`
: Contains the display name, which is used by some development tools.

<factory>
: Declares replacements for the factory classes.

<lifecycle>
: Lists the lifecycle phase listeners.

<managed-bean>
: Declares a managed bean; a managed bean is instantiated and initialized automatically by the JSF framework.

<navigation-rule>
: Creates a rule for the navigation handler.

<render-kit>
: Declares a render kit or custom renderers for the default render kit.

<validator>
: Declares the class for a validator.

Our *faces-config.xml* file is shown in Example 9-4. This simple application uses only the <render-kit>, <component>, and <lifecycle> elements.

*Example 9-4. faces-config.xml*

```
<?xml version="1.0" encoding="UTF-8"?>
<!DOCTYPE faces-config PUBLIC "-//Sun Microsystems, Inc.//DTD JavaServer Faces
   Config 1.1//EN" "http://java.sun.com/dtd/web-facesconfig_1_1.dtd">
<faces-config>
   <lifecycle>
      <phase-listener>com.oreilly.ajax.ZipCodePhaseListener</phase-listener>
   </lifecycle>
   <render-kit>
      <description>
         Render kit implementation for the Ajax JSF components
      </description>
      <renderer>
         <component-family>javax.faces.Input</component-family>
         <renderer-type>ZipCode</renderer-type>
         <renderer-class>com.oreilly.ajax.ZipCodeRenderer</renderer-class>
      </renderer>
   </render-kit>
   <component>
      <display-name>O'Reilly Zip Code</display-name>
      <component-type>oreilly.ajax.ZipCode</component-type>
      <component-class>com.oreilly.ajax.ZipCode</component-class>
   </component>
</faces-config>
```

The <lifecycle> element contains a <phase-listener> element, which defines a class that can be called at the end of each phase (in this case, ZipCodePhaseListener).

The <render-kit> element in this configuration contains one <renderer> element, which is set to com.oreilly.ajax.ZipCodeRenderer. Render kits can contain one or more renderers. The default render kit contains renderers for HTML, but render kits can be developed for other markup languages. A renderer draws a specific component. For example, a form renderer in the HTML render kit renders the `<form>` element (more specifically, the renderer's `encodeBegin()` method renders the `<form>` tag, and the `encodeEnd()` method renders the closing `</form>` tag). The *faces-config.xml* file in Example 9-4 defines a renderer that uses the `com.oreilly.ajax.ZipCodeRenderer` class to build the HTML display and Ajax code that our JSF tag needs.

The `<component>` element defines the JSF component that is used in the application. In this case, the `com.oreilly.ajax.ZipCode` class is a custom component; it is used to get the application's HTML input.

Figure 9-3 models the configuration of our application. Bear in mind that this is a very basic example; a real-world application will almost certainly have a more complex configuration containing many other elements.

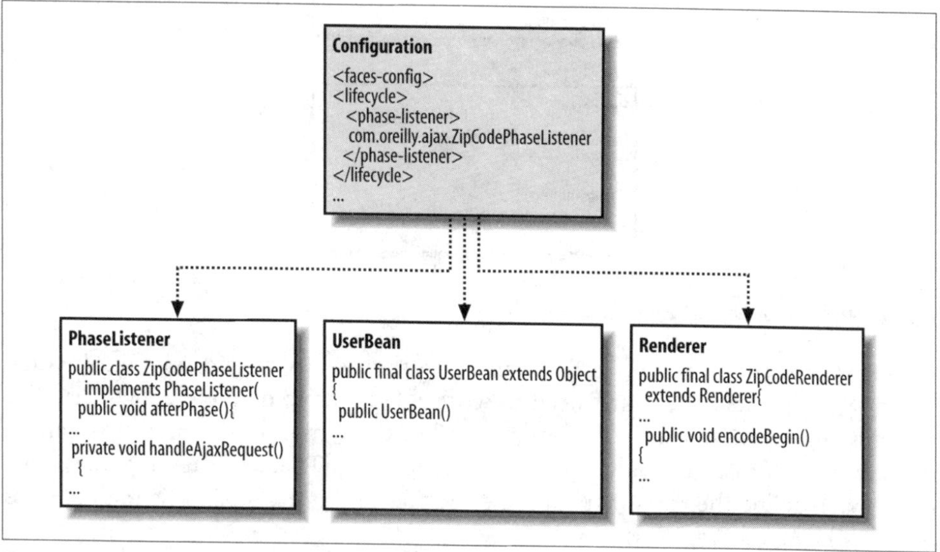


*Figure 9-3. JavaServer Faces configuration*

## Developing a Custom JSF Tag

In Chapter 7, we wrote a custom JSP tag. Now we're going to write a custom JSF tag. There are similarities between the two types of tag. For example, we use a Tag Library Definition (TLD) file to define both JSP and JSF custom tags, and we use tag handlers to handle both. However, there are also important differences:

- The JSP custom tag extends `javax.servlet.jsp.tagext.TagSupport`; the JSF custom tag extends `javax.faces.component.UIComponentBase`.
- The JSF custom tag has another class, called a renderer, which puts information into the view (in our case, a JSP page). The renderer extends `javax.faces.render.Renderer`.

Figure 9-4 shows how the tag class and the renderer fit together with the tag library and the JSP that uses the library.

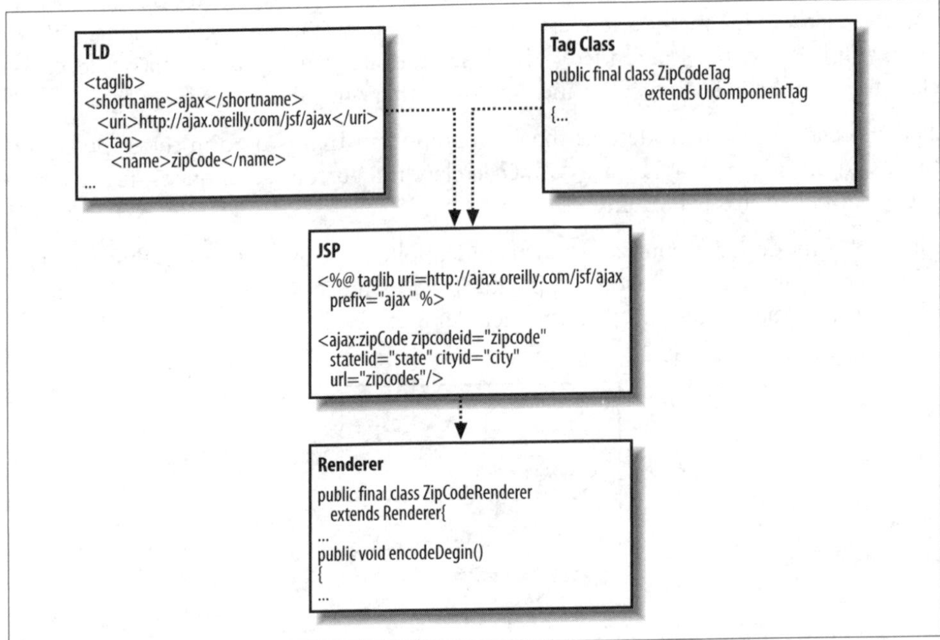


*Figure 9-4. Custom tag files and interactions*

Let's start with what we know. We want a tag to display city and state information based on a zip code. We'll first need to write a TLD file to define the tag. The TLD file must have a parent tag of `<taglib>`; within that any number of `<tag>`s can be defined. In this case, we only need to define one tag. Then, in the `<tagclass>` element, we'll define the class that supports the tag. In this example, it is the full class name of the `ZipCodeTag` class.

## Writing the TLD File

The Tag Library Definition file, presented in Example 9-5, defines a single tag: `zipCode`. This tag contains three fields: zip code, state, and city.

*Example 9-5. The TLD file for JSF*

```
<taglib>
    <tlibversion>1.0</tlibversion>
    <jspversion>1.1</jspversion>
    <shortname>ajax</shortname>
    <uri>http://ajax.oreilly.com/jsf/ajax</uri>
    <info>adds Ajax-enabled tags to your JSP</info>
```

*Example 9-5. The TLD file for JSF (continued)*

```
    <tag>
        <name>zipCode</name>
        <tagclass>com.oreilly.ajax.ZipCodeTag</tagclass>
        <bodycontent>empty</bodycontent>
        <attribute>
            <name>zipcodeId</name>
            <required>true</required>
        </attribute>
        <attribute>
            <name>stateId</name>
            <required>true</required>
        </attribute>
        <attribute>
            <name>cityId</name>
            <required>true</required>
        </attribute>
        <attribute>
            <name>url</name>
            <required>true</required>
            <rtexprvalue>true</rtexprvalue>
        </attribute>
    </tag>
</taglib>
```

This TLD file is the same as the one used in Chapter 7 to create an Ajax JSP tag. It defines four inputs for this tag: zipcodeId, stateId, cityId, and url. The <required> tags indicate that all of these inputs are required; none are optional.

The TLD works in tandem with the tag handler and the renderer to transfer data from the web page to the JSF application. We'll look at the tag handler next.

## Writing the Tag Handler

Now that we have the TLD, we need to write a tag handler. This tag handler must extend javax.faces.webapp.UIComponentTag. It's very similar to a familiar JSP tag handler, but it requires two new methods: in addition to the usual getters and setters, we need to implement the methods getRendererType( ) and getComponentType( ). The former passes the name of the tag to the renderer, and the latter passes the type to the component on the web page.

The code for our tag handler, ZipCodeTag, appears in Example 9-6.

*Example 9-6. ZipCodeTag.java*

```
package com.oreilly.ajax;

import java.io.IOException;

import javax.faces.component.UIComponent;
import javax.faces.context.FacesContext;
```

*Example 9-6. ZipCodeTag.java (continued)*

```
import javax.faces.el.ValueBinding;
import javax.faces.render.Renderer;
import javax.faces.webapp.UIComponentTag;

public final class ZipCodeTag extends UIComponentTag {
    private String zipcodeId = "0";
    private String stateId = "";
    private String cityId = "";
    private String url = "";

    public String getCityId( ) {
        return cityId;
    }
    public void setCityId(String city) {
        this.cityId = city;
    }
    public String getStateId( ) {
        return stateId;
    }
    public void setStateId(String state) {
        this.stateId = state;
    }
    public String getUrl( ) {
        return url;
    }
    public void setUrl(String url) {
        this.url = url;
    }
    public String getZipcodeId( ) {
        return zipcodeId;
    }
    public void setZipcodeId(String zipcodeId) {
        this.zipcodeId = zipcodeId;
    }
    public String getComponentType( ) {
        return "oreilly.ajax.ZipCode";
    }
    public String getRendererType( ) {
        return "ZipCode"; // ZipCodeRenderer
    }
    public void release( ) {
        zipcodeId = null;
        stateId = null;
        cityId = null;
        url = null;
    }
    protected void setProperties(UIComponent component) {
        super.setProperties(component);
        ZipCode input = null;

        try {
            input = (ZipCode) component;
```

*Example 9-6. ZipCodeTag.java (continued)*

```
        }
        catch (ClassCastException cce) {
            throw new IllegalStateException(
                    "Component "
                    + component.toString( )
                    + " not expected type. Expected: ZipCode. Perhaps you're
                    missing a tag?");
        }
        FacesContext context = getFacesContext( );
        if (cityId != null) {
            if (isValueReference(cityId)) {
                ValueBinding vb =
                        context.getApplication( ).createValueBinding(cityId);
                component.setValueBinding("cityId", vb);
            }
            else {
                input.setCityId(cityId);
            }
        }

    }
}
```

The `ZipCodeTag` class extends `UIComponentTag`, a class from the JavaServer Faces library. Most of `ZipCodeTag` should be familiar. It uses setters and getters to manage the tag's parameters: the zip code, state, and city. The JSF application uses the `release( )` method to reset the values. The `setProperties( )` method binds the tag parameters to the values passed back from the server.

The two unfamiliar methods are really very simple. The *faces-config.xml* file defines a `<component-type>`, and `ZipCodeTag.getComponentType( )` simply returns the fully qualified class name of this type as a `String`. Likewise, `getRendererType( )` simply returns the name of the renderer we'll be using (in this case, just the string `"ZipCode"`). Note that it doesn't require a fully qualified class name.

## Creating a Renderer and Render Kits

The `<render-kit>` element in the configuration file defines how the view will be rendered. A component does not directly create its output. Instead, it calls a renderer, which is contained in a render kit and is responsible for creating a particular kind of output. The default render kit, which we will use in this example, contains renderers for HTML. Other render kits might contain renderers for other markup languages and produce output for other displays, such as mobile displays.

The renderer for `ZipCodeTag`, presented in Example 9-7, uses the `encodeBegin( )` method to inject the JavaScript into the JSP page. The renderer also inserts the HTML elements that we need, such as the city, state, and zip code fields.

*Example 9-7. ZipCodeRenderer writes information directly into the web page*

```
public final class ZipCodeRenderer extends Renderer {
    public boolean getRendersChildren( ) {
        return true;
    }

    public void encodeBegin(FacesContext context, UIComponent component)
            throws IOException {
        ResponseWriter writer = context.getResponseWriter( );
        Map attributeMap = component.getAttributes( );
        Object o = attributeMap.get("zipcodeId");
        writer.startElement("script", component);
        writer.writeAttribute("type", "text/javascript", null);
        // this should be an attribute, like cityId
        String src = "scripts/ora-ajax.js";
        writer.writeAttribute("src", src, null);

        writer.endElement("script");

        writer.startElement("div", component);
        writer.writeAttribute("id", "ajaxDivId", null);
        writer.write("Hola This is a div");
        writer.endElement("div");
        writer.write("\n");
        writer.startElement("table", component);
        writer.startElement("tr", component);
        writer.startElement("td", component);
        writer.write("Zip Code: ");
        writer.endElement("td");
        writer.startElement("td", component);
        writer.startElement("input", component);
        writer.writeAttribute("onblur", "retrieveCityState( );", null);
        writer.writeAttribute("type", "text", null);
        writer.writeAttribute("id", "zipcodeId", null);
        writer.endElement("td");
        writer.endElement("tr");

        writer.startElement("tr", component);
        writer.startElement("td", component);
        writer.write("City: ");
        writer.endElement("td");
        writer.startElement("td", component);
        writer.startElement("input", component);
        writer.writeAttribute("type", "text", null);
        writer.writeAttribute("id", "cityId", null);
        writer.endElement("td");
        writer.endElement("tr");

        writer.startElement("tr", component);
        writer.startElement("td", component);
        writer.write("State: ");
        writer.endElement("td");
        writer.startElement("td", component);
        writer.startElement("input", component);
        writer.writeAttribute("type", "text", null);
```

*Example 9-7. ZipCodeRenderer writes information directly into the web page (continued)*

```
        writer.writeAttribute("id", "stateId", null);
        writer.endElement("td");
        writer.endElement("tr");
        writer.endElement("table");

        writer.write("\n");
    }

    public void encodeEnd(FacesContext context, UIComponent component) {
    }

}
```

The renderer extends `javax.faces.render.Renderer` and overrides its `encodeBegin( )` and `encodeEnd( )` methods. `encodeBegin( )` injects information at the start of the tag, and `encodeEnd( )` writes information at the end. We use `encodeBegin( )` to insert the reference to our JavaScript library, *ora-ajax.js*.

We could have hardcoded the JavaScript as a `String` and written it directly into the page, as we did in Chapter 7. There are advantages to doing this: it ensures that the JavaScript will always be there (no extra file is needed), and it prevents the JavaScript from being changed, which can introduce unexpected behavior. However, the disadvantages of hard-wiring the JavaScript are significant. One major consideration is that it is harder to change the JavaScript code when you're developing and debugging the library; instead of changing a text file, you must change a Java class, which in turn requires you to recompile and redeploy. This could be a serious disadvantage if many changes to that file are required.

The `javax.faces.context.ResponseWriter` class has some useful methods at its disposal. Methods such as `startElement( )`, `endElement( )`, and `writeAttribute( )` allow you to write markup to a client without being tied to a specific implementation. For example, in a different render kit, these methods could generate the correct markup to work with a cell phone.

Using the `ResponseWriter` is fairly simple and intuitive. In our renderer, the following code:

```
writer.startElement("td", component);
writer.write("State: ");
writer.endElement("td");
writer.startElement("td", component);
writer.startElement("input", component);
writer.writeAttribute("type", "text", null);
writer.writeAttribute("id", "stateId", null);
writer.endElement("td");
```

writes this table tag:

```
<td><input type="text" id="stateId"></td>
```

The application is just about ready to make the Ajax call. We have our TLD, our tag handler, and our renderer. All we're missing is the *ora-ajax.js* file. We'll attack that next.

## Writing the JavaScript Support File

The *ora-ajax.js* file is inserted into the HTML generated by our JSP by the `<ajax:zipCode>` tag. This file is presented in Example 9-8.

*Example 9-8. ora-ajax.js*

```
function retrieveCityState( ) {
    var zip = document.getElementById("zipcodeId");
    // the url in this case must be .faces to be detected
    var url = "ZipCode-Ajax.faces?zip=" + escape(zip.value);
    if (window.XMLHttpRequest) {
        req = new XMLHttpRequest( );
    } else {
        if (window.ActiveXObject) {
            req = new ActiveXObject("Microsoft.XMLHTTP");
        }
    }
    req.open("Get", url, true);
    req.onreadystatechange = callbackCityState;
    req.send(null);
}

function populateCityState( ) {
    var jsonData = req.responseText;
    var myJSONObject = eval("(" + jsonData + ")");
    var city = document.getElementById("cityId");
    city.value = myJSONObject.location.city;
    var state = document.getElementById("stateId");
    state.value = myJSONObject.location.state;
}

function callbackCityState( ) {
    if (req.readyState == 4) {
        if (req.status == 200) {
            if (window.XMLHttpRequest) {
                nonMSPopulate( );
            } else {
                if (window.ActiveXObject) {
                    alert("mspopulate");
                    msPopulate( );
                }
            }
        }
    }
}
```

*Example 9-8. ora-ajax.js (continued)*

```
function nonMSPopulate( ) {
    var resp = req.responseText;
    var parser = new DOMParser( );
    var dom = parser.parseFromString(resp, "text/xml");
    cityValue = dom.getElementsByTagName("city");
    var city = document.getElementById("cityId");
    city.value = cityValue[0].childNodes[0].nodeValue;
    stateValue = dom.getElementsByTagName("state");
    var state = document.getElementById("stateId");
    state.value = stateValue[0].childNodes[0].nodeValue;
}

function msPopulate( ) {
    var resp = req.responseText;
    var xmlDoc = new ActiveXObject("Microsoft.XMLDOM");
    xmlDoc.async = "false";
    xmlDoc.loadXML(resp);
    cityValue = xmlDoc.getElementsByTagName("city");
    var cityField = document.getElementById("cityId");
    cityField.value = cityValue[0].firstChild.data;
    stateValue = xmlDoc.getElementsByTagName("state");
    alert("state" + stateValue);
    var state = document.getElementById("stateId");
    state.value = stateValue[0].firstChild.data;
}
```

This JavaScript file is no different from the JavaScript support used in previous chapters of this book. The `retrieveCityState( )` method configures the `XMLHttpRequest` with a URL and callback method. The callback method, `callbackCityState( )`, determines whether or not the browser is a Microsoft product and calls the appropriate procedure to populate the form fields.

## Handling JSF Input by Extending HtmlInputText

The `ZipCode` class itself is a Java bean that transfers data between a JSF page and the application. It extends `HtmlInputText`, which handles the text from an input element such as a text field. `ZipCode` consists mostly of accessor methods for various properties, such as `cityId` and `stateId`. The important part of `ZipCode` is the constructor, which sets the `rendererType` to `"ZipCode"` through a call to the parent class's `setRendererType( )` method. That `rendererType` must be the same as that returned by `ZipCodeTag.getRendererType( )`.

The `ZipCode` class and the `ZipCodeTag` class look almost identical, but both are needed for this application. The `ZipCode` class gets input from the form, whereas the `ZipCodeTag` class configures the fields in the tag. Because the two classes are working with the same form fields, they have many of the same class variables, but they each extend different classes and have different methods (`ZipCode` extends `HtmlInputText`, and `ZipCodeTag` extends `UIComponentTag`).

ZipCode is wired into the rest of the application by the *faces-config.xml* file, which must define the component that handles zip codes. A <component> tag in *faces-config.xml* contains a <component-type> tag that assigns the name "oreilly.ajax.ZipCode". ZipCodeTag has a method called getComponentType( ) that must return a matching component type: the string "oreilly.ajax.ZipCode". The <component-type> tag is really just an ID, and it can be assigned any value as long as it matches the string returned by ZipCodeTag.getComponentType( ).

The code for the ZipCode class is presented in Example 9-9.

*Example 9-9. ZipCode.java*

```
public class ZipCode extends HtmlInputText {
    private String zipcodeId = "0";
    private String stateId = "";
    private String cityId = "";
    private String url = "";
    public ZipCode( ) {
        super( );
        setRendererType("ZipCode");
    }
    public String getCityId( ) {
        return cityId;
    }
    public void setCityId(String cityId) {
        this.cityId = cityId;
    }
    public String getStateId( ) {
        return stateId;
    }
    public void setStateId(String stateId) {
        this.stateId = stateId;
    }
    public String getUrl( ) {
        return url;
    }
    public void setUrl(String url) {
        this.url = url;
    }
    public String getZipcodeId( ) {
        return zipcodeId;
    }
    public void setZipcodeId(String zipcodeId) {
        this.zipcodeId = zipcodeId;
    }
}
```

## Writing the JSF Support for Ajax

When an Ajax request arrives, it must move through the JSF lifecycle. At the appropriate phase in the lifecycle, the request must be handed off to a service for processing. In JSF, a *phase listener* is responsible for handing requests to services at the appropriate point in the lifecycle. It listens for phase events in the lifecycle and, when an appropriate event arrives, calls the service.

A phase listener is a class that implements the PhaseListener interface, which requires beforePhase( ) and afterPhase( ) methods. The JSF framework calls these methods before and after each phase change. We'll use this mechanism to implement a ZipCodePhaseListener that executes the Ajax backend support code (Example 9-10).

*Example 9-10. The ZipCodePhaseListener class*

```
public class ZipCodePhaseListener implements PhaseListener {
    public void afterPhase(PhaseEvent event) {
        String viewId = event.getFacesContext().getViewRoot().getViewId( );
        if (viewId.indexOf("Ajax") != -1) {
            handleAjaxRequest(event);
        }
    }
    private void handleAjaxRequest(PhaseEvent event) {
        FacesContext context = event.getFacesContext( );
        HttpServletResponse response = (HttpServletResponse)
                context.getExternalContext().getResponse( );
        Object object = context.getExternalContext().getRequest( );
        if (!(object instanceof HttpServletRequest)) {
            // only handle HttpServletRequests
            return;
        }

        HttpServletRequest request = (HttpServletRequest) object;
        String zipcode = request.getParameter("zip");
        Location location = ZipcodeManager.getZipcode(zipcode);

        // actually render using XML
        StringBuffer returnXML = null;
        returnXML = new StringBuffer("\r\n<location>");
        returnXML.append("\r\n<city>"+
                        location.getCity( )+"</city>");
        returnXML.append("\r\n<state>"+
                        location.getState( )+"</state>");
        returnXML.append("\r\n</location>");
```

*Example 9-10. The ZipCodePhaseListener class (continued)*

```
        response.setContentType("text/xml");
        response.setHeader("Cache-Control", "no-cache");
        try {
            response.getWriter().write(returnXML.toString( ));
            event.getFacesContext().responseComplete( );
        }
        catch (IOException e) {
            e.printStackTrace( );
        }
    }
    public void beforePhase(PhaseEvent arg0) {
        //not used, but implemented to satisfy compiler
    }
    public PhaseId getPhaseId( ) {
        return PhaseId.RESTORE_VIEW;
    }
}
```

Everything needed to process the request is encapsulated in the `PhaseEvent`. We don't care about the `beforePhase( )` method, so it can have an empty body. The `afterPhase( )` method looks at the `PhaseEvent` to determine when it needs to process an Ajax request. `afterPhase( )` is called after each request phase, and if the string `"Ajax"` is found in the `viewId`, we know that we're processing an Ajax request and that we need to pass it off to an appropriate service.

The `viewId` is obtained by a call to `getViewId( )`, which returns the `id` of the view that sent the last request. To verify whether the request was an Ajax request, we execute a check for the string `"Ajax"` in the `viewId`:

```
if (viewId.indexOf("Ajax") != -1) {
```

For example, look at the URL in the `retrieveCityState( )` function of Example 9-8. The URL is `ZipCode-Ajax.faces`, and that is the string that the `viewId` contains. Thus, by checking the origin of the request, which is stored in the `viewId`, this JSF application is able to determine that this is an Ajax request that needs to be serviced.

This strategy for determining whether a request is an Ajax request requires that the developer use URLs containing the string `"Ajax"` only for Ajax requests. If the developer creates a normal JSF page whose name contains "Ajax," this will cause a problem: each time that page sends a request, the application will try to handle the request as an Ajax request.

When there's an Ajax request to be processed, `afterPhase( )` passes control to the `handleAjaxRequest( )` method. `handleAjaxRequest( )` gets a `FacesContext` object from the event and then gets a `ServletResponse` from the context. With the `ServletResponse` in hand, handleAjaxRequest( ) calls ZipcodeManager.getZipcode( ) to look up the city and state for the zip code; it then uses this data to build the XML response to send back to the client. Sending the response back to the client is just a matter of using the ServletResponse object to set a MIME type and any appropriate headers and then using a Writer to send the XML back to the browser.

ZipcodeManager (Example 9-11) is a utility class that looks up the state and city corresponding to a given zip code. It's a simple database lookup—nothing particularly interesting, and certainly nothing that you couldn't improve on in a more sophisticated application.

*Example 9-11. The ZipcodeManager class*

```
public class ZipcodeManager {

    static public Location getZipcode(String zip) {
        Location location = null;
        Connection con = DatabaseConnector.getConnection( );
        String sqlString = "";
        location = new Location( );
        location.setZipCode(zip); // put in original zip code

        try {
            sqlString = "SELECT CITY,STATE,ZIPCODE FROM ZIPCODES WHERE
                    ZIPCODE='"+zip+"';";
            Statement select = con.createStatement( );
            ResultSet result = select.executeQuery(sqlString);
            if (result.next( )) { // process results one row at a time
                location.setCity(result.getString(1));
                location.setState(result.getString(2));
                location.setZipCode(result.getString(3));
            }

        } catch (Exception e) {
            System.out.println("exception in login"+e.getMessage( ));
        } finally {
            if (con != null) {
                try {
                    con.close( );
                } catch (SQLException e) {
                }
            }
        }
        return location;
    }
}
```

To pass the state and city back to the caller, we use a simple Java bean class called Location. This class is shown in Example 9-12.

*Example 9-12. The Java bean Location.java*

```
public class Location {
    private String city;
    private String state;
    private String zipCode;
    public String getCity( ) {
        return city;
    }
    public void setCity(String city) {
        this.city = city;
    }
    public String getState( ) {
        return state;
    }
    public void setState(String state) {
        this.state = state;
    }
    public String getZipCode( ) {
        return zipCode;
    }
    public void setZipCode(String zipCode) {
        this.zipCode = zipCode;
    }
}
```

## Summary

This discussion has barely scratched the surface of JavaServer Faces. JSF is a very complex technology that's well beyond the scope of this chapter. But although it's a complex architecture, designed for developing components that can be manipulated with an IDE, integrating Ajaxian features into this architecture isn't that difficult. We have explored one way to incorporate JSF into a JavaServer Faces application. If you're interested in going further with JSF, check out Hans Bergsten's *JavaServer Faces* (O'Reilly).

CHAPTER 10

# Google Web Toolkit

In June 2006, Google announced a new product at the JavaOne conference: the Google Web Toolkit (GWT). GWT represents a completely new way of building Ajax applications: rather than writing HTML (or JSPs, or JSF pages) and JavaScript, with Java servlets or JSF components to handle the server side of the application, GWT lets you write the whole application, from client to server, in Java. It generates all the JavaScript automatically, based on the Java code you write. You still need to write some HTML, but GWT provides skeleton HTML as a starting point.

Being able to write the whole application in Java is an advantage, but that's far from the whole story. After all, neither HTML nor JavaScript is that difficult to write. Another major benefit is that GWT handles all cross-browser issues for you. Even better, it provides hooks for full round-trip debugging. That's right, you can debug the client code and the server code all with one IDE!

The trick to debugging the client code is the GWT client libraries. They are written in Java; when compiled, they are converted to JavaScript and HTML. In "hosted mode," the client code is still in Java and can be debugged.

## Getting Started with GWT

To get started with GWT, you must:

1. Download and install a JDK.
2. Download and install GWT, available from *http://code.google.com/webtoolkit*.
3. Write some code and build your app.

Let's start with step 3; the first two steps are trivial. Figure 10-1 shows what the sample application we will develop in this chapter will look like on the three major browsers.

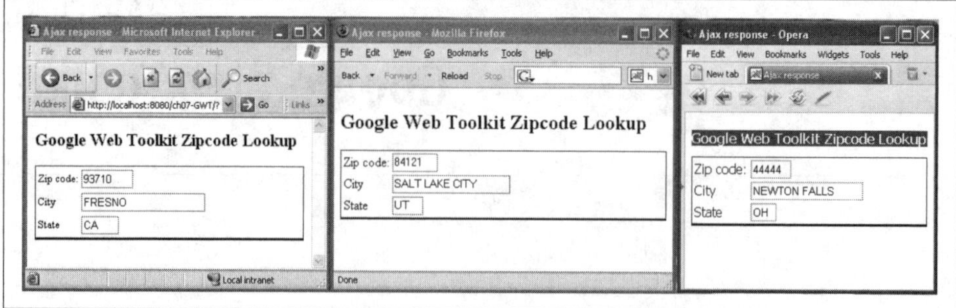


*Figure 10-1. Our sample application running in Internet Explorer, Firefox, and Opera*

Run GWT's ApplicationCreator program to get your application skeleton started. Make sure that you invoke ApplicationCreator from the directory in which you installed GWT, or use the full path to the ApplicationCreator executable:

```
C:> applicationCreator com.oreilly.client.ZipCodes
```

This command creates a *src* directory tree with two subdirectories: *src/com/oreilly/client* and *src/com/oreilly/public*. There's nothing surprising here: the subdirectories simply follow the standard Java packaging conventions. The *client* directory contains the Java class file *ZipCodes.java*, and the *public* directory contains *ZipCodes.html*. Figure 10-2 shows the directory tree that ApplicationCreator builds.

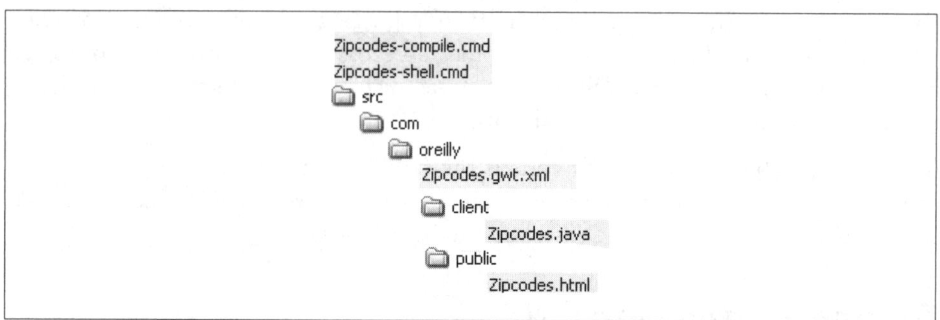


*Figure 10-2. The files created with ApplicationCreator*

The glue that holds the application together is in *ZipCodes.gwt.xml* (Example 10-1). This file contains information about how your application ties into the GWT core.

*Example 10-1. ZipCodes.gwt.xml*

```
<module>
    <!-- Inherit the core Web Toolkit stuff.                    -->
    <inherits name='com.google.gwt.user.User'/>
    <!-- Specify the app entry point class.                     -->
    <entry-point class='com.oreilly.client.ZipCodes'/>
</module
```

The *ZipCodes.gwt.xml* file also lists the servlets that we will use on the backend to answer requests. For now, we need the `<entry-point>` tag, which specifies the class that starts the application, and the main toolkit library inheritance definition tag, `<inherits>`.

In addition to the *src* directory and its contents, ApplicationCreator generates two executable files: *ZipCodes-compile.cmd* and *ZipCodes-shell.cmd*. ZipCodes-compile compiles the application into a form that GWT can use; the source code contained in *ZipCodes.java* will be converted into JavaScript that works across different browsers. The next step in development is running *ZipCodes-compile.cmd*:

```
C:> ZipCodes-compile
Output will be written into www\com.oreilly.ZipCodes
Copying all files found on public path
Compilation succeeded
```

ZipCodes-compile has now created something that GWT can run. The directory structure is now in place; you can see it in the *www* directory on the filesystem (Figure 10-3).

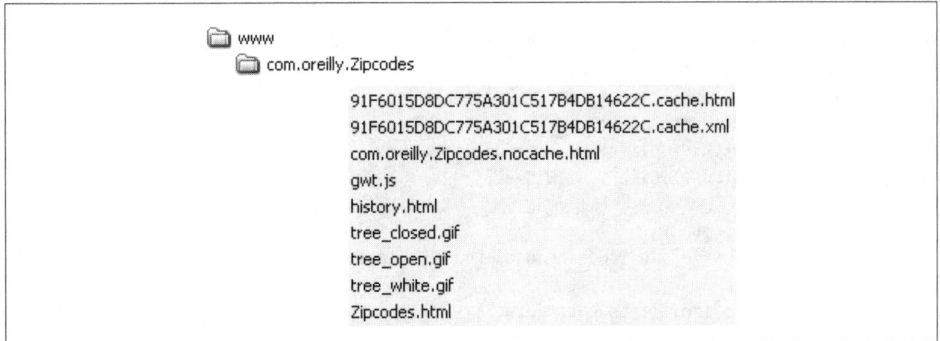


*Figure 10-3. The www directory and files created by ZipCodes-compile*

Now everything is in place to test the skeleton program that GWT has developed for you. To run and test the ZipCodes application, run *ZipCodes-shell.cmd*, which starts a web server container that allows you to run the program and test it:

```
C:> ZipCodes-shell
```

This command starts a compact version of Tomcat (*http://tomcat.apache.org*) and then launches a browser and loads the URL *ZipCodes.html*, as shown in Figure 10-4. The "Click me" button is part of the skeleton application that ApplicationCreator created. If you click this button, the text "Hello World" appears.

The fun part is just beginning. A regular Ajax application hosted by a Java application server would require several pieces to get running: HTML, JavaScript, and Java server-side code. But with GWT, the Java and JavaScript are intermingled, and the server-side code is hidden as well. The actual code looks more like that of a Swing or AWT application, as you can see in Example 10-2.

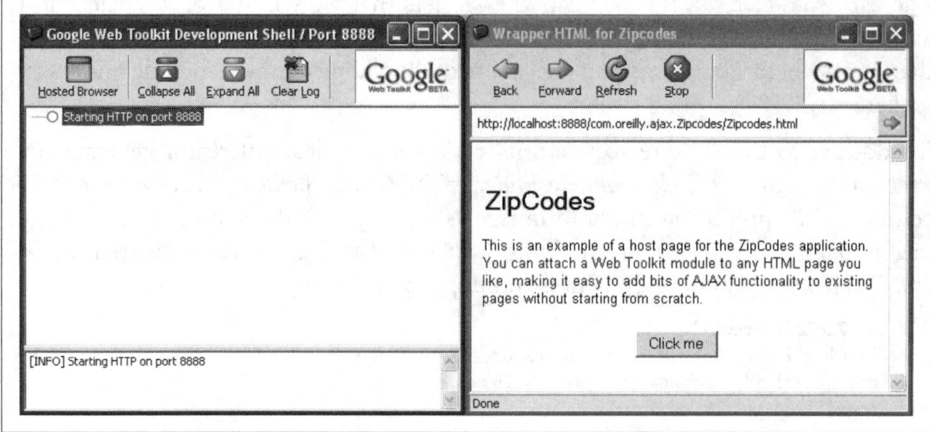


*Figure 10-4. The GWT development shell and browser*

*Example 10-2. ZipCodes.java*

```
package com.oreilly.client;

import com.google.gwt.core.client.EntryPoint;
import com.google.gwt.user.client.ui.Button;
import com.google.gwt.user.client.ui.ClickListener;
import com.google.gwt.user.client.ui.Label;
import com.google.gwt.user.client.ui.RootPanel;
import com.google.gwt.user.client.ui.Widget;

/**
 * Entry point classes define <code>onModuleLoad( )</code>.
 */
public class ZipCodes implements EntryPoint {

    /**
     * This is the entry point method.
     */
    public void onModuleLoad( ) {
        final Button button = new Button("Click me");
        final Label label = new Label( );

        button.addClickListener(new ClickListener( ) {
            public void onClick(Widget sender) {
                if (label.getText( ).equals(""))
                    label.setText("Hello World!");
                else
                    label.setText("");
            }
        });

        // Assume that the host HTML has elements defined whose
        // IDs are "slot1", "slot2". In a real app, you probably would not want
        // to hard-code IDs. Instead, you could, for example, search for all
        // elements with a particular CSS class and replace them with widgets.
```

*Example 10-2. ZipCodes.java (continued)*

```
        RootPanel.get("slot1").add(button);
        RootPanel.get("slot2").add(label);
    }
}
```

The ZipCodes class implements GWT's EntryPoint interface and overrides the onModuleLoad( ) method. The onModuleLoad( ) method adds widgets (user interface components) to divs in the HTML file; Table 10-1 lists all the widgets that GWT provides. Think of the RootPanel as the Java class that represents the area in the HTML file that corresponds to the <body> tag. To access an element within the body of an HTML document, you call RootPanel.get(elementId), passing in the element id as a string. To add a button to the client, for example, use get( ) to find the div you want and then call add( ) to add the button:

```
RootPanel.get("slot1").add(button);
```

In this case, slot1 is the id of the div that will receive the button.

To assign an action to a button or another widget, add a listener:

```
button.addClickListener(new ClickListener( ){...});
```

This looks like Swing code, but don't be fooled; this is code that uses the GWT libraries.

All of this Java code is compiled into JavaScript and HTML, and it will be the client view for your application. What that means is that you can debug this code with your Java IDE—something that has not been possible before GWT. Sure, you could use a JavaScript debugging tool like the Venkman JavaScript debugger, but using two debuggers is a bit cumbersome. Using GWT makes full round-trip debugging with a single debugger possible!

## Hosted Mode Versus Web Mode

Before building a debuggable GWT application, you need to understand the two modes in which a GWT application can run:

*Hosted mode*
: Interacting with the GWT application without JavaScript translation

*Web mode*
: Interacting with the GWT application after the client-side code has been converted from Java to HTML and JavaScript

When a GWT application is under development, it is a best practice to stay in hosted mode. Hosted-mode development is more productive because round-trip debugging is possible. Then, when the application is ready to be released, you can compile it to JavaScript and HTML and deploy it in web mode.

## Debugging the Application

GWT doesn't have a built-in debugger. Why force you to learn yet another tool? Instead, Google provides hooks that can be used by most Java IDEs, so you can use your IDE's debugger.

At this writing, IntelliJ IDEA and Eclipse users have had success debugging GWT applications; other IDEs should work if you set up the project with the startup class `com.google.gwt.dev.GWTShell`, which is located in *gwt-dev-windows.jar* (for Windows), *gwt-dev-linux.jar* (for Linux), or *gwt-dev-mac.jar* (for Mac OS X).

This chapter demonstrates the Eclipse IDE, which seems to be the unofficial de facto reference IDE of GWT. To create an Eclipse project for GWT:

1. Use the ProjectCreator script to create the project:

   ```
   C:> projectCreator -eclipse ZipCodes
   ```

2. Use the ApplicationCreator script to create the skeleton GWT application:

   ```
   C:> applicationCreator -eclipse ZipCodes com.oreilly.ajax.client.ZipCodes
   ```

Now start up Eclipse and import the project. That is done from the Eclipse File menu (File → Import → "Existing Projects into Workspace"). Browse to the directory where you created the ZipCodes project, and then make sure the checkbox next to ZipCodes is checked. Figure 10-5 shows what you should see in Eclipse when you reach this point.

Now start the project in hosted mode with debug capability (Run → Debug). You should now see the Debug window (Figure 10-6).

Select the ZipCodes application in the lefthand pane. The window will update to reflect the ZipCodes project information. Notice that the main class is `com.google.gwt.dev.GWTShell`. That class starts the Tomcat server.

It is important to make sure that both the source code and the compiled code are in the classpath. The source needs to be listed first, because in hosted mode the client Java class source is used to debug the client-side code. The debugger is actually looking for Java classes (host mode), not JavaScript (web mode), so it must find the Java source for the client in the classpath first.

Click the Debug button to start the GWT application in host mode. Two windows will appear on the desktop (Figure 10-7). First, you'll see the Google Web Toolkit Shell. This is actually a custom Tomcat application server running on port 8888. GWT then starts the application itself and launches a browser window to show the client view.

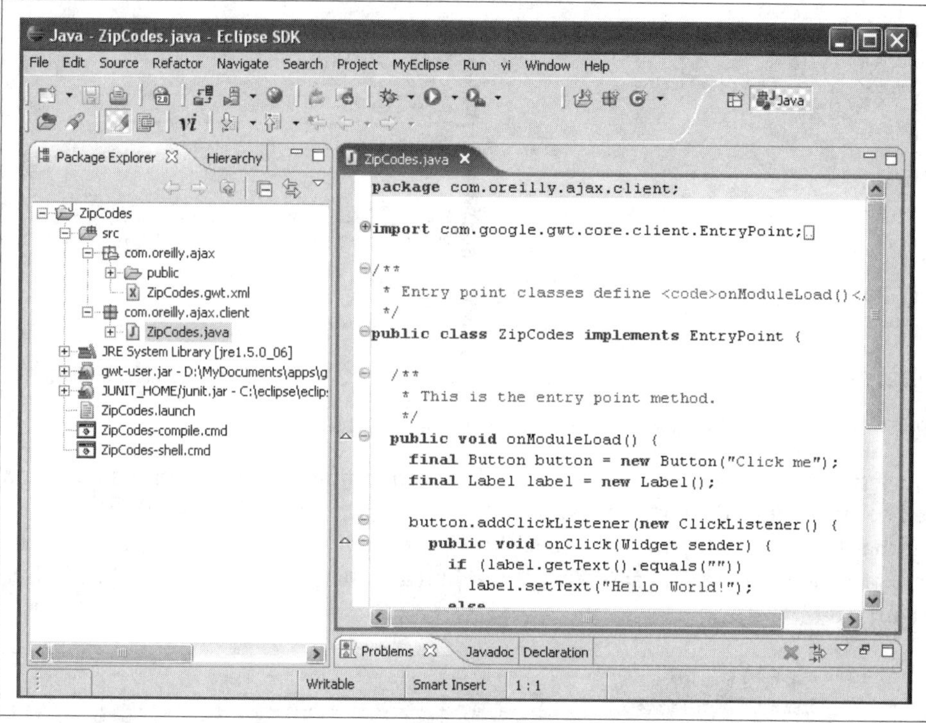


*Figure 10-5. Eclipse with the ZipCodes GWT project loaded*

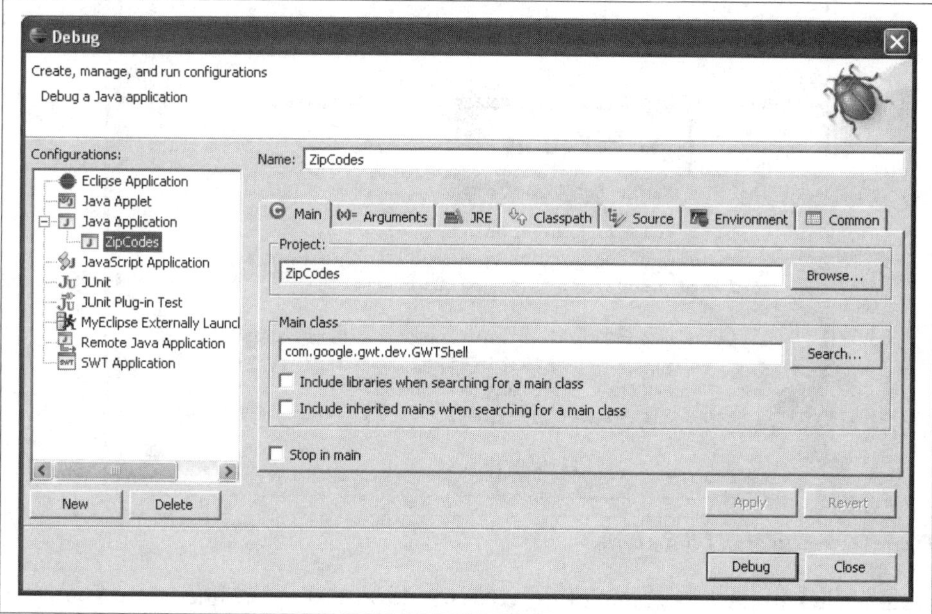


*Figure 10-6. The Eclipse debug configuration window*

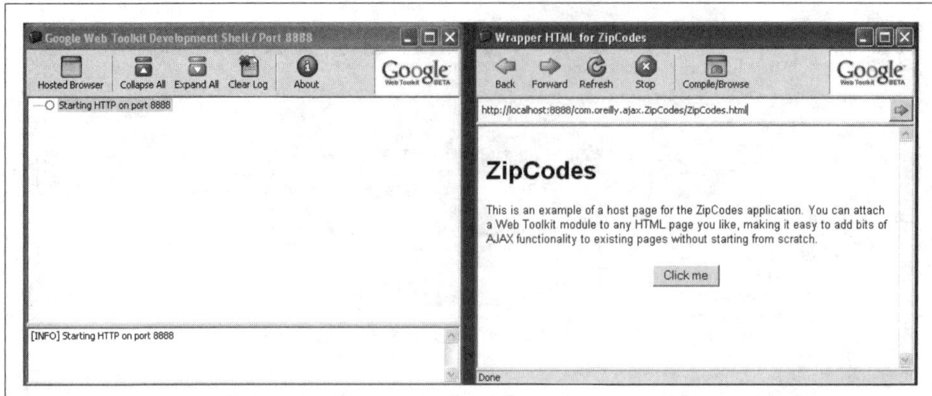


*Figure 10-7. The GWT shell and browser started through Eclipse*

Now that the debugging environment has been configured, you can get to work. Let's start by introducing a breakpoint. First, open the *ZipCodes.java* file by clicking on that file in the left pane (refer back to Figure 10-5). Then move the cursor to the line of code in `onModuleLoad( )` where the button label is set to "Hello World" (see Figure 10-8).

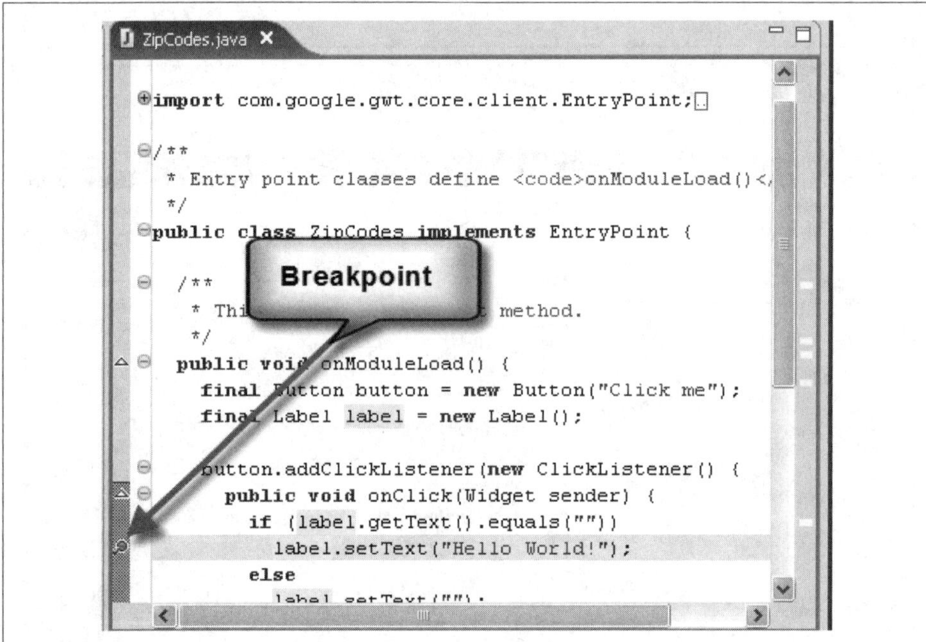


*Figure 10-8. Setting an Eclipse breakpoint*

Double-click in the left margin of the code window, next to the line where you want the breakpoint.

Now, go back to the browser window and click the "Click me" button. The code will begin executing and stop at the breakpoint that you just set. Then Eclipse will transfer control of the application to the debugger. Now change the "Hello World" text to something else, like "Goodbye cruel World!":

```
label.setText("Goodbye cruel World!");
```

Press Ctrl-S to save the file, then press F8 three times to start the execution of the file. You have to press it three times because when you change code that is being debugged, the debugger starts at the entry point to the method that was changed. The first time you press F8, Eclipse takes you back to the start of the method. The second F8 takes you to the breakpoint again, and the third F8 moves the program past the breakpoint. Figure 10-9 shows the result.

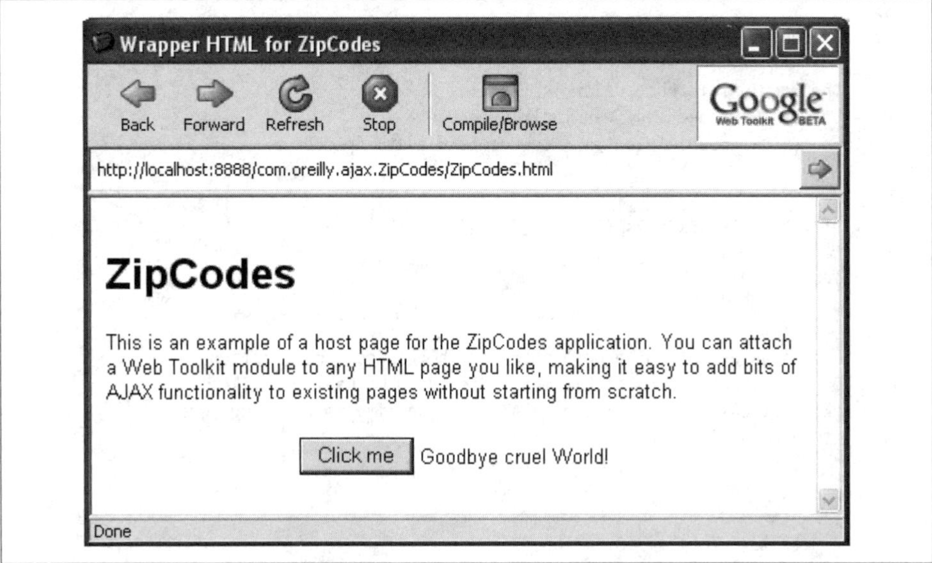


*Figure 10-9. The result of changing the label text during debugging*

This is really a breakthrough! You've started debugging a GWT application. Now you can have very productive development cycles with Ajax, thanks to complete round-trip debugging provided by the Google Web Toolkit.

## Fleshing Out the Application: The Client

Now that the simple application is in place, we need to make it do something interesting. We know how to create a skeleton, and we have a sense of how to debug, but we're a long way from having a working ZipCodes application. We'll start by working on the client.

The source code for the rudimentary client that GWT built is in the *src/com/oreilly/ajax/client/ZipCodes.java* file. This file looks a lot like a Java GUI application. There's a listener, there's a button, you can set text on elements with a call to `setText( )`, and so on. It's not all that different from AWT or Swing.

The main points to note are that the `ZipCodes` class implements `EntryPoint` and overrides the `onModuleLoad( )` method. The `onModuleLoad( )` method configures the GUI widgets, and at the end of this method, the widgets are added to elements in the HTML page. The HTML file (Example 10-3) is located in the project's *public* subdirectory.

*Example 10-3. ZipCodes.html*

```
<html>
<head>
    <title>Wrapper HTML for ZipCodes</title>

    <!-- The module reference below is the link   -->
    <!-- between HTML and your Web Toolkit module -->
    <meta name='gwt:module' content='com.oreilly.ajax.ZipCodes'>
</head>
<body>
    <script language="javascript" src="gwt.js"></script>

    <h1>ZipCodes</h1>

    <p>
        This is an example of a host page for the ZipCodes application.
        You can attach a Web Toolkit module to any HTML page you like,
        making it easy to add bits of AJAX functionality to existing pages
        without starting from scratch.
    </p>
    <table align=center>
        <tr>
            <td id="slot1"></td>
            <td id="slot2"></td>
        </tr>
    </table>
</body>
</html>
```

The *ZipCodes.html* file contains a hook to the Web Toolkit module, which is defined by the `<meta>` tag. You'll also see that the JavaScript reference to *gwt.js* is in the document's body rather than inside the `<head>` tag, where you would normally expect it. That's supposed to make it faster to load.

Finally, note that the `<td>` elements in the table have `id`s of `"slot1"` and `"slot2"`. These are the places where GWT puts the button and the label. If you look back at *ZipCodes.java* (Example 10-2), you'll see that `"slot1"` and `"slot2"` are used to identify elements in the root panel; the button and the label are added to these elements. The Java client uses these `id`s to access elements in the HTML page.

## Customizing the Client

Now let's get started with the ZipCodes client. We only need three fields: zip code, city, and state. Those fields will be in a `<div>` with the `id` of `"gridholder"` (see Example 10-4).

*Example 10-4. Modified ZipCodes.html*

```
<html xmlns="http://www.w3.org/1999/xhtml" xml:lang="en" lang="en">
<head>
    <link rel="stylesheet" type="style/css" href="gwtpage.css" />
    <title>Ajax response</title>
    <meta name="gwt:module" content="com.oreilly.ajax.ZipCodes" />
    <meta http-equiv="content-type" content= "text/html; charset=UTF-8" />
</head>
<body>
    <script language="javascript" src="gwt.js"></script>
    <h2>Ajax with the Google Web Toolkit. </h2>
    <div id="status"></div>
    <div id="gridholder"></div>
</body>
</html>
```

The status div is used to pass error messages and other information from the server, as you'll see shortly.

> You might have thought that you wouldn't need to write any HTML with GWT. It's true that the ApplicationCreator generates a skeleton HTML file for you, but you do need to edit that HTML in order to create elements that GWT can manipulate. GWT creates the JavaScript to manipulate the elements but will not create the elements themselves.

Now let's modify the `ZipCodes` class to populate the HTML page (Example 10-5).

*Example 10-5. ZipCodes updated with a grid and widgets*

```
package com.oreilly.ajax.client;

import com.google.gwt.core.client.EntryPoint;
import com.google.gwt.core.client.GWT;
import com.google.gwt.user.client.DOM;
import com.google.gwt.user.client.Element;
import com.google.gwt.user.client.rpc.AsyncCallback;
import com.google.gwt.user.client.rpc.ServiceDefTarget;
import com.google.gwt.user.client.ui.FocusListener;
import com.google.gwt.user.client.ui.Grid;
import com.google.gwt.user.client.ui.Label;
import com.google.gwt.user.client.ui.RootPanel;
import com.google.gwt.user.client.ui.TextBox;
import com.google.gwt.user.client.ui.Widget;
```

*Example 10-5. ZipCodes updated with a grid and widgets (continued)*

```
/**
 * Entry point classes define <code>onModuleLoad( )</code>.
 */
public class ZipCodes implements EntryPoint {
    private Label zipCodeLabel = new Label( );
    private TextBox zipCodeBox = new TextBox( );
    private Label stateLabel = new Label("State:");
    private TextBox stateTextBox = new TextBox( );
    private Label cityLabel = new Label("City:");
    private TextBox cityTextBox = new TextBox( );
    private Grid grid = new Grid(3, 2);
    /**
     * This is the entry point method.
     */
    public void onModuleLoad( ) {

        zipCodeLabel.setText("Zip Code:");
        zipCodeBox.setVisibleLength(5);
        zipCodeBox.setMaxLength(5);

        stateTextBox.setVisibleLength(2);
        stateTextBox.setMaxLength(2);
        cityTextBox.setMaxLength(40);
        cityTextBox.setVisibleLength(40);

        grid.setWidget(0, 0, zipCodeLabel);
        grid.setWidget(0, 1, zipCodeBox);
        grid.setWidget(1, 0, cityLabel);
        grid.setWidget(1, 1, cityTextBox);
        grid.setWidget(2, 0, stateLabel);
        grid.setWidget(2, 1, stateTextBox);

        zipCodeBox.addFocusListener(new FocusListener( ) {
            public void onFocus(Widget sender) {
            }

            public void onLostFocus(Widget sender) {
                if (zipCodeBox.getText( ).equals("")) {
                    cityTextBox.setText("??");
                    stateTextBox.setText("??");
                    displayFormattedMessage("Try a real code", "blue");
                }
                else {
                    cityTextBox.setText("");
                    stateTextBox.setText("");
                    displayFormattedMessage("This application has no services",
                                            "red");
                }
            }
        });
```

*Example 10-5. ZipCodes updated with a grid and widgets (continued)*

```
        RootPanel.get("gridholder").add(grid);
    }

    private void displayFormattedMessage(String message, String color) {
        Element el = DOM.getElementById("status");
        if (el != null) {
            DOM.setStyleAttribute(el, "color", color);
            DOM.setStyleAttribute(el, "font-family", "ariel, san-serif");
            DOM.setInnerHTML(el, message);
        }
    }
}
```

The ZipCodes class now looks like a GUI application. It has widgets and a grid, and the widgets have methods like setText( ) and listeners like the FocusListener. GWT will translate these widgets into JavaScript, but you really don't need to worry about that while developing your code. Just treat the client like a Java GUI application.

The ZipCodes class defines widgets at the beginning of the class; for this application, TextBox and Label widgets are used within a Grid layout. The widgets are configured in the onModuleLoaded( ) method: the visible length of the text fields is set with setVisibleLength( ), the maximum length of the fields is set with setMaxLength( ), and the widgets are formatted in a grid with grid.setWidget( ).

The Grid object is initialized as a three-row, two-column array of widgets:

```
private Grid grid = new Grid(3, 2);
```

The DOM library that GWT supplies is used to format a message that can be sent to the client. Look at the displayFormattedMessage( ) method. The DOM object can be used to retrieve elements from the client and set styles on the elements (for example, setting the color). Those style attributes match the styles that can be set with stylesheets. Look at a good CSS reference to see the different styles that can be set on an element.

To display the message, call setInnerHTML( ). If you are familiar with dynamically changing HTML text with JavaScript, you will recognize this call. It is very similar to setting the innerHTML parameter with JavaScript.

At this point, you can run this application in hosted mode (Figure 10-10). Try entering a zip code and then pressing the Tab key to move to the next field.

The application has no services yet, so a message is sent to the client to inform the user that the services are not yet available. The next section shows how to make a service available to the client.

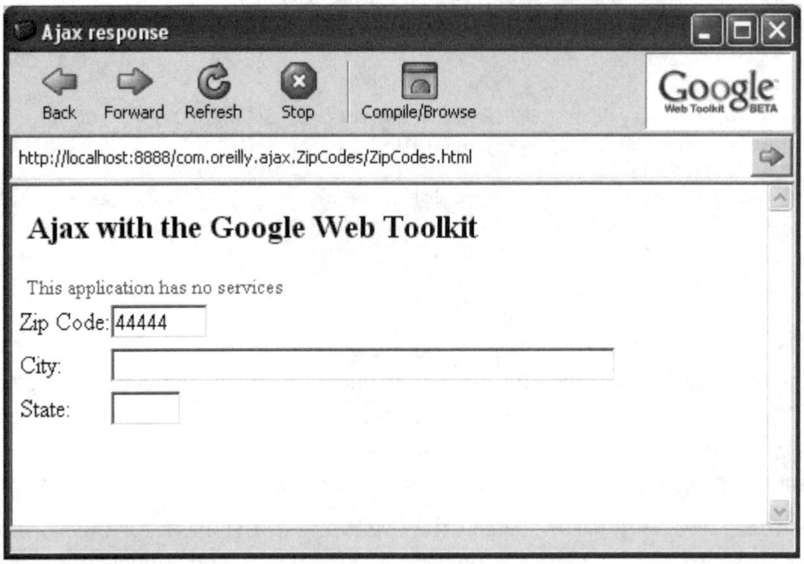

Figure 10-10. ZipCodes application client

## Supplying Services to the Client

It's no surprise that, given a zip code, we need a service to look up the city and state. But how should we do that? One slick option is to use a Remote Procedure Call (RPC), which is a mechanism that allows a computer to cause a program running on another computer to execute. GWT provides an RPC mechanism that eliminates the need to work directly with the `XMLHttpRequest` object that other Ajax applications must use.

To use GWT's RPC plumbing, you must define two Java interfaces and one class. The first interface (`ResponseService`, shown in Example 10-6) extends `com.google.gwt.user.client.rpc.RemoteService` and defines the service.

*Example 10-6. ResponseService.java*

```
package com.oreilly.ajax.client;

import com.google.gwt.user.client.rpc.RemoteService;

public interface ResponseService extends RemoteService {
    String displayResponse(String req);
}
```

This service interface must define the method `displayResponse()`.

The second interface (ResponseServiceAsync, shown in Example 10-7) specifies a method (displayResponse( )) that the client uses to call the service. That interface extends com.google.gwt.user.client.rpc.AsyncCallback.

*Example 10-7. ResponseServiceAsync.java*

```
package com.oreilly.ajax.client;

import com.google.gwt.user.client.rpc.AsyncCallback;

public interface ResponseServiceAsync {
    public void displayResponse(String s, AsyncCallback callback);
}
```

The AsyncCallback handles the response for the client.

The class that must be implemented should extend com.google.gwt.user.server.rpc.RemoteServiceServlet. We'll call this class ResponseServiceImpl; its code is presented in Example 10-8.

*Example 10-8. ResponseServiceImpl.java sits on the server*

```
package com.oreilly.ajax.server;

import com.google.gwt.user.server.rpc.RemoteServiceServlet;
import com.oreilly.ajax.client.ResponseService;

public class ResponseServiceImpl extends RemoteServiceServlet
        implements ResponseService {
    public String displayResponse(String req) {
        if (req.length( ) < 1) {
            throw new IllegalArgumentException(
                    "Blank submissions from the client are invalid.");
        }
        Zipcode zipcode = ZipcodeManager.getZipcode(req);
        String state = zipcode.getState( );
        String city = zipcode.getCity( );
        if ((state==null || state.length()<1) || (city==null || city.length( )<1))
          return null;
        String jsonString = "{\"state\":\""+state+"\", \"city\":\""+city+"\"}";
        return jsonString;
    }
}
```

The ResponseServiceImpl class extends RemoteServiceServlet, which in turn extends javax.servlet.http.HttpServlet. That means that this class is actually a servlet and will be deployed in the servlet container. For this application, the service returns a JSON-formatted string with the state set to "state" and the city set to "city".

## Connecting the Client to the Service

The client is not yet connected to the service. We can accomplish this by adding a FocusListener to the zipCodeBox element, as shown in Example 10-9. This is done with an inner class, just as you would add a listener to a widget in Swing.

*Example 10-9. The client ZipCodes class with the service connected*

```
zipCodeBox.addFocusListener(new FocusListener( ) {
    public void onFocus(Widget sender) {
    }

    public void onLostFocus(Widget sender) {
        ResponseServiceAsync respService = (ResponseServiceAsync)
                GWT.create(com.oreilly.ajax.client.ResponseService.class);
        ServiceDefTarget endpoint = (ServiceDefTarget) respService;
        endpoint.setServiceEntryPoint("/responseService");

        displayFormattedMessage("getting data...", "blue");
        AsyncCallback callback = new AsyncCallback( ) {
            public void onSuccess(Object result) {

                JSONObject jsonObject;
                try {
                    displayFormattedMessage("Parsing JSON data...", "blue");
                    jsonObject = JSONParser.parse((String) result);
                    String[] keys = jsonObject.getKeys( );
                    if (keys.length >= 2) {
                        String city = jsonObject.get("city").toString( );
                        String state = jsonObject.get("state").toString( );
                        cityTextBox.setText(city);
                        stateTextBox.setText(state);
                        displayFormattedMessage("", "blue");
                    }
                    else {
                        cityTextBox.setText("");
                        stateTextBox.setText("");
                        displayFormattedMessage("This zip code was not found in
                                                the database.", "red");
                    }

                } catch (JSONException e) {
                    displayFormattedMessage("Error parsing JSON data \n"
                                            + e.getMessage( ), "red");
                }
            }

            public void onFailure(Throwable caught) {

                displayFormattedMessage(
                        "Server request raised an error; Java exception : " +
                        caught == null ? "An unknown exception"
                        : caught.getMessage( ), "red");
            }
        };
```

*Example 10-9. The client ZipCodes class with the service connected (continued)*

```
        try {
            displayFormattedMessage("getting request", "green");
            respService.displayResponse(zipCodeBox.getText( ), callback);
        } catch (Exception e) {
            displayFormattedMessage("Server request raised an error: "
                                   + e.getMessage( ), "red");
        } finally {
            displayFormattedMessage("", "green");
        }
    }
});
```

The work of detecting that the zip code field has lost focus is done in the `onLostFocus( )` method of the `FocusListener`. The `onFocus( )` method must be implemented to satisfy the `FocusListener` interface, but the body of the method can be left blank because this application doesn't do anything when the `zipCodeBox` element comes in focus.

The entry point for the Ajax service is added to the `ResponseServiceAsync` object by passing the service's URL—in this case, */responseService*—into `setServiceEntryPoint( )`.

Then, in the `try` block at the end of the `onLostFocus( )` method, the response service (`respService`) configures the service, passing in the text of the `zipCodeBox` and the `AsyncCallback` object:

```
respService.displayResponse(zipCodeBox.getText( ), callback);
```

The `callback` parameter was set earlier to the instantiated `AsyncCallback` object.

The `AsyncCallback` interface defines what happens to the client when the Ajax call is returned. This is the callback function that `XMLHttpRequest` uses, but because we are using GWT, the details of that call are hidden from the developer.

The `AsyncCallback` interface has two methods that this application must implement: `onFailure( )` and `onSuccess( )`. The `onSucess( )` method is invoked when the Ajax call returns successfully. This is handled by decoding the JSON object, which should contain the city and state information. The city and state are displayed by calls to the `setText( )` method on the `cityTextBox` and the `stateTextBox`.

If there is an error, the `onFailure( )` method is invoked and the application displays an error message.

The project directory structure should now look like Figure 10-11.

We have modified the `ZipCodes` class to use the new service. The new service is implemented by the `com.oreilly.ajax.server.ResponseServiceImpl` class; the interfaces to the service are `ResponseService` and `ResponseServiceAsync`, which are both in the client package.

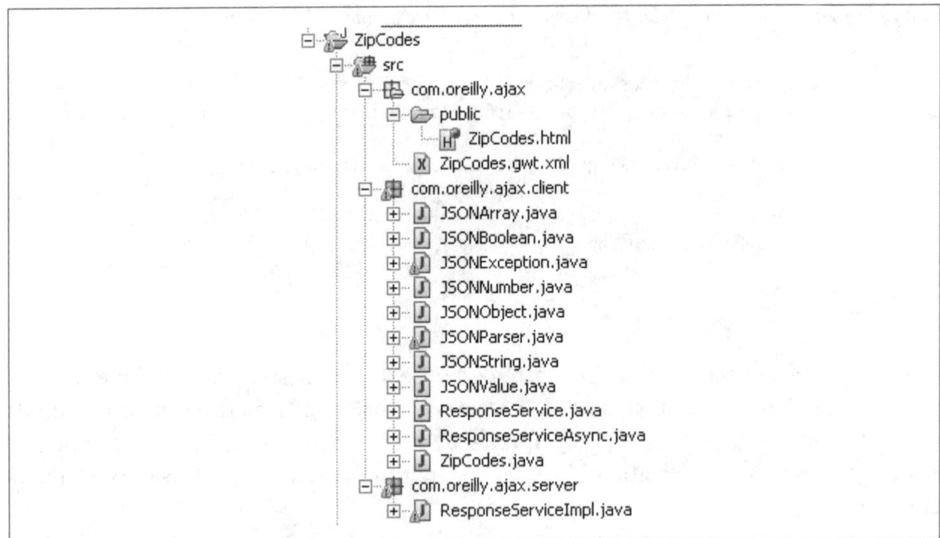


*Figure 10-11. ZipCodes project with services*

Figure 10-11 also shows some JSON support classes that are part of the client package. JSON support is not currently implemented in GWT. To facilitate use of JSON, download the JSON RPC example from *http://code.google.com/webtoolkit/documentation/examples*. Then copy the JSON classes into the application's client package. The ZipCodes application needs JSON to handle the data passed asynchronously to the `onSuccess( )` method of the `AsyncCallback` object.

## Connecting the Service to the Servlet URL

One last item must be addressed: we must connect the service to the */responseService* URL. That's handled in *ZipCodes.gwt.xml* (Example 10-10).

*Example 10-10. ZipCodes.gwt.xml with the servlet configuration*

```
<module>
    <!-- Inherit the core Web Toolkit stuff.                    -->
    <inherits name='com.google.gwt.user.User'/>
    <!-- Specify the app entry point class.                     -->
    <entry-point class='com.oreilly.ajax.client.ZipCodes'/>
    <!-- GWT's RPC Servlet path                                 -->
    <servlet path='/responseService'
            class='com.oreilly.ajax.server.ResponseServiceImpl'/>
</module>
```

With the `<servlet>` tag added to *ZipCodes.gwt.xml*, the entire application is ready for testing.

## Testing ZipCodes with the Service

Start the hosted application from Eclipse, using the Run → Debug menu command. The GWT development shell should start up, along with a browser window that displays the ZipCodes client. Enter a zip code in the zip code field and press Tab. Figure 10-12 shows the result.

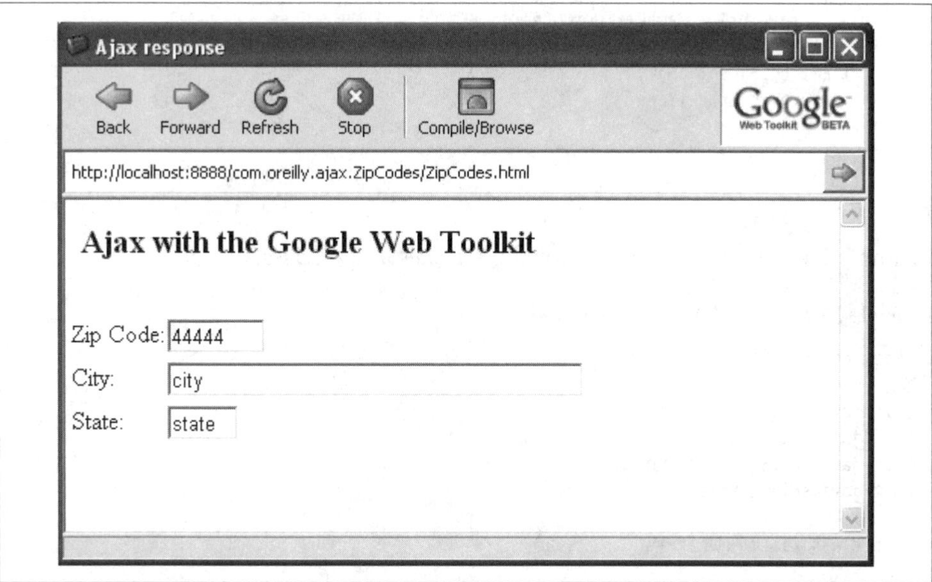


*Figure 10-12. ZipCodes application with a service*

We've got a client—but we don't have a backend service, so all we have is bogus data. (Remember that `ResponseServiceImpl` in Example 10-8 returns the hardcoded values "state" and "city".) All we need now is a way to look up the state and city information in the database, just like we've done in previous chapters.

Adding the `DatabaseConnector` class, the `ZipcodeManager` class, and the POJO `Zipcode` class should do the trick. Those classes were described earlier in this book, but the source code is provided here for reference. The `DatabaseConnector` class is reproduced in Example 10-11.

*Example 10-11. DatabaseConnector.java*

```
public class DatabaseConnector {

    public static Connection getConnection( ) {
        Connection con = null;
        String driver = "com.mysql.jdbc.Driver";
```

*Example 10-11. DatabaseConnector.java (continued)*

```
        try {
            Class.forName(driver).newInstance( );
        } catch (Exception e) {
            System.out.println("Failed to load mySQL driver.");
            return null;
        }
        try {
            con = DriverManager.getConnection(
                    "jdbc:mysql:///AJAX?user=ajax&password=polygon");
        } catch (Exception e) {
            e.printStackTrace( );
        }
        return con;
    }
}
```

Example 10-12 presents the code for the ZipcodeManager class.

*Example 10-12. ZipcodeManager.java*

```
package com.oreilly.ajax.server;

import java.sql.Connection;
import java.sql.ResultSet;
import java.sql.SQLException;
import java.sql.Statement;

public class ZipcodeManager {

    static public Zipcode getZipcode(String zip) {
        Zipcode zipcode = null;
        Connection con = DatabaseConnector.getConnection( );
        String sqlString = "";
        zipcode = new Zipcode( );
        zipcode.setZipcode(zip);// put in original zip code

        try {
            sqlString = "SELECT CITY,STATE,ZIPCODE FROM ZIPCODES WHERE
                        ZIPCODE='"+ zip + "';";
            Statement select = con.createStatement( );
            ResultSet result = select.executeQuery(sqlString);
            if (result.next( )) { // process results one row at a time
                zipcode.setCity(result.getString(1));
                zipcode.setState(result.getString(2));
                zipcode.setZipcode(result.getString(3));
            }

        } catch (Exception e) {
            System.out.println("exception in login, "
                    + "you might need the mysql jar in the lib directory: "
                    + e.getMessage( ));
        } finally {
            if (con != null) {
```

*Example 10-12. ZipcodeManager.java (continued)*

```
                try {
                    con.close( );
                } catch (SQLException e) {
                }
            }
        }
    return zipcode;
    }
}
```

Finally, the Zipcode class is presented in Example 10-13.

*Example 10-13. Zipcode.java*

```
package com.oreilly.ajax.server;

public class Zipcode {
    String city;
    String state;
    String zipcode;

    public Zipcode( ) {
        zipcode = "";
        city = "";
        state = "";
    }

    public String getCity( ) {
        return city;
    }

    public void setCity(String city) {
        this.city = city;
    }

    public String getState( ) {
        return state;
    }

    public void setState(String state) {
        this.state = state;
    }

    public String getZipcode( ) {
        return zipcode;
    }

    public void setZipcode(String zipcode) {
        this.zipcode = zipcode;
    }
}
```

Figure 10-13 shows what the project looks like after these classes have been added to the server package.

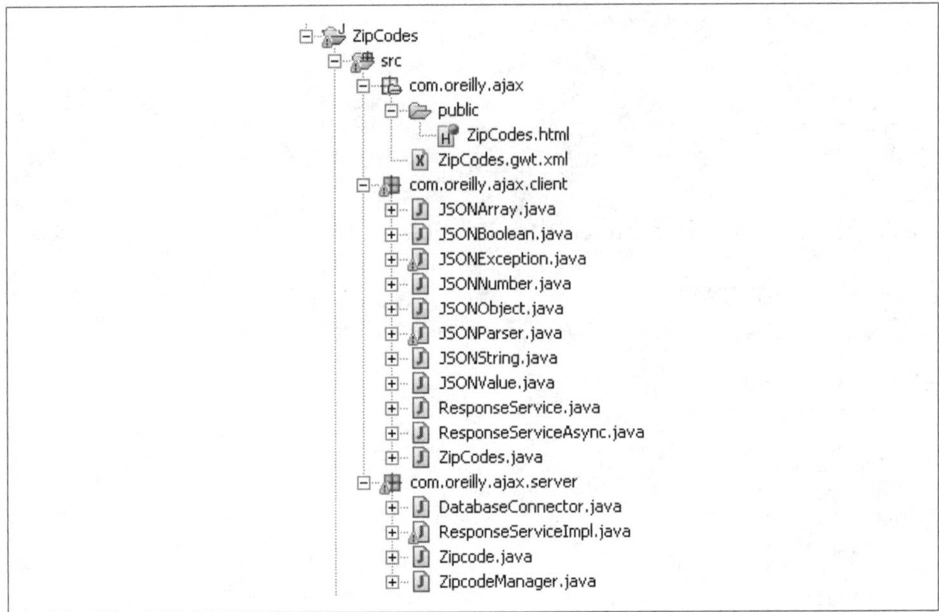


*Figure 10-13. The complete and final ZipCodes project*

Now connect the `ZipcodeManager` to the `displayResponse( )` method of the `ResponseServiceImpl` class. The `ZipcodeManager.getZipcode( )` method returns a POJO `Zipcode` that contains the city and state corresponding to the zip code:

```
public String displayResponse(String req) {
    if (req.length( ) < 1) {
        throw new IllegalArgumentException(
                "Blank submissions from the client are invalid.");
    }
    Zipcode zipcode = ZipcodeManager.getZipcode(req);
    String state = zipcode.getState( );
    String city = zipcode.getCity( );
    if ((state==null || state.length()<1) || (city==null || city.length( )<1))
        return null;
    String jsonString = "{\"state\":\""+state+"\", \"city\":\""+city+"\"}";
    return jsonString;
}
```

In order for the application to connect to the database, the MySQL connector must be in the classpath. If you haven't done it already, download the connector from *http://www.mysql.org* and add the *.jar* file to the Classpath tab of Eclipse's Debug window (Run → Debug).

That completes the plumbing for the ZipCodes application. Now it should be fully functional; Figure 10-14 shows the result. Try setting breakpoints in the client and in the service to verify that you can fully debug the application. It almost seems too good to be true!

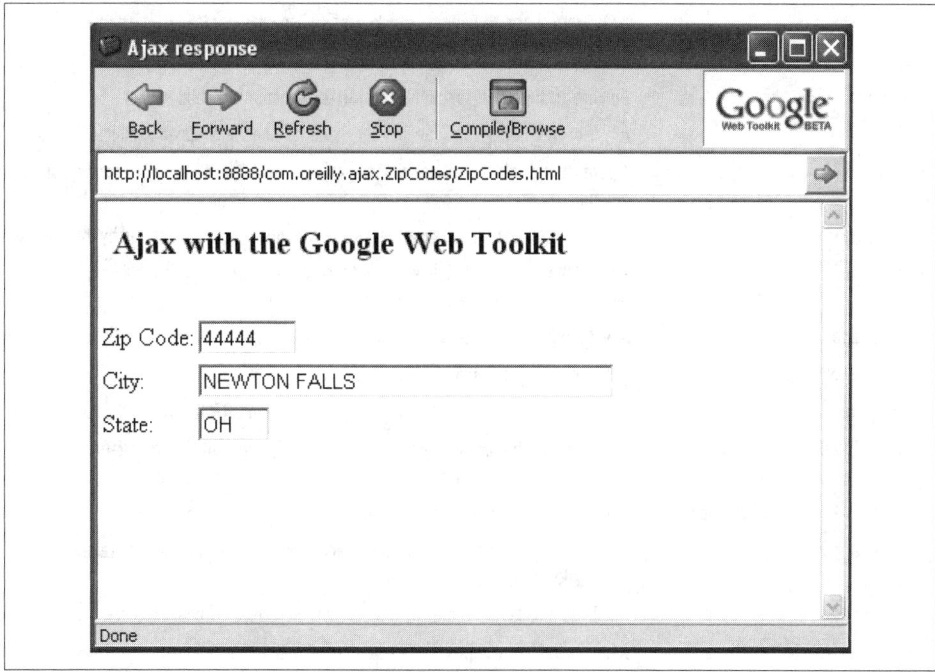


*Figure 10-14. Final client for the ZipCodes application*

Well, you made it! You should now be familiar with all the basics for building an Ajax application with the Google Web Toolkit. For more examples, refer to the GWT home page at *http://code.google.com*.

# GWT Widgets

Table 10-1 lists some of the widgets that can be used with GWT and their corresponding HTML element types.

*Table 10-1. GWT widgets*

| Widget | Description |
| --- | --- |
| `AbsolutePanel` | A panel that positions all of its children absolutely, allowing them to overlap |
| `Button` | A standard push-button widget |
| `ButtonBase` | The abstract base class for `Button`, `CheckBox`, and `RadioButton` |

*Table 10-1. GWT widgets (continued)*

| Widget | Description |
|---|---|
| CellPanel | A panel whose child widgets are contained within the cells of a table |
| ChangeListenerCollection | A helper class for implementers of the SourcesChangeEvents interface |
| CheckBox | A standard checkbox widget (also serves as a base class for RadioButton) |
| ClickListenerCollection | A helper class for implementers of the SourcesClickEvents interface |
| ComplexPanel | An abstract base class for panels that can contain multiple child widgets |
| Composite | A type of widget that can wrap another widget, hiding the wrapped widget's methods |
| DeckPanel | A panel that displays all of its child widgets in a "deck," where only one can be visible at a time |
| DialogBox | A form of pop-up that has a caption area at the top and can be dragged by the user |
| DockPanel | A panel that lays out its child widgets "docked" at its outer edges and allows its last widget to take up the remaining space in its center |
| FileUpload | A widget that wraps the HTML <input type="file"> element |
| FlexTable | A flexible table that creates cells on demand |
| FlowPanel | A panel that formats its child widgets using the default HTML layout behavior |
| FocusListenerAdapter | An adapter to simplify focus event listeners that do not need all events defined on the FocusListener interface |
| FocusListenerCollection | A helper class for implementers of the SourcesFocusEvents interface |
| FocusPanel | A simple panel that makes its contents focusable and adds the ability to catch mouse and keyboard events |
| FocusWidget | An abstract base class for most widgets that can receive keyboard focus |
| FormHandlerCollection | A helper class for widgets that accept FormHandlers |
| FormPanel | A panel that wraps its contents in an HTML <form> element |
| FormSubmitCompleteEvent | An Event object containing information about form submission events |
| FormSubmitEvent | An Event object containing information about form submission events |
| Frame | A widget that wraps an <IFRAME> element, which can contain an arbitrary web site |
| Grid | A rectangular grid that can contain text, HTML, or a child widget within its cells |
| HorizontalPanel | A panel that lays out all of its widgets in a single horizontal column |
| HTML | A widget that can contain arbitrary HTML |
| HTMLPanel | A panel that contains HTML and can attach child widgets to identified elements within that HTML |
| HTMLTable | A widget that contains the common table algorithms for Grid and FlexTable |
| Hyperlink | A widget that serves as an "internal" hyperlink |
| Image | A widget that displays the image at a given URL |
| KeyboardListenerAdapter | An adapter to simplify keyboard event listeners that do not need all events defined on the KeyboardListener interface |
| KeyboardListenerCollection | A helper class for implementers of the SourcesKeyboardEvents interface |

*Table 10-1. GWT widgets (continued)*

| Widget | Description |
| --- | --- |
| `Label` | A widget that contains arbitrary text, *not* interpreted as HTML |
| `ListBox` | A widget that presents a list of choices to the user, either as a listbox or as a drop-down list |
| `LoadListenerCollection` | A helper class for implementers of the `SourcesLoadEvents` interface |
| `MenuBar` | A standard menu bar widget |
| `MenuItem` | A widget that can be placed in a `MenuBar` |
| `MouseListenerAdapter` | An adapter to simplify mouse event listeners that do not need all events defined on the `MouseListener` interface |
| `MouseListenerCollection` | A helper class for implementers of the `SourcesMouseEvents` interface |
| `NamedFrame` | A *frame* that has a "name" associated with it |
| `Panel` | An abstract base class for all panels, which are widgets that can contain other widgets |
| `PasswordTextBox` | A text box that visually masks its input to prevent eavesdropping |
| `PopupListenerCollection` | A helper class for implementers of the `SourcesPopupEvents` interface |
| `PopupPanel` | A panel that can "pop up" over other widgets |
| `RadioButton` | A mutually exclusive selection radio button widget |
| `RootPanel` | The panel to which all other widgets must ultimately be added |
| `ScrollListenerCollection` | A helper class for implementers of the `SourcesScrollEvents` interface |
| `ScrollPanel` | A simple panel that wraps its contents in a scrollable area |
| `SimplePanel` | An abstract base class for panels that contain only one widget |
| `StackPanel` | A panel that stacks its children vertically, displaying only one at a time, with a header for each one that the user can click to display it |
| `TabBar` | A horizontal bar of folder-style tabs, most commonly used as part of a `TabPanel` |
| `TableListenerCollection` | A helper class for implementers of the `SourcesTableEvents` interface |
| `TabListenerCollection` | A helper class for implementers of the `SourcesTabEvents` interface |
| `TabPanel` | A panel that represents a tabbed set of pages, each of which contains another widget |
| `TextArea` | A text box that allows multiple lines of text to be entered |
| `TextBox` | A standard single-line text box |
| `TextBoxBase` | An abstract base class for all text-entry widgets |
| `Tree` | A standard hierarchical tree widget |
| `TreeItem` | An item that can be contained within a `Tree` |
| `TreeListenerCollection` | A helper class for implementers of the `SourcesClickEvents` interface |
| `UIObject` | The base class for all user-interface objects |
| `VerticalPanel` | A panel that lays out all of its widgets in a single vertical column |
| `Widget` | The base class for the majority of user-interface objects |

# Index



We'd like to hear your suggestions for improving our indexes. Send email to *index@oreilly.com*.

## About the Author

**Steven Douglas Olson** has been a software developer for 20 years, starting in 1984 with Fortran, Pascal, Basic, and, later, C at a company called Signetics. In 1991, he went to work for Novell, writing C. He began dabbling in Java, and in 1995 was one of the first to join the Java development group at Novell. Since then, he has consulted or worked directly for eight other companies writing primarily in Java. Currently, he works as a consultant in Salt Lake City, where his programming adventures continue.

## Colophon

The animal on the cover of *Ajax on Java* is a cotton-top tamarin (*Saguinus oedipus*), a small-bodied monkey characterized by the fan of long, white hair on its head. Tamarins are divided into three groups based on facial hair. The cotton-top is marked by thin hair on its black-skinned face such that its face appears naked. This puts it squarely into the bare-face group, as opposed to the hairy-face or mottled-face group. Tamarins have claw-like nails resembling those of a squirrel rather than flat nails like other primates, which they use to cling, run, and leap through trees. They can do this with great ease due to their size: cotton-tops weigh less than one pound and reach only nine inches in height.

Cotton-top tamarins are found in a small area of northwest Colombia. Their range is bound by the Cauca and Magdalena Rivers and the Atlantic coast; however, they are currently found only in parks and reserves throughout this area. A group of tamarins maintains a fixed territory within its home range, which it chooses based on fruit availability. Other sources of nourishment for the tamarin include insects, plant exudates, nectar, and occasionally reptiles and amphibians. Most groups appear to be monogamous, with only one reproductively active male and female. Cotton-tops, like other members of their subfamily (*callitrichines*), primarily give birth to non-identical twins. As its scientific name indicates, the male tamarin seems to have an Oedipus complex, yet the mother does not allow this relationship to be consummated.

The cover image is from *Lydekker's Royal History*. The cover font is Adobe ITC Garamond. The text font is Linotype Birka; the heading font is Adobe Myriad Condensed; and the code font is LucasFont's TheSans Mono Condensed.

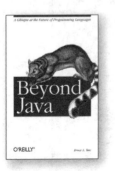